ASPEN PUBLISHERS

Casenote™ Legal Briefs

HEALTH LAW

Keyed to Courses Using

Furrow, Greaney, Johnson, Jost, and Schwartz's
Health Law
Sixth Edition

Wolters Kluwer
Law & Business

AUSTIN BOSTON CHICAGO NEW YORK THE NETHERLANDS

a Wolters Kluwer business
http://lawschool.aspenpublishers.com

To contact Customer Care, e-mail customer.care@aspenpublishers.com, call 1-800-234-1660, fax 1-800-901-9075, or mail correspondence to:

Aspen Publishers
Attn: Order Department
P.O. Box 990
Frederick, MD 21705

Printed in the United States of America.

1 2 3 4 5 6 7 8 9 0

ISBN 978-0-7355-8266-8

About Wolters Kluwer Law & Business

Wolters Kluwer Law & Business is a leading provider of research information and workflow solutions in key specialty areas. The strengths of the individual brands of Aspen Publishers, CCH, Kluwer Law International and Loislaw are aligned within Wolters Kluwer Law & Business to provide comprehensive, in-depth solutions and expert-authored content for the legal, professional and education markets.

CCH was founded in 1913 and has served more than four generations of business professionals and their clients. The CCH products in the Wolters Kluwer Law & Business group are highly regarded electronic and print resources for legal, securities, antitrust and trade regulation, government contracting, banking, pension, payroll, employment and labor, and health-care reimbursement and compliance professionals.

Aspen Publishers is a leading information provider for attorneys, business professionals and law students. Written by preeminent authorities, Aspen products offer analytical and practical information in a range of specialty practice areas from securities law and intellectual property to mergers and acquisitions and pension/benefits. Aspen's trusted legal education resources provide professors and students with high-quality, up-to-date and effective resources for successful instruction and study in all areas of the law.

Kluwer Law International supplies the global business community with comprehensive English-language international legal information. Legal practitioners, corporate counsel and business executives around the world rely on the Kluwer Law International journals, loose-leafs, books and electronic products for authoritative information in many areas of international legal practice.

Loislaw is a premier provider of digitized legal content to small law firm practitioners of various specializations. Loislaw provides attorneys with the ability to quickly and efficiently find the necessary legal information they need, when and where they need it, by facilitating access to primary law as well as state-specific law, records, forms and treatises.

Wolters Kluwer Law & Business, a unit of Wolters Kluwer, is headquartered in New York and Riverwoods, Illinois. Wolters Kluwer is a leading multinational publisher and information services company.

Format for the Casenote Legal Brief

Nature of Case: This section identifies the form of action (e.g., breach of contract, negligence, battery), the type of proceeding (e.g., demurrer, appeal from trial court's jury instructions) or the relief sought (e.g., damages, injunction, criminal sanctions).

Palsgraf v. Long Island R.R. Co.

Injured bystander (P) v. Railroad company (D)

N.Y. Ct. App., 248 N.Y. 339, 162 N.E. 99 (1928).

NATURE OF CASE: Appeal from judgment affirming verdict for plaintiff seeking damages for personal injury.

FACT SUMMARY: Helen Palsgraf (P) was injured on R.R.'s (D) train platform when R.R.'s (D) guard helped a passenger aboard a moving train, causing his package to fall on the tracks. The package contained fireworks which exploded, creating a shock that tipped a scale onto Palsgraf (P).

RULE OF LAW

The risk reasonably to be perceived defines the duty to be obeyed.

FACTS: Helen Palsgraf (P) purchased a ticket to Rockaway Beach from R.R. (D) and was waiting on the train platform. As she waited, two men ran to catch a train that was pulling out from the platform. The first man jumped aboard, but the second man, who appeared as if he might fall, was helped aboard by the guard on the train who had kept the door open so they could jump aboard. A guard on the platform also helped by pushing him onto the train. The man was carrying a package wrapped in newspaper. In the process, the man dropped his package, which fell on the tracks. The package contained fireworks and exploded. The shock of the explosion was apparently of great enough strength to tip over some scales at the other end of the platform, which fell on Palsgraf (P) and injured her. A jury awarded her damages, and R.R. (D) appealed.

ISSUE: Does the risk reasonably to be perceived define the duty to be obeyed?

HOLDING AND DECISION: (Cardozo, C.J.) Yes. The risk reasonably to be perceived defines the duty to be obeyed. If there is no foreseeable hazard to the injured party as the result of a seemingly innocent act, the act does not become a tort because it happened to be a wrong as to another. If the wrong was not willful, the plaintiff must show that the act as to her had such great and apparent possibilities of danger as to entitle her to protection. Negligence in the abstract is not enough upon which to base liability. Negligence is a relative concept, evolving out of the common law doctrine of trespass on the case. To establish liability, the defendant must owe a legal duty of reasonable care to the injured party. A cause of action in tort will lie where harm, though unintended, could have been averted or avoided by observance of such a duty. The scope of the duty is limited by the range of danger that a reasonable person could foresee. In this case, there was nothing to suggest from the appearance of the parcel or otherwise that the parcel contained fireworks. The guard could not reasonably have had any warning of a threat to Palsgraf (P), and R.R. (D) therefore cannot be held liable. Judgment is reversed in favor of R.R. (D).

DISSENT: (Andrews, J.) The concept that there is no negligence unless R.R. (D) owes a legal duty to take care as to Palsgraf (P) herself is too narrow. Everyone owes to the world at large the duty of refraining from those acts that may unreasonably threaten the safety of others. If the guard's action was negligent as to those nearby, it was also negligent as to those outside what might be termed the "danger zone." For Palsgraf (P) to recover, R.R.'s (D) negligence must have been the proximate cause of her injury, a question of fact for the jury.

ANALYSIS

The majority defined the limit of the defendant's liability in terms of the danger that a reasonable person in defendant's situation would have perceived. The dissent argued that the limitation should not be placed on liability, but rather on damages. Judge Andrews suggested that only injuries that would not have happened but for R.R.'s (D) negligence should be compensable. Both the majority and dissent recognized the policy-driven need to limit liability for negligent acts, seeking, in the words of Judge Andrews, to define a framework "that will be practical and in keeping with the general understanding of mankind." The Restatement (Second) of Torts has accepted Judge Cardozo's view.

Quicknotes

FORESEEABILITY A reasonable expectation that change is the probable result of certain acts or omissions.

NEGLIGENCE Conduct falling below the standard of care that a reasonable person would demonstrate under similar conditions.

PROXIMATE CAUSE The natural sequence of events without which an injury would not have been sustained.

Party ID: Quick identification of the relationship between the parties.

Fact Summary: This is included to refresh your memory and can be used as a quick reminder of the facts.

Rule of Law: Summarizes the general principle of law that the case illustrates. It may be used for instant recall of the court's holding and for classroom discussion or home review.

Facts: This section contains all relevant facts of the case, including the contentions of the parties and the lower court holdings. It is written in a logical order to give the student a clear understanding of the case. The plaintiff and defendant are identified by their proper names throughout and are always labeled with a (P) or (D).

Concurrence/Dissent: All concurrences and dissents are briefed whenever they are included by the casebook editor.

Analysis: This last paragraph gives you a broad understanding of where the case "fits in" with other cases in the section of the book and with the entire course. It is a hornbook-style discussion indicating whether the case is a majority or minority opinion and comparing the principal case with other cases in the casebook. It may also provide analysis from restatements, uniform codes, and law review articles. The analysis will prove to be invaluable to classroom discussion.

Issue: The issue is a concise question that brings out the essence of the opinion as it relates to the section of the casebook in which the case appears. Both substantive and procedural issues are included if relevant to the decision.

Holding and Decision: This section offers a clear and in-depth discussion of the rule of the case and the court's rationale. It is written in easy-to-understand language and answers the issue presented by applying the law to the facts of the case. When relevant, it includes a thorough discussion of the exceptions to the case as listed by the court, any major cites to the other cases on point, and the names of the judges who wrote the decisions.

Quicknotes: Conveniently defines legal terms found in the case and summarizes the nature of any statutes, codes, or rules referred to in the text.

Note to Students

Aspen Publishers is proud to offer *Casenote Legal Briefs*—continuing thirty years of publishing America's best-selling legal briefs.

Casenote Legal Briefs are designed to help you save time when briefing assigned cases. Organized under convenient headings, they show you how to abstract the basic facts and holdings from the text of the actual opinions handed down by the courts. Used as part of a rigorous study regimen, they can help you spend more time analyzing and critiquing points of law than on copying bits and pieces of judicial opinions into your notebook or outline.

Casenote Legal Briefs should never be used as a substitute for assigned casebook readings. They work best when read as a follow-up to reviewing the underlying opinions themselves. Students who try to avoid reading and digesting the judicial opinions in their casebooks or online sources will end up shortchanging themselves in the long run. The ability to absorb, critique, and restate the dynamic and complex elements of case law decisions is crucial to your success in law school and beyond. It cannot be developed vicariously.

Casenote Legal Briefs represents but one of the many offerings in Aspen's Study Aid Timeline, which includes:

- *Casenote Legal Briefs*
- *Emanuel Law Outlines*
- *Examples & Explanations* Series
- *Introduction to Law* Series
- Emanuel *Law in a Flash* Flashcards
- Emanuel *CrunchTime* Series

Each of these series is designed to provide you with easy-to-understand explanations of complex points of law. Each volume offers guidance on the principles of legal analysis and, consulted regularly, will hone your ability to spot relevant issues. We have titles that will help you prepare for class, prepare for your exams, and enhance your general comprehension of the law along the way.

To find out more about Aspen Study Aid publications, visit us online at *http://lawschool.aspenpublishers.com* or email us at *legaledu@wolterskluwer.com.* We'll be happy to assist you.

Free access to Briefs online!

Download cases from this Casenote Legal Brief. Simply fill out this form for full access to this useful feature provided by Loislaw. Learn more about Loislaw services on the inside front cover of this book or visit *www.loislawschool.com.*

Name	**Phone** ( )	
Address		**Apt. No.**
City	**State**	**ZIP Code**
Law School	**Year** (check one) ☐ **1st** ☐ **2nd** ☐ **3rd**	

Cut out the UPC found on the lower left-hand corner of the back cover of this book. Staple the UPC inside this box. Only the original UPC from the book cover will be accepted. No photocopies or store stickers are allowed.

Attach UPC inside this box.

Email (Print legibly or you may not get access!)
Title of this book (course subject)
Used with which casebook (provide author's name)

Mail the completed form to:

Aspen Publishers, Inc.
Legal Education Division
Casenote Online Access
130 Turner Street, Building 3, 4th Floor
Waltham, MA 02453-8901

I understand that online access is granted solely to the purchaser of this book for the academic year in which it was purchased. Any other usage is not authorized and will result in immediate termination of access. Sharing of codes is strictly prohibited.

Signature ______________________________

Upon receipt of this completed form, you will be emailed codes with which to access the briefs for this Casenote Legal Brief. Online briefs are not available for all titles. For a full list of Casenote Legal Brief titles, please visit *http://lawschool.aspenpublishers.com.*

Make a photocopy of this form and your UPC for your records.

For detailed information on the use of the information you provide on this form, please see the PRIVACY POLICY at www.aspenpublishers.com.

How to Brief a Case

A. Decide on a Format and Stick to It

Structure is essential to a good brief. It enables you to arrange systematically the related parts that are scattered throughout most cases, thus making manageable and understandable what might otherwise seem to be an endless and unfathomable sea of information. There are, of course, an unlimited number of formats that can be utilized. However, it is best to find one that suits your needs and stick to it. Consistency breeds both efficiency and the security that when called upon you will know where to look in your brief for the information you are asked to give.

Any format, as long as it presents the essential elements of a case in an organized fashion, can be used. Experience, however, has led *Casenotes* to develop and utilize the following format because of its logical flow and universal applicability.

NATURE OF CASE: This is a brief statement of the legal character and procedural status of the case (e.g., "Appeal of a burglary conviction").

There are many different alternatives open to a litigant dissatisfied with a court ruling. The key to determining which one has been used is to discover *who is asking this court for what.*

This first entry in the brief should be kept as *short as possible.* Use the court's terminology if you understand it. But since jurisdictions vary as to the titles of pleadings, the best entry is the one that addresses who wants what in this proceeding, not the one that sounds most like the court's language.

RULE OF LAW: A statement of the general principle of law that the case illustrates (e.g., "An acceptance that varies any term of the offer is considered a rejection and counteroffer").

Determining the rule of law of a case is a procedure similar to determining the issue of the case. Avoid being fooled by red herrings; there may be a few rules of law mentioned in the case excerpt, but usually only one is *the* rule with which the casebook editor is concerned. The techniques used to locate the issue, described below, may also be utilized to find the rule of law. Generally, your best guide is simply the chapter heading. It is a clue to the point the casebook editor seeks to make and should be kept in mind when reading every case in the respective section.

FACTS: A synopsis of only the essential facts of the case, i.e., those bearing upon or leading up to the issue.

The facts entry should be a short statement of the events and transactions that led one party to initiate legal proceedings against another in the first place. While some cases conveniently state the salient facts at the beginning of the decision, in other instances they will have to be culled from hiding places throughout the text, even from concurring and dissenting opinions. Some of the "facts" will often be in dispute and should be so noted. Conflicting evidence may be briefly pointed up. "Hard" facts must be included. Both must be *relevant* in order to be listed in the facts entry. It is impossible to tell what is relevant until the entire case is read, as the ultimate determination of the rights and liabilities of the parties may turn on something buried deep in the opinion.

Generally, the facts entry should not be longer than three to five *short* sentences.

It is often helpful to identify the role played by a party in a given context. For example, in a construction contract case the identification of a party as the "contractor" or "builder" alleviates the need to tell that that party was the one who was supposed to have built the house.

It is always helpful, and a good general practice, to identify the "plaintiff" and the "defendant." This may seem elementary and uncomplicated, but, especially in view of the creative editing practiced by some casebook editors, it is sometimes a difficult or even impossible task. Bear in mind that the *party presently* seeking something from this court may not be the plaintiff, and that sometimes only the cross-claim of a defendant is treated in the excerpt. Confusing or misaligning the parties can ruin your analysis and understanding of the case.

ISSUE: A statement of the general legal question answered by or illustrated in the case. For clarity, the issue is best put in the form of a question capable of a "yes" or "no" answer. In reality, the issue is simply the Rule of Law put in the form of a question (e.g., "May an offer be accepted by performance?").

The major problem presented in discerning what is *the* issue in the case is that an opinion usually purports to raise and answer several questions. However, except for rare cases, only one such question is really the issue in the case. Collateral issues not necessary to the resolution of the matter in controversy are handled by the court by language known as *"obiter dictum"* or merely *"dictum."* While dicta may be included later in the brief, they have no place under the issue heading.

To find the issue, ask *who wants what* and then go on to ask *why did that party succeed or fail in getting it.* Once this is determined, the "why" should be turned into a question.

The complexity of the issues in the cases will vary, but in all cases a single-sentence question should sum up the issue. *In a few cases,* there will be two, or even more rarely, three issues of equal importance to the resolution of the case. Each should be expressed in a single-sentence question.

Since many issues are resolved by a court in coming to a final disposition of a case, the casebook editor will reproduce the portion of the opinion containing the issue or issues most relevant to the area of law under scrutiny. A noted law professor gave this advice: "Close the book; look at the title on the cover." Chances are, if it is Property, you need not concern yourself with whether, for example, the federal government's treatment of the plaintiff's land really raises a federal question sufficient to support jurisdiction on this ground in federal court.

The same rule applies to chapter headings designating sub-areas within the subjects. They tip you off as to what the text is designed to teach. The cases are arranged in a casebook to show a progression or development of the law, so that the preceding cases may also help.

It is also most important to remember to *read the notes and questions* at the end of a case to determine what the editors wanted you to have gleaned from it.

HOLDING AND DECISION: This section should succinctly explain the rationale of the court in arriving at its decision. In capsulizing the "reasoning" of the court, it should always include an application of the general rule or rules of law to the specific facts of the case. Hidden justifications come to light in this entry; the reasons for the state of the law, the public policies, the biases and prejudices, those considerations that influence the justices' thinking and, ultimately, the outcome of the case. At the end, there should be a short indication of the disposition or procedural resolution of the case (e.g., "Decision of the trial court for Mr. Smith (P) reversed").

The foregoing format is designed to help you "digest" the reams of case material with which you will be faced in your law school career. Once mastered by practice, it will place at your fingertips the information the authors of your casebooks have sought to impart to you in case-by-case illustration and analysis.

B. Be as Economical as Possible in Briefing Cases

Once armed with a format that encourages succinctness, it is as important to be economical with regard to the time spent on the actual reading of the case as it is to be economical in the writing of the brief itself. This does not mean "skimming" a case. Rather, it means reading the case with an "eye" trained to recognize into which "section" of your brief a particular passage or line fits and having a system for quickly and precisely marking the case so that the passages fitting any one particular part of the brief can be easily identified and brought together in a concise and accurate manner when the brief is actually written.

It is of no use to simply repeat everything in the opinion of the court; record only enough information to trigger your recollection of what the court said. Nevertheless, an accurate statement of the "law of the case," i.e., the legal principle applied to the facts, is absolutely essential to class preparation and to learning the law under the case method.

To that end, it is important to develop a "shorthand" that you can use to make margin notations. These notations will tell you at a glance in which section of the brief you will be placing that particular passage or portion of the opinion.

Some students prefer to underline all the salient portions of the opinion (with a pencil or colored underliner marker), making marginal notations as they go along. Others prefer the color-coded method of underlining, utilizing different colors of markers to underline the salient portions of the case, each separate color being used to represent a different section of the brief. For example, blue underlining could be used for passages relating to the rule of law, yellow for those relating to the issue, and green for those relating to the holding and decision, etc. While it has its advocates, the color-coded method can be confusing and time-consuming (all that time spent on changing colored markers). Furthermore, it can interfere with the continuity and concentration many students deem essential to the reading of a case for maximum comprehension. In the end, however, it is a matter of personal preference and style. Just remember, whatever method you use, underlining must be used sparingly or its value is lost.

If you take the marginal notation route, an efficient and easy method is to go along underlining the key portions of the case and placing in the margin alongside them the following "markers" to indicate where a particular passage or line "belongs" in the brief you will write:

N (NATURE OF CASE)
RL (RULE OF LAW)
I (ISSUE)
HL (HOLDING AND DECISION, relates to the RULE OF LAW behind the decision)
HR (HOLDING AND DECISION, gives the RATIONALE or reasoning behind the decision)
HA (HOLDING AND DECISION, APPLIES the general principle(s) of law to the facts of the case to arrive at the decision)

Remember that a particular passage may well contain information necessary to more than one part of your brief, in which case you simply note that in the margin. If you are using the color-coded underlining method instead of margin notation, simply make asterisks or checks in the margin next to the passage in question in the colors that indicate the additional sections of the brief where it might be utilized.

The economy of utilizing "shorthand" in marking cases for briefing can be maintained in the actual brief writing process itself by utilizing "law student shorthand" within the brief. There are many commonly used words and phrases for which abbreviations can be substituted in your briefs (and in your class notes also). You can develop abbreviations that are personal to you and which will save you a lot of time. A reference list of briefing abbreviations can be found on page xii of this book.

C. Use Both the Briefing Process and the Brief as a Learning Tool

Now that you have a format and the tools for briefing cases efficiently, the most important thing is to make the time spent in briefing profitable to you and to make the most advantageous use of the briefs you create. Of course, the briefs are invaluable for classroom reference when you are called upon to explain or analyze a particular case. However, they are also useful in reviewing for exams. A quick glance at the fact summary should bring the case to mind, and a rereading of the rule of law should enable you to go over the underlying legal concept in your mind, how it was applied in that particular case, and how it might apply in other factual settings.

As to the value to be derived from engaging in the briefing process itself, there is an immediate benefit that arises from being forced to sift through the essential facts and reasoning from the court's opinion and to succinctly express them in your own words in your brief. The process ensures that you understand the case and the point that it illustrates, and that means you will be ready to absorb further analysis and information brought forth in class. It also ensures you will have something to say when called upon in class. The briefing process helps develop a mental agility for getting to the *gist* of a case and for identifying, expounding on, and applying the legal concepts and issues found there. The briefing process is the mental process on which you must rely in taking law school examinations; it is also the mental process upon which a lawyer relies in serving his clients and in making his living.

Abbreviations for Briefs

acceptance	acp
affirmed	aff
answer	ans
assumption of risk	a/r
attorney	atty
beyond a reasonable doubt	b/r/d
bona fide purchaser	BFP
breach of contract	br/k
cause of action	c/a
common law	c/l
Constitution	Con
constitutional	con
contract	K
contributory negligence	c/n
cross	x
cross-complaint	x/c
cross-examination	x/ex
cruel and unusual punishment	c/u/p
defendant	D
dismissed	dis
double jeopardy	d/j
due process	d/p
equal protection	e/p
equity	eq
evidence	ev
exclude	exc
exclusionary rule	exc/r
felony	f/n
freedom of speech	f/s
good faith	g/f
habeas corpus	h/c
hearsay	hr
husband	H
in loco parentis	ILP
injunction	inj
inter vivos	I/v
joint tenancy	j/t
judgment	judgt
jurisdiction	jur
last clear chance	LCC
long-arm statute	LAS
majority view	maj
meeting of minds	MOM
minority view	min
Miranda warnings	Mir/w
Miranda rule	Mir/r
negligence	neg
notice	ntc
nuisance	nus
obligation	ob
obscene	obs
offer	O
offeree	OE
offeror	OR
ordinance	ord
pain and suffering	p/s
parol evidence	p/e
plaintiff	P
prima facie	p/f
probable cause	p/c
proximate cause	px/c
real property	r/p
reasonable doubt	r/d
reasonable man	r/m
rebuttable presumption	rb/p
remanded	rem
res ipsa loquitur	RIL
respondeat superior	r/s
Restatement	RS
reversed	rev
Rule Against Perpetuities	RAP
search and seizure	s/s
search warrant	s/w
self-defense	s/d
specific performance	s/p
statute of limitations	S/L
statute of frauds	S/F
statute	S
summary judgment	s/j
tenancy in common	t/c
tenancy at will	t/w
tenant	t
third party	TP
third party beneficiary	TPB
transferred intent	TI
unconscionable	uncon
unconstitutional	unconst
undue influence	u/e
Uniform Commercial Code	UCC
unilateral	uni
vendee	VE
vendor	VR
versus	v
void for vagueness	VFV
weight of the evidence	w/e
weight of authority	w/a
wife	W
with	w/
within	w/i
without prejudice	w/o/p
without	w/o
wrongful death	wr/d

Table of Cases

CHAPTER 1

Introduction

Quick Reference Rules of Law

Katskee v. Blue Cross/Blue Shield of Nebraska

Patient (P) v. Insurer (D)

Neb. Sup. Ct., 245 Neb. 808, 515 N.W.2d 645 (1994).

NATURE OF CASE: Appeal of summary judgment dismissing action for breach of contract.

FACT SUMMARY: Blue Cross/Blue Shield of Nebraska (D) refused to cover a surgery to remove organs from Katskee (P), a patient who was genetically predisposed to cancer.

RULE OF LAW

An ambiguous insurance policy will be construed in favor of the insured.

FACTS: Katskee (P) was referred by her gynecologist to another doctor to consult on her family history of breast and ovarian cancer. Although Katskee (P) did not have cancer at the time, the doctor determined that she was in an extremely high risk category. Katskee (P) filed a claim with Blue Cross/Blue Shield of Nebraska (D) to cover a scheduled hysterectomy and other procedures. Blue Cross (D) declined to pay for the surgery. Katskee's (P) policy provided coverage for treatments that were "medically necessary" to treat an illness. Katskee (P) proceeded with the surgery and then filed suit against Blue Cross (D) for breach of contract. The court granted summary judgment to Blue Cross (D), and Katskee (P) appealed.

ISSUE: Will an ambiguous insurance policy be construed in favor of the insured?

HOLDING AND DECISION: (White, J.) Yes. An ambiguous insurance policy will be construed in favor of the insured. An insurance policy is construed like any other contract. In this case, there is some uncertainty as to what constitutes an illness as mentioned in the policy. According to Katskee's (P) cancer specialist, women from families with a prevalent cancer history have more than a 50 percent chance of developing breast or ovarian cancer. The general population has roughly a 1 percent risk of the same cancers. While her surgery was prophylactic in that it was to prevent a possible future cancer, given the weight of the odds against her, Katskee's (P) genetic condition is properly defined as an illness. Reversed and remanded.

ANALYSIS

As the sensitivity and technology used in medical diagnoses improve, conditions that precede illnesses will be caught with greater frequency. The question for insurers will be how remote a risk will activate coverage. In particular, genetic advances will find an ever-growing list of risk factors for cancers and other diseases.

Quicknotes

SUMMARY JUDGMENT Judgment rendered by a court in response to a motion by one of the parties, claiming that the lack of a question of material fact in respect to an issue warrants disposition of the issue without consideration by the jury.

Berry v. Cardiology Consultants, P.A.

Estate of deceased (P) v. Doctor (D)

Del. Super. Ct., 909 A.2d 611 (2006).

NATURE OF CASE: Motion for a new trial.

FACT SUMMARY: Howard Scott Berry died, ostensibly from side effects associated with a medication prescribed for his heart condition. Following a jury verdict in favor of the doctors and associates, the plaintiffs moved for a new trial, arguing that a chart showing the dosage and regimen for the medication should not have been admitted into evidence, since it was not relevant to the issue of standard of care.

RULE OF LAW

An algorithm is relevant to the issue of standard of care if it provides an analytical path demonstrating that a particular drug was an appropriate medication and a description of an appropriate drug regimen.

FACTS: Howard Scott Berry was a patient of Dr. Andrew Doorey (D), a cardiologist, for twelve years. After several heart attacks and surgeries, Berry experienced atrial fibrillation. He was given Amiodarone under the direction of the surgical staff, and Doorey (D) reviewed the decision. During a post-operative appointment with Doorey (D), Berry was given a prescription for Amiodarone, though it was never filled. Doorey (D) testified that he explained the appropriate dosage and regimen. Approximately two months later, Berry returned to the hospital with pulmonary complaints. Another cardiologist determined that the pulmonary issues may have resulted from use of Amiodarone, as it was a known side effect. Berry died approximately two months later, and the certificate of death says that the immediate cause of death was Acute Pneumonitis and Amiodarone Toxicity. Berry's estate (P) argued that the amount of Amiodarone administered to Berry was more than double that permitted by the standard of care, according to expert testimony and the Cardiac Surgery Service Manual, which contained the algorithm for post-cardiac surgery atrial fibrillation. That algorithm states that the appropriate dosage in such a case is 400 mg for 5-7 days, and then 200 mg per day. The amount given to Berry was greater than that indicated on the algorithm. A jury returned a verdict in favor of the defendants, and the plaintiffs moved for a new trial, arguing that the algorithm should not have been admitted because it was a learned treatise.

ISSUE: Is an algorithm relevant to the issue of standard of care if it provides an analytical path demonstrating that a particular drug was an appropriate medication and a description of an appropriate drug regimen?

HOLDING AND DECISION: (Del Pesco, J.) Yes. An algorithm is relevant to the issue of standard of care if it provides an analytical path demonstrating that a particular drug was an appropriate medication and a description of an appropriate drug regimen? The algorithm—essentially a chart showing the appropriate dosage and regimen for Amiodarone—was not followed by the cardiac surgeon, because the guidelines do not set standards to which he or she is bound. Rather, the algorithm provides guidelines for the rest of the staff to follow in the event the surgeon is unavailable, in order to ensure a prompt response to any problems that arise. Further, the algorithm showed that the drug was the appropriate medication for Mr. Berry's condition. The evidence was admissible, and the jury's verdict in favor of the defendants was not against the weight of the evidence. Motion for new trial is denied.

ANALYSIS

Note that the drug in this case was not referenced in the Physician's Desk Reference as applicable to Berry's case, but that the defendants offered expert testimony that it was used widely by doctors in cases such as Berry's. Governmental guidance regarding the prescription and use of certain drugs is not always available, and it is not uncommon for the U.S. Food and Drug Administration to remain silent on the issue, thus leaving it to scholars and health care professionals to use it as they see fit, though under the agency's watchful eye.

Quicknotes

FOOD AND DRUG ADMINISTRATION A federal agency responsible for establishing safety and quality standards for foods, drugs, and cosmetics.

Newman v. Sathyavaglswaran

Parents (P) v. county coroner (D)

287 F.3d 786 (9th Cir. 2002).

NATURE OF CASE: Action alleging improper government taking without due process.

FACT SUMMARY: Robert Newman and Barbara Obarski (Parents) (P) brought suit pursuant to 42 U.S.C. § 1983 after the Los Angeles County Coroner (Coroner) (D) extracted the corneas of their deceased children without notification or consent of the Parents (P).

RULE OF LAW

The next of kin of the deceased has a constitutionally protected property right in the disposition of the body of the decedent.

FACTS: To help provide the State of California's nonprofit eye banks with a sufficient supply of corneal tissue for transplantation, the legislature adopted California Government Code (CGC) § 27492.47. The code provides, in pertinent part, that the coroner is authorized to "remove and release or authorize the removal and release of corneal eye tissue from a body within the coroner's custody . . . if the coroner has no knowledge of objection to the removal." The section also immunizes the coroner from civil and criminal liability for the removal of such tissue, provided there was no objection to the removal of the tissue. Robert Newman and Barbara Obarski (Parents) (P) each had children who died in 1997, and after their deaths the Los Angeles County Coroner (Coroner) (D) obtained possession of their bodies. The Coroner (D), following the provisions of § 27492.47, removed the corneas from the children without attempting to notify the Parents (P) or obtain their consent. The Parents (P) learned of the Coroner's (D) actions in 1999 and subsequently filed suit under 42 U.S.C. § 1983 alleging an unconstitutional taking of property without due process of law in violation of the Fourteenth Amendment. The district court dismissed and this appeal ensued.

ISSUE: Does the next of kin of the deceased have a constitutionally protected property right in the disposition of the body of the decedent?

HOLDING AND DECISION: [Judge not stated in casebook excerpt.] Yes, the next of kin of the deceased has a constitutionally protected property right in the disposition of the body of the decedent. While there is no question that each individual has a fundamental right to the possession and control of his own person, it is not as clear whether the Due Process Clause extends to the rights of kin in relation to possession and control of a deceased relative's body. A dead body has traditionally been viewed as not being the subject of property rights, and it is clear that California has a significant state interest in obtaining corneas and other tissue for transplantation. However, following traditional common-law principles, this court recognizes that preservation of the dignity of the human body is also firmly rooted in both social and legal traditions. The Uniform Anatomical Gift Act (UAGA), adopted by California in 1968, grants the next of kin the right to transfer body parts for medical purposes and limits such transfers to preclude the sale of body parts. Consent for such transfers is required, and the prohibition of ascribing a positive monetary value to the body does not negate the classification of the body of a deceased as being property. To help increase the supply of certain tissues for transplantation, some states passed "presumed consent" laws, such as CGC § 27491.47 to allow removal of tissue so long as no objection to the removal is known. The "no knowledge of objection" clause implies that informed consent will be obtained and acknowledges the property rights of the deceased's next of kin. Consequently, § 27491.47 is not unconstitutional on its face. The case is reversed so the Coroner's (D) application of his statutory authority in this situation can be fully examined to determine if an unconstitutional taking in violation of due process occurred. Reversed and remanded.

ANALYSIS

Legislative attempts at redistributing the property rights held by a deceased's next of kin, even when there is a compelling state interest to do so, cannot override the fundamental right of due process. While the need for tissue for transplantation meets a shortfall of available tissue each year, our society holds paramount individual liberties and the autonomy of an individual's right to maintain control over his or her body. This right essentially passes on to the next of kin at the time of death, and provides one of only several unique situations where a third party is allowed standing to raise the constitutional right of another.

Quicknotes

DUE PROCESS CLAUSE Clauses found in the Fifth and Fourteenth Amendments to the United States Constitution providing that no person shall be deprived of "life, liberty, or property, without due process of law."

Jacobson v. Massachusetts

Noncompliant citizen (D) v. State (P)

197 U.S. 11 (1905).

NATURE OF CASE: Review of conviction for refusal to be vaccinated.

FACT SUMMARY: A state statute requiring vaccination was alleged to be unconstitutional.

RULE OF LAW
The scope of the state's police power includes the authority to enact reasonable regulations to protect public health and safety.

FACTS: A Massachusetts statute authorized cities to require that all city residents be vaccinated. The city of Cambridge adopted such a regulation.

ISSUE: Does the scope of the state's police power include the authority to enact reasonable regulations to protect public health and safety?

HOLDING AND DECISION: (Harlan, J.) Yes. The scope of the state's police power includes the authority to enact reasonable regulations to protect public health and safety. The liberty secured by the Constitution to every person within its jurisdiction does not import an absolute right in each person to be, at all times and in all circumstances, wholly free from restraint. There are manifold restraints to which every person is necessarily subject for the common good. The means employed by Cambridge to stamp out smallpox have a real and substantial relation to the protection of the public health and the public safety. Nothing clearly appears that would justify this court in holding the statute to be unconstitutional. Affirmed.

ANALYSIS

This case has never been repudiated. The Court suggested that at times there simply is no liberty interest in conduct that may put others at risk. In the early part of the twentieth century, courts were extremely deferential to a state's power to protect the public health.

Quicknotes

LIBERTY INTEREST A right conferred by the Due Process Clauses of the state and federal constitutions.

CHAPTER 2

Quality Control Regulation

Quick Reference Rules of Law

In re Williams

Medical board (P) v. Physician (D)

Ohio Sup. Ct., 60 Ohio St. 3d, 573 N.E.2d 638 (1991).

NATURE OF CASE: Review of medical board finding against a physician.

FACT SUMMARY: Dr. Williams (D) dispensed, with some controversy, controlled substances in weight control programs.

RULE OF LAW
While a medical board need not in every case present expert testimony to support a charge against a physician, the charge must be supported by some reliable, probative, and substantial evidence.

FACTS: Dr. Williams (D) dispensed controlled substances in conjunction with weight control programs. At the time in question, the drugs were legally dispensed. However, Dr. Williams's (D) practices were disfavored by many in the medical community. Dr. Williams (D) was brought before the medical board on charges. The only evidence offered was by an expert for Dr. Williams (D). The expert testified that the activities of Dr. Williams (D) did not fall below the acceptable standard of medical practice. The board found against Dr. Williams (D). He then sought judicial review of the board's decision.

ISSUE: Must a medical board present expert testimony to support a charge against an accused physician?

HOLDING AND DECISION: (Brown, J.) No. While a medical board need not in every case present expert testimony to support a charge against a physician, the charge must be supported by some reliable, probative, and substantial evidence. Medical review boards have broad discretion to resolve evidentiary conflicts. However, where the medical community disagrees as to a particular practice and no law governs the issue, the board may not substitute its own opinions as evidence. The board is not compelled to meet expert with expert; it may evaluate evidence presented in various forms to reach a decision. But in this case, the board heard no contradictory evidence to rebut Dr. Williams's (D) expert. The board may not set aside the requirement for probative evidence simply because it personally disagrees with a medical practice. If its finding in this case were affirmed, it would mean that a doctor would have no access to meaningful review of board decisions. Reversed.

DISSENT: (Wright, J.) The board does not need experts to tell it what constitutes acceptable medical practice.

ANALYSIS

Controversy remains as to whether expert testimony is required to support a charge of violating standards of practice. The problem is compounded by the presence of laypersons on medical boards. Whether they can properly evaluate expert testimony is uncertain, further slowing resolution of this issue.

Quicknotes

DUTY OF CARE A principle of negligence requiring an individual to act in such a manner as to avoid injury to a person to whom he or she owes an obligatory duty.

MALPRACTICE A failure to perform one's professional duties during the course of a client relationship, either intentionally or negligently, or the poor or improper discharge of one's professional obligations.

Hoover v. The Agency for Health Care Administration

Physician (P) v. Administrative agency (D)

Fla. Dist. Ct. App., 676 So. 2d 1380 (1996).

NATURE OF CASE: Appeal of a Board of Medicine decision to revoke a license to practice medicine.

FACT SUMMARY: The Board of Medicine (D) ignored reasonable findings of fact and recommendations made by a hearing officer when deciding to revoke Dr. Hoover's (P) medical license.

RULE OF LAW

An administrative review board must give substantial weight to a hearing officer's findings before supplanting the findings and revoking a license to practice medicine.

FACTS: The Agency for Health Care Administration (D) filed an administrative complaint against Dr. Hoover (P) for excessively prescribing controlled substances. Dr. Hoover (P) denied the charge and requested a hearing. At the hearing, the Agency (D) presented two physicians as experts. The experts had not examined any patient or patient record; the sole basis of their testimony was from pharmacy records. Dr. Hoover (P) testified in great detail about her diagnoses and courses of treatment. The hearing officer recommended that the complaint be dismissed. The Agency (D) excepted to the finding, and the Board of Medicine (D) set aside the hearing officer's findings and penalized Dr. Hoover (P). Dr. Hoover (P) appealed.

ISSUE: Must an administrative review board give substantial weight to a hearing officer's findings before supplanting the findings and revoking a license to practice medicine?

HOLDING AND DECISION: (Jorgenson, J.) Yes. An administrative review board must give substantial weight to a hearing officer's findings before supplanting the findings and revoking a license to practice medicine. So long as an administrative officer bases findings on competent substantial evidence, there are no grounds to set aside the officer's findings. In this case, the hearing officer weighed the detailed and extensive testimony of Dr. Hoover (P) against the opinions of two experts who had not so much as read a single patient file. After examining federal guidelines, subsequent legislation in the state, and all the evidence in the proceeding, the hearing officer made a reasonable recommendation to the Board of Medicine (D), which it rejected. Reversed.

ANALYSIS

The majority of actions before state medical boards concern the prescription of drugs. There are multiple issues surrounding controlled substances. First, there are cases where doctors are prescribing themselves drugs. Second, there is the concern that doctors might deal in drugs by selling prescriptions. Contending against these concerns is the problem of pain management in severely ill patients.

Quicknotes

MALPRACTICE A failure to perform one's professional duties during the course of a client relationship, either intentionally or negligently, or the poor or improper discharge of one's professional obligations.

State Board of Registration for the Healing Arts v. McDonagh

Administrative agency (P) v. Physician (D)

Mo. Sup. Ct., 123 S.W.3d 146 (2003).

NATURE OF CASE: Appeal of an administrative decision.

FACT SUMMARY: The State Board of Registration for the Healing Arts (Board) (P) appealed from the Administrative Hearing Commission's (AHC) rejection of the Board's (P) thirteen-count complaint against Dr. McDonagh's (D) medical license based upon his use of unconventional treatments for atherosclerosis.

RULE OF LAW

The relevant standard of care for disciplining a practitioner's medical license, when based upon allegations of negligence, is that same degree of skill and learning used by members of the profession in similar circumstances.

FACTS: Dr. McDonagh (D), a licensed osteopathic physician and surgeon, employed the use of ethylene diamine tetraacetic acid (EDTA) in the treatment of atherosclerosis and other diseases. The Food and Drug Administration (FDA) licensed EDTA only for the treatment of heavy metal poisoning in what is known as chelation therapy where it binds to the metal and facilitates its removal from the body. However, "off-label" use of medications is not prohibited by the FDA and is common practice among physicians, and the American College for Advancement in Medicine (ACAM) endorsed chelation therapy for treatment of vascular diseases and developed a protocol for its safe administration. Two published controlled studies in the early 1990s, however, indicated that such treatment was ineffective in treating vascular disease and the American Medical Association (AMA) adopted a position statement calling the treatment "an experimental process without proven efficacy." Effective in 2001, the State Board of Registration for the Healing Arts (Board) (P) adopted a rule stating the therapy was of no medical value, but that it would not seek disciplinary action against a physician using the technique, provided that the patients had given the appropriate informed consent. Dr. McDonagh (D) continued the practice during the early 1990s, following ACAM's protocol and securing the informed consent of his patients. Ultimately the Board (P), after receiving inquiries about Dr. McDonagh's (D) treatments, filed a thirteen-count complaint alleging that he endangered his patients with this unconventional therapy. After hearing, the AHC found no evidence to discipline Dr. McDonagh's (D) license. The circuit court affirmed and the Board (P) appealed to the state Supreme Court.

ISSUE: Is the relevant standard of care for disciplining a practitioner's medical license, when based upon allegations of negligence, that same degree of skill and learning used by members of the profession in similar circumstances?

HOLDING AND DECISION: (Stith, J.) Yes. The relevant standard of care for disciplining a practitioner's medical license, when based upon allegations of negligence, is that same degree of skill and learning used by members of the profession in similar circumstances. The parties' arguments concern the sufficiency of the evidence that Dr. McDonagh's (D) use of EDTA chelation therapy constituted "repeated negligence," as the term is statutorily defined in the Missouri Revised Statutes § 334.100.2(5). The Board (P) argues that the appropriate standard of care required the doctor to treat his patients in the manner practiced in the profession in general. Dr. McDonagh (D), and his experts at the hearing, argued that he should be measured against the manner in which physicians employing chelation therapy practice. The statute is clear that the standard to be employed is that same degree of skill and learning used by members of the profession in similar circumstances. The AHC relied on Dr. McDonagh's (D) expert witnesses, who were arguing the incorrect standard of care. Consequently, the decision of the AHC is reversed and the case is remanded for reconsideration while employing the proper standard of care.

CONCURRENCE: (Wolff, J.) It should be noted that no evidence established that the off-label chelation therapy with EDTA was dangerous or harmful to the doctor's patients. There was no evidence that Dr. McDonagh (D) was negligent in the manner in which he employed this therapy or that he failed to obtain informed consent from his patients. More pertinent, perhaps, is when the Board (P) finally adopted its rule declaring this therapy to have no value, it also declared that it would not seek disciplinary action against a physician prescribing it. The Board (P) should dismiss its action.

ANALYSIS

The practice of unconventional or experimental therapies provides a challenge for state licensing boards. The state board is charged with the duty of policing physicians and protecting the public, but the medical profession has the dual responsibility to push the envelope with new or alternative treatments in the hopes of discovering new cures. It would appear that when evaluating whether a physician was negligent with the prescription of alternative treatments that the standard of care remains the time-tested maxim of employing that "same degree of skill and learning used

Continued on next page.

by members of the profession in like or similar circumstances." However, there does appear to be a higher requirement in terms of obtaining informed consent from the patients before proceeding with such controversial treatment regimes. The Board (P) in this case is essentially given a second opportunity to prove their case applying the appropriate standard of care, but the concurrence implies that if the Board (P) proceeds in its action that a second round of appellate review may be unfavorable to their position.

Quicknotes

DUTY OF CARE A principle of negligence requiring an individual to act in such a manner as to avoid injury to a person to whom he or she owes an obligatory duty.

NEGLIGENCE Conduct falling below the standard of care that a reasonable person would demonstrate under similar conditions.

State Board of Nursing and State Board of Healing Arts v. Ruebke

Administrative agencies (P) v. Midwife (D)

Kan. Sup. Ct., 259 Kan. 599, 913 P.2d 142 (1996).

NATURE OF CASE: Appeal of a trial court denial of a temporary injunction.

FACT SUMMARY: Various nursing and medical groups (P) sought an injunction against Ruebke (D) for the practice of lay midwifery.

RULE OF LAW

The practice of lay midwifery does not constitute the practice of nursing and medicine for the purpose of statutory professional regulation.

FACTS: Ruebke (D) worked as a lay midwife, comprehensively assisting pregnant women with prenatal care, delivery, and post-partum care. She followed a thorough set of standards to ensure safe practice, and she regularly consulted with physicians. The State Board of Healing Arts (P) and the State Board of Nursing (P) sought a temporary injunction to stop Ruebke's (D) alleged practice of medicine and nursing. A gynecologist testified that many of Ruebke's (D) assessments were obstetrical diagnoses, and a nurse testified that Ruebke (D) practiced nursing functions during deliveries. The trial court found that the two acts cited by the Boards (P) were unconstitutionally vague and that, even if the acts were constitutional, Ruebke's (D) acts fell within exceptions to them. The trial court denied the injunction. The State Board of Nursing (P) and the State Board of Healing Arts (P) appealed the decision.

ISSUE: Does the practice of lay midwifery constitute the practice of nursing and medicine for the purpose of statutory professional regulation?

HOLDING AND DECISION: (Larson, J.) No. The practice of lay midwifery does not constitute the practice of nursing and medicine for the purpose of statutory professional regulation. Where a statute can be construed as constitutional without subverting legislative intent, it is always preferable to do so. In this case, it is not clear whether the state regulations are intended to cover midwifery. The healing arts are defined in the act in terms of pathologies and abnormal conditions. Pregnancy and delivery, if without major complications, are merely a continuation of normal human conditions. It appears consistent with legislative intent to conclude that midwifery was not precluded by the regulation of the healing arts. The acts are not unconstitutionally vague by this interpretation, but they do not apply to restrict lay midwifery. Affirmed in part and reversed in part.

ANALYSIS

States disagree widely as to how midwifery should be treated. Nursing boards have attempted to carve out the field of midwifery from medicine by certifying nurses as nurse-midwives. Various courts have separated the act of assisting at a birth with the act of delivering a child, a rather tenuous distinction. However, with the trend in medicine toward low-cost alternatives, midwives will likely gain increased favor for low-risk births.

Quicknotes

INJUNCTION A court order requiring a person to do or prohibiting that person from doing a specific act.

MALPRACTICE A failure to perform one's professional duties during the course of a client relationship, either intentionally or negligently, or the poor or improper discharge of one's professional obligations.

Sermchief v. Gonzales

Nurses (P) v. Administrative agency (D)

Mo. Sup. Ct., 660 S.W.2d 683 (1983).

NATURE OF CASE: Appeal from order denying declaratory and injunctive relief.

FACT SUMMARY: Several nurses (P) contended that their employer's practice of permitting them to perform medical acts such as taking histories and conducting diagnostic procedures did not constitute unauthorized practice of medicine.

RULE OF LAW

A nurse may perform certain medical procedures without having engaged in unauthorized practice of medicine.

FACTS: The Missouri Action Agency provided medical services at several locations, largely to low-income individuals. Protocols of the Agency allowed nurses to perform procedures such as taking histories, conducting examinations, performing lab tests, dispensing certain medications, and giving family planning information. The Missouri State Board of Registration for the Healing Arts (D) threatened to cite the nurses for unauthorized practice of medicine and the physicians at the clinic for aiding and abetting. Several of these nurses and doctors filed an action seeking a declaratory judgment that they were not in violation of the law and an injunction against the Board (D) prohibiting it from prosecuting a case against them. The trial court, holding that the clinic allowed unauthorized medical practice, denied relief. An appeal was taken.

ISSUE: May a nurse perform certain medical procedures without having engaged in unauthorized practice of medicine?

HOLDING AND DECISION: (Welliver, J.) Yes. A nurse may perform certain medical procedures without having engaged in unauthorized practice of medicine. Section 334.010 of Missouri's revised statutes prohibits unauthorized medical practice. Section 334.155 exempts nurses lawfully performing their professional duties. Where nursing ends and medical practice begins has always been unclear. However, in 1975 the Missouri legislature revised § 335.016.8, which defines the scope of legitimate nursing duties. It is uniformly agreed that these revisions broadened the scope of what a nurse can do. It removed the requirement that all nursing be done under a physician's direct supervision. Also, the statute uses the language "including, but not limited to" in giving examples of what a nurse can do. In light of this legal framework, it is clear that what the nurses (P) did in their clinic fell well within tolerable limits of nursing. Reversed and remanded.

ANALYSIS

The court's decision here was rather narrow. It did not attempt to define the outer scope of what a nurse can do; it merely held that the tasks performed by the nurses in this case were acceptable. The court felt that trying to make rigid rules as to exactly what constitutes the practice of medicine was inappropriate in the context of this case.

Quicknotes

MALPRACTICE A failure to perform one's professional duties during the course of a client relationship, either intentionally or negligently, or the poor or improper discharge of one's professional obligations.

CHAPTER 3

Quality Control Regulation of Health Care Institutions

Quick Reference Rules of Law

Mauceri v. Chassin

Referral provider (P) v. Health department (D)

N.Y. Sup. Ct., 156 Misc. 2d 802, 594 N.Y.S.2d 605 (1993).

NATURE OF CASE: Suit seeking to overturn a Department of Health finding of unlicensed health care referrals in violation of the law.

FACT SUMMARY: Mauceri (P) operated a business from her home that consisted of providing patients with referrals to home health aides.

RULE OF LAW
The provision of names of home health aides constitutes the arranging of home health care services as defined by statute.

FACTS: Mauceri (P) ran a business from her home that consisted of providing patients and their families with the names of home health aides. She did not investigate the qualifications of the aides, create any care plans, or maintain medical records. Subsequent to a complaint that Mauceri (P) was arranging medical services without a license, the Department of Health (D) ruled that Mauceri (P) would have to receive a license pursuant to Article 36 of the Public Health Law. Mauceri (P) filed suit, contending that her services fell outside the statutory definition.

ISSUE: Does the provision of names of home health aides constitute the arranging of home health care services as defined by statute?

HOLDING AND DECISION: [Judge not stated in casebook excerpt.] Yes. The provision of names of home health aides constitutes the arranging of home health care services as defined by statute. The construction given to a statute by the agency charged with implementing it should be upheld if not irrational. In this case, the Department of Health (D) has determined that the statute, which requires licensing to arrange "home health aide services," applies directly to Mauceri (P). The fact that Mauceri (P) does not herself provide or supervise the services does not mean that she is not arranging them for clients. The Department's (D) interpretation is completely rational, and, as a result, Mauceri (P) will be enjoined from operating her service until such time as she is licensed.

ANALYSIS

One argument for requiring licensing for agencies arranging home health care is that it provides a method to oversee the quality of individuals referred by the agencies. However, in this case, there was no evidence to suggest that Mauceri (P) made any warranty or representation about the quality of the health aides she listed for referral. Thus, the counter-argument to oversight of quality is that consumers can examine the credentials of any individual that is referred to them by an agency.

Quicknotes

PUBLIC HEALTH LAW Home care services agencies must comply with statutory licensing requirements.

In re the Estate of Michael Patrick Smith v. Heckler

Nursing home residents (P) v. Administrative agency (D)

747 F.2d 583 (10th Cir. 1984).

NATURE OF CASE: Appeal from denial of injunction to compel compliance with federal statute.

FACT SUMMARY: A class of nursing home patients (P) challenged the federal health department (D) practice of enforcing compliance with the Medicaid Act by focusing on homes' facilities rather than patient care.

RULE OF LAW

The federal health department must enforce compliance with the Medicaid Act by focusing on patient care.

FACTS: A class action suit was filed on behalf of nursing home patients (P) residing in Colorado against Heckler (D), the Secretary of Health and Human Services. In essence, the suit alleged that Heckler (D) was under a duty to enforce compliance with the federal Medicaid Act by considering the quality of care actually provided to patients (P) rather than by looking only to the facilities offered by such homes. The district court concluded that Heckler (D) was acting consistently with the statute in effecting a "facility-oriented" compliance review, and dismissed. An appeal was taken.

ISSUE: Must the federal health department enforce compliance with the Medicaid Act by focusing on patient care?

HOLDING AND DECISION: (McKay, J.) Yes. The Department of Health and Human Services (D) must enforce compliance with the Medicaid Act by focusing on patient care. Nothing in the Medicaid Act indicates that Congress intended the physical facilities to be the end product of the Act. Rather, the Act repeatedly focuses on the care to be provided. For example, the Act provides that health standards are to be developed and maintained and also provides that states must inform the Secretary of what methods they use to ensure quality care. In light of this, the Secretary must look to patient care actually rendered. The current review system, as implemented by Heckler (D), which looks to facilities only and, therefore, only to the potential of care, is insufficient. Reversed and remanded.

ANALYSIS

The Medicaid Act is found at 42 U.S.C. § 1396. The purpose of the Act is to assist states in providing quality care to the disabled. To receive funding, a state must submit to the Department of Health and Human Services a plan that meets the Act's requirements. These requirements were at issue here.

Quicknotes

MEDICAID ACT Makes federal funding contingent on a state's plan for medical assistance to aged, blind, or disabled individuals.

Fairfax Nursing Home, Inc. v. U.S. Dep't of Health & Human Services

Skilled nursing facility (D) v. Government agency (P)

300 F.3d 835 (7th Cir. 2002), *cert. denied*, 537 U.S. 1111 (2003).

NATURE OF CASE: Appeal of an administrative decision assessing monetary penalties.

FACT SUMMARY: Fairfax Nursing Home, Inc. (D) appeals the decision by the Center for Medicare and Medicaid Services (CMS) assessing a civil monetary penalty (CMP) for failure to comply with Medicare regulations governing the care of respirator-dependent residents.

RULE OF LAW

The correct legal standard for imposition of the highest civil monetary penalty for violating Medicare regulations is a provider's noncompliance with one or more requirements for participation in the program that "has caused, or is likely to cause, serious injury, harm, impairment or death to a resident."

FACTS: Fairfax Nursing Home, Inc. (D) is a skilled nursing facility (SNF) participating in the Medicaid and Medicare programs. Regulation of such SNFs includes unannounced surveys at least every 15 months. Any violations that are discovered can result in the imposition of CMPs. Over a 105-day period beginning on December 20, 1996, through April 3, 1997, at least five violations were documented concerning Fairfax's (D) provision of respiratory care to residents in the SNF who were ventilator-dependent. In three of these incidents, negligent and incomplete care and follow-up resulted in the death of the resident, and in the other two, the resident's health and safety were placed in jeopardy. All of the incidents were violations of 42 C.F.R. § 483.25(k) pertaining to the care of ventilator-dependent residents. After an administrative hearing, a CMP of $3,050 per day for each of the 105 days was imposed. Fairfax (D) brought this appeal.

ISSUE: Is the correct legal standard for imposition of the highest civil monetary penalty for violating Medicare regulations a provider's noncompliance with one or more requirements for participation in the program that "has caused, or is likely to cause, serious injury, harm, impairment or death to a resident?"

HOLDING AND DECISION: (Ripple, J.) Yes. The correct legal standard for imposition of the highest civil monetary penalty (CMP) for violating Medicare regulations is a provider's noncompliance with one or more requirements for participation in the program that "has caused, or is likely to cause, serious injury, harm, impairment or death to a resident." By contrast, there is a lower standard where the CMP ranges between $50 and $3,000 per day, and Fairfax (D) argues that the Administrative Law Judge (ALJ) incorrectly imposed the higher CMP while applying this lower standard. The lower standard for the lower penalties involves "deficiencies that do not constitute immediate jeopardy, but either caused actual harm or have the potential for causing more than minimal harm." Fairfax (D) points to the ALJ's use of the word "potential" in its findings to substantiate its claim. However, the findings of the ALJ are replete with explicit and lengthy descriptions of how Fairfax's (D) actions had caused, or were likely to cause, serious injury, harm, impairment or death to a resident. In fact, three residents died and the other two likely faced serious harm as a result of Fairfax's (D) negligent practices. There was substantial evidence to support the findings of the ALJ and the decision is affirmed.

ANALYSIS

While there is controversy surrounding the effectiveness of "unannounced" surveys, they are the primary regulatory enforcement tool employed to monitor health care providers who are participating in government Medicaid and Medicare programs. Criticisms include that the timing of the inspections is too predictable, allowing deficiencies to be covered up during the inspection period. The fact that these inspections are usually delegated by the Department of Health and Human Services to local Departments of Health due to relative limitations in resources also remains a point of contention. The standards for imposing the CMPs, themselves, appear to be subjective and open to debate, explaining Fairfax's (D) willingness to pursue an appeal, despite the fact that three of its residents had actually died in connection with its violations. It appears to be a discretionary call for the ALJ as to what separates "minimal harm actually caused" from "the likeliness to cause serious harm." In this case, the argument failed for Fairfax (D).

Quicknotes

MEDICAID ACT Makes federal funding contingent on a state's plan for medical assistance to aged, blind, or disabled individuals.

CHAPTER 4

The Professional-Patient Relationship

Quick Reference Rules of Law

Esquivel v. Watters

Patient (P) v. Health care provider (D)

Kan. Ct. App., 154 P.3d 1184 (2007).

NATURE OF CASE: Appeal of summary judgment in favor of the health care provider.

FACT SUMMARY: Michelle Esquivel (P) went to South Central Kansas Regional Medical Center (SCKRMC) (D) for a free sonogram, which was only to determine the unborn baby's sex. An abnormality was discovered, but not disclosed to Esquivel (P) by SCKRMC (D). She sued SCKRMC (D) when her baby died after birth, and the court granted summary judgment for SCKRMC (D). Esquivel (P) appealed.

RULE OF LAW

A patient-health care provider relationship does not exist where the provider does not undertake to advise the patient, or treat the patient, regarding any medical condition, disease, or illness.

FACTS: Michelle Esquivel (P) went to South Central Kansas Regional Medical Center (SCKRMC) (D) for a free sonogram. She signed a consent form stating that the purpose for the procedure was only to determine the sex of the unborn baby, and that it was not to determine fetal abnormalities. The form also contained a release clause for any cause of action that could arise from the procedure. The technician discovered that Esquivel's (P) baby's bowel was outside the body, a condition known as gastroschisis. He did not inform Esquivel (P) of the problem, because he is not a doctor and was not qualified to make a diagnosis. He took the sonogram pictures and sent them to a radiologist, but the radiologist refused to look at them because the sonogram was only for gender determination and not for diagnosis. The technician also reported the irregularity to Esquivel's (P) obstetrician, but did not send the sonogram pictures or a written report to him. The obstetrician told his nurse to call Esquivel (P), who tried for ten days, eventually leaving a message with a man the nurse believed to be Esquivel's (P) husband. Esquivel (P) missed her next prenatal appointment, and by the time of her next appointment, five weeks later, the obstetrician had forgotten about the problem. She had another appointment approximately one month later, and the doctor again forgot. Esquivel's (P) baby was born by emergency caesarean section after Esquivel (P) became ill, and the baby's condition was terminal. After he died, the Esquivels (P) sued SCKRMC (D). The district court granted summary judgment in favor of SCKRMC (D) because the clinic did not owe the Esquivels (P) a duty upon which they based their claims, and their claims were barred by the release signed by Esquivel (P) before the sonogram. The Esquivels (P) appealed.

ISSUE: Does a patient-health care provider relationship exist where the provider does not undertake to advise the patient, or treat the patient, regarding any medical condition, disease, or illness?

HOLDING AND DECISION: [Judge not stated in casebook excerpt.] No. A patient-health care provider relationship does not exist where the provider does not undertake to advise the patient, or treat the patient, regarding any medical condition, disease, or illness. In this case, SCKRMC (D) only undertook to do a sonogram for the specific purpose of determining her unborn baby's sex. The provider's duty was therefore limited to performing the sonogram in a non-negligent manner, and no negligence in the performance of the sonogram is alleged.

ANALYSIS

Note in the court's discussion of the issue that courts disagree about whether there is a duty to notify even in the absence of a physician-patient relationship, even though a physician-patient relationship is usually a prerequisite to a malpractice suit against a doctor. But note also that once a physician-patient relationship is established, the higher duty of care is always applied.

Quicknotes

SUMMARY JUDGMENT Judgment rendered by a court in response to a motion made by one of the parties, claiming that the lack of a question of material fact in respect to an issue warrants disposition of the issue without consideration by the jury.

Millard v. Corrado

Patient (P) v. Physician (D)

Mo. Ct. App., 14 S.W.3d 42 (1999).

NATURE OF CASE: Appeal of summary judgment in favor of physician in negligence action.

FACT SUMMARY: A surgeon's delay in transferring a car crash victim to a facility equipped to handle trauma surgery resulted in permanent harm to the victim. She sued.

RULE OF LAW

The absence of a physician-patient relationship does not preclude an action based on negligence where the physician's allegedly negligent acts or omissions do not involve a matter of medical science, and public policy favors the recognition of a duty or the harm is particularly foreseeable.

FACTS: While on call as a general surgeon at Audrain Medical Center, Joseph Corrado (D) asked an orthopedist who did not have surgical privileges at the hospital to cover his responsibilities while he attended a meeting, but did not notify the emergency department. That day, Marjorie Millard (P) was brought to AMC, which held itself out as providing a 24-hour emergency room care with a physician on duty and a general surgeon on call. Corrado (D) was paged twice. Thirty-eight minutes after the first page, he telephoned. After a brief discussion with another physician, Corrado (D) agreed Millard (P) should be transferred. Nearly two hours later—and 150 minutes after Corrado's (D) initial page—emergency surgery on Millard (P) began at the University of Missouri Medical Center. Millard (P) suffered the loss of a kidney as well as her gall bladder, colon, and part of her small intestine. The trial court granted summary judgment in favor of Corrado (D), finding that (1) Millard (P) failed to state a general negligence claim against Corrado (D) and (2) there was insufficient evidence of a physician-patient relationship between Millard (P) and Corrado (D).

ISSUE: Does the absence of a physician-patient relationship preclude an action based on negligence where the physician's allegedly negligent acts or omissions do not involve a matter of medical science, and public policy favors the recognition of a duty or the harm is particularly foreseeable?

HOLDING AND DECISION: [Judge not stated in casebook excerpt.] No. The absence of a physician-patient relationship does not preclude an action based on negligence where the physician's allegedly negligent acts or omissions do not involve a matter of medical science, and public policy favors the recognition of a duty or the harm is particularly foreseeable. The existence of a duty is determined by applying a six-factor test outlined in *Hoover's Dairy Inc. v. Mid-America Dairymen Inc.*, 700 S.W.2d 426 (Mo. 1985). The factors include (1) whether there is a social consensus about the existence of a duty, (2) the foreseeability of harm, (3) the moral blame of harmful conduct, (4) deterrence considerations, (5) the cost of the loss, (6) and the economic burden upon the actor. A social consensus on the importance of life-saving medical care is shown by a state regulation that on-call physicians arrive at the hospital within 30 minutes of an emergency-room page, and it was foreseeable that the lack of timely care would endanger patients. Had Corrado (D) notified the hospital of his unavailability, Millard's (P) ambulance may have been rerouted rather than arriving at AMC, placing her at a hospital able to offer emergency surgery much sooner. In addition, a reasonable jury could find that Corrado's (D) telephone discussion about Millard's (P) transfer created a physician-patient relationship, a prerequisite for a medical negligence claim. Some courts have recognized physician-patient relationships in the absence of personal contact in circumstances similar to this.

CONCURRENCE: (Crahan, J.) The plaintiffs failed to allege in their complaint that the transfer itself was negligent. All damages allegedly arose from Corrado's (D) general negligence—failure to tell the hospital he would be unavailable to fulfill his call duty, which resulted in a delay in Millard's (P) medical care.

ANALYSIS

This case stands for the rule that Missouri physicians "on call" to hospital emergency departments owe potential patients the legal duty to provide reasonable notice when unavailable, and may be sued for the breach of that duty. But it also raises the question whether a telephone discussion between two doctors about an emergency room intake created a physician-patient relationship—essentially implying that the physician-patient relationship can arise without any direct interaction between physician and patient.

Quicknotes

NEGLIGENCE Conduct falling below the standard of care that a reasonable person would demonstrate under similar conditions.

SUMMARY JUDGMENT Judgment rendered by a court in response to a motion made by one of the parties, claiming that the lack of a question of material fact in respect to an issue warrants disposition of the issue without consideration by the jury.

Mills v. Pate

Patient (P) v. Doctor (D)

Tex. Ct., App., 225 S.W.3d 277 (2006).

NATURE OF CASE: Appeal of no-evidence summary judgment.

FACT SUMMARY: A cosmetic surgeon made representations about the results a patient would enjoy if she agreed to surgery, and the results were not as represented. The patient sued under a theory of breach of express warranty.

RULE OF LAW

Where a physician promises particular surgical results, he or she may be held liable for breach of that express warranty if the breach of warranty claim is not based on the physician's breach of the accepted standard of medical care.

FACTS: Ms. Mills (P) told Dr. Pate (D), a physician able to perform liposuction, that she wanted to remove the fat bulges she had on her abdomen, hips, and thighs. He specified to her that liposuction would achieve the results she sought. She experienced pain following the surgery and was dissatisfied with the results, and she retained a plastic surgeon to fix problems caused by the liposuction and a follow-up surgery done by Pate (D). After her successful surgery with another surgeon, Mills (P) sued Pate (D), alleging among other things that he made representations to her about the quality or characteristics of his services, specifically (1) that she was a suitable candidate for surgery, and (2) that after liposuction, she would look beautiful and that she would have smooth skin without ripples, bulges, or bags. She claimed he breached the warranty because the services he provided did not conform to his representations. Pate (D) moved to dismiss her claim, arguing that her breach of warranty claim was an attempt to recast her negligence claims as a breach of contract claim, and that there was no evidence to support her claims.

ISSUE: Where a physician promises particular surgical results, may he or she be held liable for breach of that express warranty if the breach of warranty claim is not based on the physician's breach of the accepted standard of medical care?

HOLDING AND DECISION: [Judge not stated in casebook excerpt.] Yes. Where a physician promises particular surgical results, he or she may be held liable for breach of that express warranty if the breach of warranty claim is not based on the physician's breach of the accepted standard of medical care. Mills (P) presented evidence to support her common-law claim for breach of express warranty. Pate's (D) remarks, the promised results, and injuries she suffered raised genuine issues of material fact as to each challenged element of her breach of express warranty claim. Pate's (D) representations about the quality or characteristics of the services were related to their patient-client relationship, but were separable from her negligence claims and do not require a determination as to whether Pate (D) failed to meet the accepted standard of medical care for cosmetic surgery. Therefore, Mills's (P) breach of warranty claim is not an improper attempt to recast her informed consent claim. There is some evidence that Pate's (D) particular representations were actionable as an express warranty claim, in that his representations did not conform to the character and quality of the services promised, they formed the basis of the parties' first bargain for the first surgery, and injury resulted. The trial court erred in granting a no-evidence summary judgment as to Mills's (P) breach of express warranty claim. Reversed and remanded.

ANALYSIS

When analyzing a fact pattern for possible causes of action in cases such as this, be sure to consider breach of warranty claims, but remember to think of the issues separately: quality of care versus quality of the results as promised. A physician who botches an operation can be liable under both theories, but they must be pleaded separately, and will involve distinct fact patterns.

Quicknotes

BREACH OF EXPRESS WARRANTY The breach of an express promise made by one party to a contract on which the other party may rely, relieving that party from the obligation of determining whether the fact is true and indemnifying the other party from liability if that fact is shown to be false.

NEGLIGENCE Conduct falling below the standard of care that a reasonable person would demonstrate under similar conditions.

SUMMARY JUDGMENT Judgment rendered by a court in response to a motion made by one of the parties, claiming that the lack of a question of material fact in respect to an issue warrants disposition of the issue without consideration by the jury.

Tunkl v. Regents of Univ. of California

Decedent's widow (P) v. Hospital owners (D)

Cal. Sup. Ct., 60 Cal. 2d 92, 383 P.2d 441 (1963).

NATURE OF CASE: Appeal of denial of damages for malpractice.

FACT SUMMARY: Prior to admission to a nonprofit hospital, Tunkl's (P) decedent signed a release waiving any malpractice action.

RULE OF LAW

A release waiving any malpractice liability of a nonprofit hospital is unenforceable.

FACTS: Tunkl's (P) decedent was admitted to the UCLA Medical Center, a nonprofit and largely research-based medical facility, as part of a research project. Prior to admission, he signed a liability waiver. While in the hospital, he was allegedly injured due to physician malpractice. The decedent brought an action for personal injury, into which Tunkl (P) substituted as administratrix following the decedent's demise. A jury held the release valid and returned a defense verdict. The court of appeal affirmed, and the California Supreme Court granted review.

ISSUE: Is a release waiving malpractice liability of a nonprofit hospital enforceable?

HOLDING AND DECISION: (Tobriner, J.) No. A release waiving malpractice liability of a nonprofit hospital is unenforceable. Under Civil Code § 1668, a contract purporting to exculpate a party from his own negligence will not stand if it involves "the public interest." A contract will involve such interest if the party seeking exculpations engaged in performing a service of great public importance, which is often a practical necessity for some. A contract for hospital services certainly falls within this definition. Here, however, it is argued that the section should not be applied to a nonprofit charitable hospital. However, this court has already abolished charitable immunity; to the extent a charity is negligent, it may be liable. Since the basis for the jury verdict was the unenforceable contract, the matter must be retried. Reversed.

ANALYSIS

Generally speaking, courts have been quite hostile to attempts by health care providers to limit their malpractice liability. General releases are almost never honored and arbitration provisions have only been partially successful. Whatever liability limitations exist do so by virtue of legislative action.

Quicknotes

CAL. CIVIL CODE § 1668 Provides that all contracts which have for their object to exempt anyone for his own fraud, willful injury to another, or violation of law, are against the policy of the state.

Shorter v. Drury

Decedent's widower (P) v. Physician (D)

Wash. Sup. Ct., 103 Wash. 2d 645, 695 P.2d 116 (1985).

NATURE OF CASE: Review of award of damages for malpractice/wrongful death.

FACT SUMMARY: Prior to a surgical procedure, Shorter's (P) decedent, being religiously opposed to blood transfusions, signed a document releasing medical providers from liability arising from injuries resulting therefrom.

RULE OF LAW

When a patient refuses advised medical treatment, a document releasing medical providers from liability resulting from such refusal is valid.

FACTS: Shorter's (P) decedent carried a fetus that had died but not miscarried. The fetus had to be surgically removed. Shorter's (P) decedent, a Jehovah's Witness, was opposed to blood transfusions on religious grounds and made it clear she did not want a transfusion. She signed a standard refusal to permit a transfusion, which contained a clause releasing the providers of responsibility for consequences thereof. During the procedure, the decedent began to bleed internally. She continued to refuse a transfusion, and she bled to death. Shorter (P) sued for malpractice. The jury held Drury (D), the surgeon, negligent. Finding 75% of the damages to be the result of the decedent's refusal of a transfusion, the jury awarded a net amount of $103,000, 25% of the gross verdict of $412,000. Shorter (P) appealed.

ISSUE: When a patient refuses advised medical treatment, will a document releasing medical providers from liability resulting from such refusal be valid?

HOLDING AND DECISION: (Dolliver, J.) Yes. When a patient refuses advised medical treatment, a document releasing medical providers from liability resulting from such refusal is valid. A release of liability from negligence in a matter involving the public interest is unenforceable. The provision of medical services is such a matter. However, this is not the end of the analysis. A release of liability pursuant to a refusal to accept a transfusion is not an attempt to release a medical provider from the effects of his negligence. It is merely an insistence that the party refusing the transfusion bear the consequences of his own conscious decision. To hold otherwise would have the likely effect of medical providers refusing to treat such a patient at all, which is not a result consistent with the policy goal of encouraging access to medical treatment. For these reasons, the jury's 75% discount of Shorter's (P) award was valid. Affirmed.

ANALYSIS

A variety of religious denominations refuse some or all medical treatment. What to do in such situations has long been a thorny issue in health law, especially when minors are involved. It is one thing for a competent adult to refuse treatment; it is another for a parent to deny treatment to a child. These situations have implications going beyond health law, spilling over into constitutional and criminal law.

Quicknotes

MALPRACTICE A failure to perform one's professional duties during the course of a client relationship, either intentionally or negligently, or the poor or improper discharge of one's professional obligations.

WRONGFUL DEATH An action brought by the beneficiaries of a deceased person, claiming that the deceased's death was the result of wrongful conduct by the defendant.

Canterbury v. Spence

Patient (P) v. Physician (D)

464 F.2d 772 (D.C. Cir. 1972).

NATURE OF CASE: Appeal from directed verdict.

FACT SUMMARY: Canterbury (P) contended that, prior to spinal surgery, surgeon Spence (D) did not disclose the possible consequence of paralysis, which he subsequently developed.

RULE OF LAW

Prior to a medical procedure, a physician must disclose to a patient all risks which a reasonable person would consider significant in deciding whether to undergo the procedure.

FACTS: Canterbury (P), then a minor, presented himself to orthopedist Spence (D), complaining of upper back pain. Following a diagnostic procedure, Spence (D) concluded that Canterbury (P) had a ruptured intervertebral disc, and that a laminectomy was indicated. Canterbury (P) underwent the procedure, which at first seemed successful. However, while still hospitalized, he fell out of bed, and began experiencing paralysis and incontinence thereafter, conditions which persisted. Canterbury (P) brought a malpractice action against Spence (D). One contention was that he had not been advised of the risk of paralysis. At the close of his case, the district court granted Spence's (D) motion for directed verdict as Canterbury (P) had produced no expert testimony that advice of such risk had been required. Canterbury (P) appealed.

ISSUE: Prior to a medical procedure, must a physician disclose to a patient all risks which a reasonable person would consider significant in deciding whether to undergo the procedure?

HOLDING AND DECISION: (Robinson, J.) Yes. Prior to a medical procedure, a physician must disclose to a patient all risks which a reasonable person would consider significant in deciding whether to undergo the procedure. It is universally accepted that, prior to a surgical procedure, a patient must consent thereto. It is further accepted that such consent must be informed, as the average lay patient lacks the expertise to make unassisted judgments regarding the propriety of any particular medical treatment. The risks of a particular procedure are clearly an element that must be disclosed. However, the question arises as to what risks must be disclosed. Many courts have held, and the district court below agreed, that the key to this question is what is standard in the medical community for the type of procedure involved. This court does not agree. First, as a practical matter, no particular custom will exist on a profession-wide basis. Further, such a rule would delegate to the medical community a decision which should be made by individual physicians. Rather, the standard should be one of reasonableness: would a reasonable patient consider a particular risk significant in evaluating whether or not to undergo a procedure? This "reasonable patient" standard is consistent with the general thrust of tort and malpractice law and does not require expert testimony. Therefore, Canterbury's (P) failure to introduce such testimony was not fatal to his case. A jury should determine whether the disclosure was sufficient based on the facts. Reversed and remanded.

ANALYSIS

The jurisdictions are split on the standard to be applied in this area. A majority still adopt the medical community standard; the type of standard elucidated here remains the minority view. Consequently, in most states, expert testimony will be required in a case dealing with a lack of informed consent.

Quicknotes

NONSUIT Judgment against a party who fails to make out a case.

Johnson v. Kokemoor

Patient (P) v. Physician (D)

Wis. Sup. Ct., 199 Wis. 2d 615, 545 N.W.2d 495 (1996).

NATURE OF CASE: Appeal from the court of appeals reversal of a jury verdict.

FACT SUMMARY: Johnson (P) brought suit against Kokemoor (D), a neurosurgeon, alleging her consent to surgery was fraudulently induced by Kokemoor's (D) misrepresentations.

RULE OF LAW

It is not an abuse of discretion for a trial court to admit physician-specific evidence in a case involving the doctrine of informed consent.

FACTS: Johnson (P) underwent a CT scan to determine the cause of her severe headaches. She was diagnosed with having a large basilar artery bifurcation aneurysm, a brain aneurysm located in the posterior circulation of Johnson's (P) brain. [An aneurysm occurs when there is a weakness in the wall of a blood vessel allowing a bubble-like protrusion to form. Complications from aneurysms can occur as a result of the aneurysm rupturing or when blood clots form within the aneurysm and are released into the general circulation.] Kokemoor (D), the neurosurgeon, consulted on Johnson's (P) condition and recommended immediate surgery to "clip" or remove the aneurysm to prevent any complications from developing. Kokemoor (D) while obtaining Johnson's (P) consent for the surgery allegedly misrepresented the level of urgency for the surgery, misrepresented his level of experience with performing this particular surgery, and misrepresented the level of risks and complications that could occur as a result of having the surgery. Johnson (P), who had no neurological impairments prior to the surgery, suffered a cerebral hemorrhage after the operation. As a result, she became an "incomplete" quadriplegic. Johnson (P) was unable to walk, lost all bowel and bladder control, had only limited use of her upper extremities, and suffered impairment to her vision and speech. At trial, Johnson (P) introduced evidence to establish that Kokemoor (D), while having experience with clipping aneurysms in the anterior circulation of the brain, had very limited experience with posterior aneurysms and had no experience with clipping Johnson's (P) specific type of aneurysm. Kokemoor (D) had represented to Johnson (P) that he had performed the surgery "dozens of times." Additionally, Kokemoor (D) had advised Johnson (P) that the associated risks of surgery, death or serious impairment were only 2 percent and stated that the surgery was less risky than the diagnostic tests that were performed prior to surgery. Johnson's (P) experts testified that this type of surgery carried a risk rate of 15 percent for an experienced surgeon and as high as 30 percent risk for a surgeon operating at Kokemoor's (D) skill level. Finally, Johnson (P) introduced evidence to establish that a reasonable physician in Kokemoor's (D) position would have provided a referral to a more experienced physician and recommended that Johnson (P) undergo the procedure at a health care facility with greater resources to manage her case post-operatively. The jury returned a verdict in favor of Johnson (P), but the court of appeals reversed, finding it was an abuse of discretion for the trial court to allow the physician-specific evidence to be admitted.

ISSUE: Is it an abuse of discretion for a trial court to admit physician-specific evidence in a case involving the doctrine of informed consent?

HOLDING AND DECISION: (Abrahamson, J.) No. It is not an abuse of discretion for a trial court to admit physician-specific evidence in a case involving the doctrine of informed consent. The doctrine of informed consent requires disclosure of all of the viable alternatives and risks of the proposed treatment. To succeed on a claim for breach of the duty to provide the patient with informed consent the plaintiff must demonstrate that the relevant risk(s) were not disclosed, that the patient would have refused treatment had the risks been disclosed, and that the patient suffered the injury which was not disclosed when undergoing the recommended treatment. Kokemoor (D) argues that he satisfied his duty to "generally" inform Johnson (P) of the risk associated with the surgery. He further argues that the doctrine of informed consent requires only that general information be provided and that the specific data admitted into evidence is irrelevant to the doctrine's application. However, the discrepancy between the percentage risks presented to Johnson (P) versus those supplied by expert testimony and learned treatises supports the materiality of this information. It would defy logic to say this information was not pertinent to Johnson's (P) decision. The relative specific risks and the availability of more experienced physicians and treatment centers all present viable alternatives that a patient needs to know when choosing a course of treatment and a doctor who will provide that treatment. Moreover, it was Kokemoor (D) who elected to present statistical data on risks to the patient in the first instance and he cannot now complain that the evidence did not support his presentation. The court of appeals decision is reversed and the case remanded to the circuit court. There was no abuse of discretion with the admission of the evidence in question.

Continued on next page.

ANALYSIS

Failure to obtain informed consent can leave a physician vulnerable to a charge of battery. To succeed on a claim based solely on lack of informed consent is extremely rare because it is difficult for a plaintiff to satisfy the element that they would have refused treatment had they been presented with all of the risks, or the totality of the magnitude of those risks. When a medical procedure is required, it will rarely be refused based upon risks. *Johnson* represents the classic case where such a claim can succeed because of the magnitude of the disparity associated between the risks presented to the patient versus the actual risks. It should be noted that courts, in general, are reluctant to admit evidence on specific risk percentages because of the firm belief that medicine is not an exact science and that presentation of hard numbers will improperly influence the jury. In this case, the court found the specific data to be material.

Quicknotes

ABUSE OF DISCRETION A determination by an appellate court that a lower court's decision was based on an error of law.

DOCTRINE OF INFORMED CONSENT Consent to a particular occurrence requiring full notification as to the consequences of that consent.

Arato v. Avedon

Decedent's family (P) v. Physician (D)

Cal. Sup. Ct., 5 Cal. 4th 1172, 858 P.2d 598 (1993).

NATURE OF CASE: Appeal from reversal of jury verdict for the defendants in an action for negligent medical management.

FACT SUMMARY: After Arato's death from pancreatic cancer, his family (P) sued his physicians (D), alleging that they had not given Arato adequate information about his life expectancy to enable him to make an informed choice as to proposed medical treatment.

RULE OF LAW

A physician is under a legal duty to disclose to a patient all material information to enable the patient to make an informed decision regarding the proposed operation or treatment.

FACTS: During surgery, physicians detected a tumor on Arato's pancreas. Removal of the tumor and a pathological examination confirmed a malignancy. Oncology practitioners, including Avedon (D), advised chemotherapy and radiation therapy. The Aratos (P) were told that most victims of pancreatic cancer die of the disease and that, should the cancer return, Arato's condition would be judged incurable. Arato was not informed, however, of specific statistical mortality rates. After Arato's death, his wife (P) filed suit, alleging that his physicians (D) had not adequately disclosed information necessary for Arato's informed consent for his treatment and that he otherwise would have opted out of the treatment and otherwise occupied himself in his final days. The jury found for Avedon (D) and the other physicians (D). The court of appeals reversed. The physicians (D) appealed.

ISSUE: Is a physician under a legal duty to disclose to a patient all material information to enable the patient to make an informed decision regarding the proposed operation or treatment?

HOLDING AND DECISION: (Arabian, J.) Yes. A physician is under a legal duty to disclose to a patient all material information to enable the patient to make an informed decision regarding the proposed operation or treatment. However, there is no need to mandate that physicians disclose specific life expectancy probabilities to every patient. Furthermore, a physician's obligations, which prohibit misrepresenting the nature of the patient's medical condition, do not include a duty to disclose every contingency that might affect the patient's nonmedical rights and interests. A physician is not the patient's financial adviser. Arato's wish to be told the truth does not in itself heighten the duty of disclosure imposed on physicians as a matter of law. Reversed and remanded with directions to affirm the judgment of the trial court.

ANALYSIS

The disclosure requirement of the informed consent doctrine protects a patient's freedom to exercise control over his or her own body. This principle of self-determination embraces all aspects of medical decision-making by the competent patient. However, statistical morbidity values derived from population groups are inherently unreliable and offer little assurance regarding the fate of the individual patient.

Quicknotes

DOCTRINE OF INFORMED CONSENT Consent to a particular occurrence requiring full notification as to the consequences of that consent.

Moore v. Regents of the University of California

Patient (P) v. Hospital owners (D)

Cal. Sup. Ct., 51 Cal. 3d 120, 793 P.2d 479 (1990).

NATURE OF CASE: Review of dismissal of action for damages for medical malpractice and conversion.

FACT SUMMARY: Several physicians extracted tissue from Moore (P) with the intent of conducting research thereon in hope of achieving financial gain.

RULE OF LAW

A physician's intent to use a person's body tissue for potentially profitable research must be disclosed.

FACTS: Moore (P) underwent treatment at UCLA Medical Center for a form of leukemia. His treating physicians, Golde (D) and Quan (D), recognized that his tissue had certain unique properties that warranted research. They suspected that a patentable cell line could be derived therefrom. Pursuant to this, various types of tissue were removed from Moore (P) including his spleen, ostensibly for treatment only but also for research as well. Several years later, a patent was issued to Golde (D) and Quan (D) on a cell line derived solely from Moore's (P) tissue. Moore (P) brought a lawsuit, alleging various causes of action including conversion and failure to obtain informed consent. The state supreme court granted review.

ISSUE: Must a physician's intent to use a person's body tissue for potentially profitable research be disclosed?

HOLDING AND DECISION: [Judge not stated in casebook excerpt.] Yes. A physician's intent to use a person's body tissue for potentially profitable research must be disclosed. A person of normal competency has a right to determine whether to consent to medical treatment. A physician has a fiduciary duty to disclose all information material to the patient's decision in this regard. When a physician has an economic interest in the results of treatment upon a patient, the potential for conflicting loyalties exists, and this might cloud the physician's judgment regarding the appropriate types of treatment to provide. The normal analysis of risk versus benefit to the patient may become skewed, and the patient has a right to know this. Hence, the intent to use a patient's tissue for profitable research must be disclosed. Here, Golde (D) had formed an intent, prior to the removal of at least some of Moore's (P) tissue, to use it in profit-seeking research. As he did not disclose this to Moore (P), he breached his duty to obtain Moore's (P) informed consent. [Moore's (P) conversion claim is rejected.]

ANALYSIS

The present case was very closely watched in the scientific and health communities. Through his conversion cause of action, Moore (P) had sought to establish a proprietary interest in his tissue. The ramifications of such a claim on research had caused some consternation among researchers. Moore's (P) conversion cause of action was unsuccessful in the California Supreme Court.

Quicknotes

CAUSE OF ACTION A fact or set of facts the occurrence of which entitles a party to seek judicial relief.

CONVERSION The act of depriving an owner of his property without permission or justification.

DOCTRINE OF INFORMED CONSENT Consent to a particular occurrence requiring full notification as to the consequences of that consent.

FIDUCIARY RELATIONSHIP Person holding a legal obligation to act for the benefit of another.

Canterbury v. Spence

Patient (P) v. Physician (D)

464 F.2d 772 (D.C. Cir. 1972).

NATURE OF CASE: Appeal from directed verdict for defendants.

FACT SUMMARY: Canterbury (P) alleged that Spence's (D) failure to disclose the risks of a medical procedure was negligent.

RULE OF LAW

When proving whether a patient would have forgone medical treatment if the physician had disclosed the medical risk involved, the conduct of a prudent person in the patient's position must be considered.

FACTS: Canterbury (P) alleged that he would not have agreed to a certain medical procedure if he had known all of the risks involved and that Spence (D) had been negligent in failing to disclose all such risks. Spence (D) argued that speculation, in hindsight, as to what Canterbury (P) would have done, was self-serving and unfair.

ISSUE: When proving whether a patient would have foregone medical treatment if the physician had disclosed the medical risk involved, must the conduct of a prudent person in the patient's position be considered?

HOLDING AND DECISION: [Judge not stated in casebook excerpt.] Yes. When proving whether a patient would have forgone medical treatment if the physician had disclosed the medical risk involved, the conduct of a prudent person in the patient's position must be considered. The causality issue should be resolved on an objective basis. Canterbury's (P) testimony must not be allowed to dominate the findings. The jury must also consider the reasonableness of his testimony.

ANALYSIS

The court here was concerned with the unfairness of the subjective patient test. The risk to the patient must be material to the patient in question. But the court must consider what a reasonable patient would have done under such circumstances.

Quicknotes

INFORMED CONSENT An individual's consent to a particular occurrence following full disclosure of the consequences of that decision.

NEGLIGENCE Conduct falling below the standard of care that a reasonable person would demonstrate under similar conditions.

RISK Danger of damage to or loss of property.

Tisdale v. Pruitt, Jr., M.D.

Patient (P) v. Physician (D)

S.C. Ct. App., 302 S.C. 238, 394 S.E.2d 857 (1990).

NATURE OF CASE: Appeal of award of damages for medical malpractice.

FACT SUMMARY: Tisdale's (P) silence and acquiescence in an incorrect procedure performed on her by Pruitt, Jr., M.D. (D) was inferred by him as consent to the procedure.

RULE OF LAW

A patient's acquiescence to a medical procedure may not be tantamount to consent.

FACTS: Tisdale (P) suffered a "missed abortion," meaning that her fetus died but did not miscarry. Her regular doctor, pursuant to insurance company demands, sent her to Pruitt, Jr., M.D. (D) for a second opinion regarding the necessity of a removal of the fetus. Pruitt (D), not realizing that Tisdale (P) came to his office for only a second opinion, performed the procedure himself. Tisdale (P) sued for failure to secure informed consent. At trial, Pruitt (D) testified that he had taken Tisdale's (P) silence and acquiescence as a sign of consent. The jury returned a verdict for Tisdale (P) of $5,000 compensatory and $25,000 punitive damages. Pruitt (D) appealed.

ISSUE: May a patient's acquiescence to a medical procedure be tantamount to consent?

HOLDING AND DECISION: (Littlejohn, J.) No. A patient's acquiescence to a medical procedure may not be tantamount to consent. A doctor is under a duty affirmatively to apprise a patient, prior to a serious medical procedure of (1) the diagnosis, (2) the nature of the contemplated procedure, (3) the risks involved, (4) the probability of success, (5) the risks of foregoing the procedure, and (6) the existence of any alternatives to the procedure. This requires affirmative communication between doctor and patient. For a physician to simply infer consent by a patient's not protesting when he performs a surgical procedure falls grossly short of a physician's standard of care and warrants compensation for any physical or emotional damages flowing therefrom. Affirmed.

ANALYSIS

In this case, the statute of limitations had run on battery. Consequently, the punitive damages were based on the lack of informed consent cause of action only. Usually, such a cause of action will not support punitive damages. However, where gross negligence or recklessness exists, such damages are available.

Quicknotes

ACQUIESCENCE Passive or implied consent.

MEDICAL MALPRACTICE Conduct on the part of a doctor falling below that demonstrated by other doctors of ordinary skill and competency under the circumstances, resulting in damages.

PUNITIVE DAMAGES Damages exceeding the actual injury suffered for the purposes of punishment of the defendant, deterrence of the wrongful behavior or comfort to the plaintiff.

STANDARD OF CARE A uniform degree of behavior against which a person's conduct can be measured when determining liability in negligence cases.

Canterbury v. Spence

Patient (P) v. Physician (D)

464 F.2d 772 (D.C. Cir. 1972).

NATURE OF CASE: Appeal from directed verdict for defendants.

FACT SUMMARY: Canterbury (P) alleged that his physician, Spence (D), had failed to adequately disclose the risks involved in a certain medical procedure.

RULE OF LAW

A physician bears the burden of going forward with evidence pertaining to a privilege not to disclose.

FACTS: The court discussed two exceptions to the physician's duty to disclose risks to a patient.

ISSUE: Does a physician bear the burden of going forward with evidence pertaining to a privilege not to disclose?

HOLDING AND DECISION: [Judge not stated in casebook excerpt.] Yes. A physician bears the burden of going forward with evidence pertaining to a privilege not to disclose. There are two exceptions to the general rule of disclosure. When a patient is unconscious or otherwise unable to consent, and harm is imminent and outweighs any harm threatened by the proposed treatment, a physician may proceed without the patient's consent. Likewise, when a physician determines that communication of the risk information would present a harm to the patient's well-being, disclosure may be dispensed with. In both cases, however, disclosure to a close relative in order to secure consent to the proposed treatment is appropriate.

ANALYSIS

The court here reasoned that the physician must bear the burden pertaining to a privilege not to disclose because he would have the necessary evidence. Once the patient established his prima facie case, the physician had to raise the privilege. Consent may be presumed in some cases involving medical emergencies.

Quicknotes

BURDEN OF PROOF The duty of a party to introduce evidence to support a fact that is in dispute in an action.

INFORMED CONSENT An individual's consent to a particular occurrence following full disclosure of the consequences of that decision.

PRIMA FACIE CASE An action where the plaintiff introduces sufficient evidence to submit the issue to the judge or jury for determination.

PRIVILEGE A benefit or right conferred upon a person or entity beyond those conferred upon the general public.

Humphers v. First Interstate Bank of Oregon

Biological mother (P) v. Physician's estate (D)

Or. Sup. Ct., 298 Or. 706, 696 P.2d 527, *en banc* (1985).

NATURE OF CASE: Review of partial reversal of order dismissing action for damages for unauthorized release of confidential information.

FACT SUMMARY: Humphers (P) sought to hold the estate (D) of the late Mackey, a doctor, liable for his having divulged information which allowed her daughter, who had been given up for adoption at birth, to find her.

RULE OF LAW

A physician who divulges information about a patient that allows her adopted-out child to locate her may be liable in damages therefor.

FACTS: Humphers (P), then known as Elwess, gave birth to a girl. The attending physician was Mackey. The baby was given up for adoption the next day. Twenty-one years later, the daughter sought out Mackey, and with his help was able to gain access to the sealed adoption papers. She was then able to locate Humphers (P). Humphers (P) was distressed by this. Mackey having since died, Humphers (P) subsequently filed a lawsuit against his estate (D), administered by First Interstate Bank (D), seeking damages under a variety of theories. The trial court sustained the estate's (D) demurrer an all counts. The court of appeals reversed on two counts based, respectively, on invasion of privacy and breach of contractual obligation of secrecy. The Oregon Supreme Court granted review.

ISSUE: May a physician who divulges information about a patient that allows her adopted-out child to locate her be liable in damages therefor?

HOLDING AND DECISION: (Linde, J.) Yes. A physician who divulges information about a patient that allows her adopted-out child to locate her may be liable in damages therefor. Under a general invasion of privacy theory, this is not so. This court does not believe that simply knowing facts about a person's location and telling them to another constitutes an invasion of privacy. However, with respect to a physician's obligations to keep confidences, matters are different. Oregon Revised Statute § 677.190(5) imposes upon a physician a duty to maintain confidences, on pain of loss of licensure or other disciplinary action. It is no great logical leap to allow a civil action for violation of this duty. Beyond this, other laws and regulations mandate confidentiality of adoption records. For these reasons, a failure to keep such confidences may result in tort liability. Affirmed in part, reversed in part, and remanded.

ANALYSIS

Billions of medical records exist in the United States. Parties other than the patient may wish to gain access to a patient's records for any number of reasons. All records enjoy some level of protection from scrutiny; generally, at the very least, a subpoena is necessary for access to be gained. Particularly sensitive records, such as those relating to substance abuse or sexual matters, often require a court order to be inspected.

Quicknotes

PATIENT-PHYSICIAN PRIVILEGE Right of physician to refuse testimony as to communications made between him and his patient for purposes of treatment.

SUBPOENA A mandate issued by court to compel a witness to appear at trial.

Doe v. Medlantic Health Care Group, Inc.

Employee/patient (P) v. Employer/hospital (D)

D.C. Ct. App., 814 A.2d 939 (2003).

NATURE OF CASE: Appeal of entry of a judgment for appellee.

FACT SUMMARY: Doe (P) brought suit against Medlantic Health Care Group, Inc. (D) alleging invasion of privacy and breach of a confidential relationship for negligent disclosure of his positive Human Immunodeficiency Virus (HIV) status.

RULE OF LAW

The obligation of confidentiality associated with the patient-provider relationship carries with it a stricter duty than that of a reasonable person to honor the trust and confidence created by the special relationship.

FACTS: Doe (P) held two jobs, one with a federal agency and the other as a janitor for a company providing cleaning services for the State Department. One of Doe's (P) co-workers at the State Department, Tijuana Goldring (Goldring), also worked at Washington Hospital Center (WHC), the medical institution where Doe (P) was being treated for HIV. Shortly after a visit to the clinic, Doe (P) learned that his co-workers at the State Department knew of his illness and he found himself being subjected to extreme ridicule because of it. Once Doe (P) realized that Goldring was the source of the rumors concerning his medical condition, he filed suit against Goldring for invasion of privacy and against Medlantic Health Care Group, Inc. (D), the owner of WHC, for breach of confidential relationship. Goldring was later dismissed from the suit, the jury having found that Goldring's disclosure was not within the scope of her employment at WHC. The jury, however, ruled in favor of Doe (P) against Medlantic (D) awarding damages of $250,000 on the breach of confidential relationship claim. The trial judge, however, granted a motion for judgment for defendant finding that Doe's (P) claim was time barred by the relevant statute of limitations. Doe (P) appealed.

ISSUE: Does the obligation of confidentiality associated with the patient-provider relationship carry with it a stricter duty than that of a reasonable person to honor the trust and confidence created by the special relationship?

HOLDING AND DECISION: (Ruiz, J.) Yes. The obligation of confidentiality associated with the patient-provider relationship carries with it a stricter duty than that of a reasonable person to honor the trust and confidence created by the special relationship. The tort of a breach of a confidential relationship consists of the "unconsented, unprivileged disclosure to a third party of nonpublic information that the defendant has learned within a confidential relationship." There was sufficient evidence presented at trial to permit the jury to find that Medlantic (D) failed to observe the "utmost caution" in preserving the confidentiality of Doe's (P) medical records. There was substantial evidence of the staff members' routine failure to comply with hospital privacy protocol and with dissemination of private information without verifying the identity of the person requesting the information or the veracity of the reason for their request. Enough causal evidence established Goldring's link as the source of the unauthorized disclosure and of the hospital's lapse in protecting Doe's (P) privacy to support the jury's verdict. The trial court's judgment is reversed and the case is remanded for reinstatement of the jury's verdict.

ANALYSIS

The casebook author uses this case to illustrate the level of duty associated with the tort of breach of a confidential relationship. This duty of care is the equivalent of a fiduciary relationship. The duty as a fiduciary carries with it a standard higher than that of simple negligence or the reasonable person standard. A fiduciary must exercise the utmost degree of honesty, forthrightness, loyalty, and fidelity within the confines of the special relationship to the client. While this case is not utilized for this purpose, it should be noted that the court of appeals reversed and remanded with instructions for the trial judge to reinstate the jury verdict based upon the trial judge's error with regard to granting defendant's motion. The appellate court applied a discovery rule to the statute of limitations finding that the cause of action accrued when the plaintiff is deemed to be on inquiry notice, or "that notice which a plaintiff would have possessed **after** due investigation." The trial court erred by failing to credit Doe (P) with the reasonable inferences derived from the evidence when the jury reasonably concluded that Doe (P) was not on notice until May 20, 1996, making his claim timely filed. In deviating from the jury's findings, the trial judge improperly invaded the province of the fact-finding role of the jury. While the sufficiency of the evidence was discussed in relation to supporting the merits of Doe's (P) claim, it was not determinant as to the procedural context for ordering the jury's verdict to be reinstated.

Continued on next page.

Quicknotes

DUTY OF CARE A principle of negligence requiring an individual to act in such a manner as to avoid injury to a person to whom he or she owes an obligatory duty.

FIDUCIARY RELATIONSHIP Person holding a legal obligation to act for the benefit of another.

INVASION OF PRIVACY The violation of an individual's right to be protected against unwarranted interference in his personal affairs, falling into one of four categories: (1) appropriating the individual's likeness or name for commercial benefit; (2) intrusion into the individual's seclusion; (3) public disclosure of private facts regarding the individual; and (4) disclosure of facts placing the individual in a false light.

STATUTE OF LIMITATIONS A law prescribing the period in which a legal action may be commenced.

Herman v. Kratche

Patient (P) v. Health care provider (D)

Ohio Ct. App., 2006 WL 3240680 (2006).

NATURE OF CASE: Appeal of summary judgment in favor of health care provider.

FACT SUMMARY: Mrs. Herman (P) received medical treatment and records of her treatment to her employer without her consent. She sued the Solon Family Health Center (Clinic) (D) for unauthorized disclosure, invasion of privacy, and intentional infliction of emotional distress. The court granted summary judgment for Dr. Kratche (D) and the Clinic (D).

RULE OF LAW

(1) An independent tort exists for the unauthorized, unprivileged disclosure to a third party of nonpublic medical information that a physician or hospital has learned within a physician-patient relationship. (2) An independent tort exists for invasion of privacy where a physician or hospital discloses to a third party, without authorization, nonpublic medical information that the physician or hospital has learned within the physician-patient relationship.

FACTS: Mrs. Herman (P) received medical treatment from Dr. Kratche (D) at the Solon Family Health Center (Clinic) (D) and the Clinic (D) sent records of her treatment to her employer, Nestle USA Inc., without her consent, even though the treatment was not work-related. The Clinic (D) claimed it mistakenly believed her visits were related to workers' compensation claims from 1993 as a Nestle employee, but she corrected the misconception, and the Clinic (D) inadvertently continued to disclose her medical information. She sued the Clinic (D) for unauthorized disclosure, invasion of privacy, and intentional infliction of emotional distress. The court granted summary judgment for Kratche (D) and the Clinic (D).

ISSUE:

(1) Does an independent tort exist for the unauthorized, unprivileged disclosure to a third party of nonpublic medical information that a physician or hospital has learned within a physician-patient relationship?

(2) Does an independent tort exist for invasion of privacy where a physician or hospital discloses to a third party, without authorization, nonpublic medical information that the physician or hospital has learned within the physician-patient relationship?

HOLDING AND DECISION: [Judge not stated in casebook excerpt.]

(1) Yes. An independent tort exists for the unauthorized, unprivileged disclosure to a third party of nonpublic medical information that a physician or hospital has learned within a physician-patient relationship. The Clinic (D) had a fiduciary duty to keep Herman's (P) medical information confidential, and it breached that duty, and the breach became the proximate cause of her damages as soon as Nestle opened the records. The tortious conduct occurred the moment the information was disclosed to the unauthorized third party, her employer, and whatever duties the third party may have—even if it too has the duty to keep the information confidential—is irrelevant to whether it was authorized to receive the information in the first place. Further, the Health Insurance Portability and Accountability Act of 1996 (HIPAA), which aims to protect the privacy of an individual's personal health information, does not cover Nestle, because it is not a "health plan," "healthcare clearinghouse," or "healthcare provider." And while HIPAA permits a covered entity to disclose an individual's personal health information to an employer for workers' compensation purposes without consent, that exception doesn't apply here because the Clinic (D) made the disclosures inadvertently, and did not state they were for a purpose permitted by HIPAA.

(2) Yes. An independent tort exists for invasion of privacy where a physician or hospital discloses to a third party, without authorization, nonpublic medical information that the physician or hospital has learned within the physician-patient relationship. When the Clinic (D) mistakenly mailed Herman's (P) information to Nestle, it wrongfully intruded into her private life. There is a genuine issue of material fact as to whether the Clinic's (D) wrongful intrusion into her private information would cause a person of ordinary sensibilities outrage, mental suffering, shame, or humiliation, and summary judgment was therefore inappropriate.

ANALYSIS

HIPPA's main purpose is to protect the privacy and confidentiality of personal health information, which contemplates the importance of privacy not only to a person's personal dignity, but also so that a person can trust the healthcare system, thereby increasing its efficiency. Neither purpose of the Act was served by the Clinic's (D) disclosure to Nestle in this case.

Quicknotes

EMOTIONAL DISTRESS Extreme personal suffering which results from another's conduct and for which damages may be sought.

Continued on next page.

INVASION OF PRIVACY The violation of an individual's right to be protected against unwarranted interference in his personal affairs, falling into one of four categories: (1) appropriating the individual's likeness or name for commercial benefit; (2) intrusion into the individual's seclusion; (3) public disclosure of private facts regarding the individual; or (4) disclosure of facts placing the individual in a false light.

SUMMARY JUDGMENT Judgment rendered by a court in response to a motion made by one of the parties, claiming that the lack of a question of material fact in respect to an issue warrants disposition of the issue without consideration by the jury.

TORT A legal wrong resulting in a breach of duty by the wrongdoer, causing damages as a result of the breach.

WORKERS' COMPENSATION Fixed awards provided to employees for job-related injuries.

Acosta v. Byrum et al.

Patient (P) v. Physician (D)

N.C. Ct. App., 638 S.E.2d 246 (2006).

NATURE OF CASE: Appeal of dismissal of complaint against a physician.

FACT SUMMARY: The trial court dismissed Heather D. Acosta's (P) complaint for negligent infliction of emotional distress against Dr. David R. Faber (D) because the complaint did not cite the specific provision of the Health Insurance Portability and Accountability Act of 1996 (HIPAA) that he violated.

RULE OF LAW

A complaint for negligent infliction of emotional distress that is based on the unauthorized disclosure of nonpublic medical information need not refer to a specific provision of HIPAA that was violated by the disclosure.

FACTS: Heather D. Acosta (P) was both an employee and a patient of Psychiatric Associates, a company owned by Dr. David R. Faber (D). Acosta (P) claimed that the company's office manager, Robin Byrum (D), held "severe personal animus" toward her. She alleged that Faber (D) improperly allowed Byrum (D) to use his access code to retrieve Acosta's (P) confidential health records, which Byrum (D) then provided to unnamed third parties without Acosta's (P) consent. Acosta (P) sued Byrum (D) for invasion of privacy and intentional infliction of emotional distress, and Faber (D) for negligent infliction of emotional distress. The trial court dismissed Acosta's (P) complaint against Faber (D) for failing to state a valid claim for negligent infliction of emotional distress (NIED). The trial court found that Acosta (P) failed to cite the exact HIPAA regulation that was violated and failed to allege that Faber's (D) actions proximately caused Acosta's (P) emotional distress.

ISSUE: Must a complaint for negligent infliction of emotional distress that is based on the unauthorized disclosure of nonpublic medical information refer to a specific provision of HIPAA that was violated by the disclosure?

HOLDING AND DECISION: [Judge not stated in casebook excerpt.] No. A complaint for negligent infliction of emotional distress that is based on the unauthorized disclosure of nonpublic medical information need not refer to a specific provision of HIPAA that was violated by the disclosure. Acosta (P) cited HIPAA as evidence of the appropriate standard of care in her negligence claim, and the Act is inapplicable beyond providing evidence of the duty of care owed by Faber (D) with respect to the privacy of Acosta's (P) medical records. Acosta (P) was not required to cite the exact rule or regulation in her complaint, but was only required to provide Faber (D) notice of how she plans to establish the duty that was negligently breached, which she did.

ANALYSIS

Remember that HIPAA Privacy Standards do not provide a private right to sue. Complaints for violation of HIPAA must be made to the Secretary of Health and Human Services. However, HIPAA can be used in civil litigation as a source of standard practice, because it creates a standard of care for the handling of confidential information.

Quicknotes

INVASION OF PRIVACY The violation of an individual's right to be protected against unwarranted interference in his personal affairs, falling into one of four categories: (1) appropriating the individual's likeness or name for commercial benefit; (2) intrusion into the individual's seclusion; (3) public disclosure of private facts regarding the individual; or (4) disclosure of facts placing the individual in a false light.

NEGLIGENCE Conduct falling below the standard of care that a reasonable person would demonstrate under similar conditions.

NEGLIGENT INFLICTION OF EMOTIONAL DISTRESS Violation of the duty of care owed to another that occurs when an individual creates a foreseeable risk of injury to the other person, causing that person emotional distress.

CHAPTER 5

Liability of Health Care Professionals

Quick Reference Rules of Law

Hall v. Hilbun

Decedent's husband (P) v. Surgeon (D)

Miss. Sup. Ct., 466 So. 2d 856 (1985).

NATURE OF CASE: Review of directed defense verdict in medical malpractice action.

FACT SUMMARY: In Hall's (P) malpractice action, nonlocal physicians were not allowed to render expert opinions due to their lack of familiarity with local medical standards.

RULE OF LAW

A physician's duty of care to a patient is to be judged by national, not local, standards.

FACTS: Hall's (P) wife underwent surgery for lower digestive tract blockage. The surgeon was Hilbun (D). Following the procedure, while Hall's (P) wife was in the recovery room, Hilbun (D) retired for the evening. He left no particular instructions to the nurses. Meanwhile, Hall's (P) wife was moved to a private room. About 14 hours later, she died from cardiopulmonary failure. Hall (P) sued for medical malpractice/wrongful death. At trial, Hall (P) sought to introduce the testimony of one Dr. Hoerr, a retired Cleveland physician. The trial court excluded much of Hoerr's testimony on the grounds that he was unfamiliar with local standards. The same occurred with another proffered expert witness, Dr. Sachs. At the close of trial, the court entered a directed defense verdict. Hall (P) appealed.

ISSUE: Is a physician's duty of care to a patient to be judged by national standards?

HOLDING AND DECISION: (Robertson, J.) Yes. A physician's duty of care to a patient is to be judged by national, not local, standards. For years, courts have followed the "locality rule" in medical malpractice cases. This rule holds that the standard of care owed a patient by a physician would be judged by reference to local standards. However, this rule has become obsolete. Medical practice has become increasingly "nationalized" in scope. Medical school admission standards are largely the same across the country. Physicians are much more mobile than before. Medical education and literature are available nationwide. Beyond that, the needs of a patient are largely the same for any particular medical condition, no matter where the patient is geographically located. For these reasons, a physician's standard of care should be measured by local standards only to the extent that some localities have greater resources than others. Apart from that, the standard of care owed by a physician to a patient should be judged by the medical community on a nationwide basis. [Here, the testimony of Drs. Hoerr and Sachs was improperly excluded.] Reversed and remanded.

ANALYSIS

The court's decision here did not constitute a complete abrogation of the locality rule. While expert witnesses no longer had to be "locals," the court did recognize that some localities simply do not have the facilities enjoyed by others. For this reason, a nonlocal expert would have to be aware of what facilities would be at a doctor's disposal before rendering an opinion regarding that doctor's standard of care.

Quicknotes

DIRECTED VERDICT A verdict ordered by the court in a jury trial.

DUTY OF CARE A principle of negligence requiring an individual to act in such a manner as to avoid injury to a person to whom he or she owes an obligatory duty.

STANDARD OF CARE A uniform degree of behavior against which a person's conduct can be measured when determining liability in negligence cases.

Hinlicky v. Dreyfuss

Estate (P) v. Doctors (D)

N.Y. Ct. App., 6 N.Y.3d 636, 848 N.E.2d 1285 (2006).

NATURE OF CASE: Appeal of trial court's admission of evidence.

FACT SUMMARY: In a malpractice case, the trial court admitted physician guidelines into evidence to demonstrate the process followed by the treating physicians. The plaintiffs appealed.

RULE OF LAW

An algorithm is properly admitted into evidence if it is offered not for its truth, and not to set a standard of care, but to illustrate a physician's decision-making process.

FACTS: Marie Hinlicky had surgery to remove plaque buildup in her carotid artery. It was successful, but she suffered a heart attack and died 25 days later. The administrator of her estate (P) filed a medical malpractice case charging with negligence internist Robert O. Frank (D), surgeon David C. Dreyfuss (D), and anesthesiologists Riverside Associates (D). Dr. Ilioff (D), an anesthesiologist, was the last to examine Mrs. Hinlicky before her surgery. He did not send her for a preoperative cardiac evaluation, basing his decision in part on a set of clinical guidelines published in 1996 by the American Heart Association and the American College of Cardiology. The guidelines are in the form of a flow diagram, or algorithm, which provides a list of variables, the presence or absence of each pointing toward surgery or cardiac evaluation. Ilioff (D) went through each step of the chart and based on his assessment of the variables, concluded that there was no need for a cardiac evaluation. The jury was asked to determine whether each defendant was negligent for failing to order preoperative cardiac clearance, and the jury found for the defendants. The appellate division affirmed, finding that the trial court properly admitted the algorithm into evidence because it was offered not for its truth, and not to set a standard of care, but to illustrate the physician's decision-making process.

ISSUE: Is an algorithm properly admitted into evidence if it is offered not for its truth, and not to set a standard of care, but to illustrate a physician's decision-making process?

HOLDING AND DECISION: [Judge not stated in casebook excerpt.] Yes. An algorithm is properly admitted into evidence if it is offered not for its truth, and not to set a standard of care, but to illustrate a physician's decision-making process. Without objection, Ilioff (D) testified that the process he used was consistent with the algorithm, and that he had incorporated the process set forth in the algorithm into his practice. The trial court then stated it was admitting the algorithm to illustrate Ilioff's (D) evaluation process. The plaintiff's argument that there is no meaningful distinction between offering the algorithm to prove its truth and offering it to illustrate the decision-making process of a party who state he adopted it into his practice is rejected, because the plaintiff never requested a limiting instruction. If the plaintiff had been concerned that the purpose for admitting the algorithm was not demonstrative but substantive, he should have said so. Affirmed.

ANALYSIS

This court focused quite a bit on procedural problems associated with the plaintiff's case. If the plaintiff had asked for a limiting instruction with respect to the algorithm, it would have been granted, and may have changed the outcome, since, as the court noted, a jury might draw unsupported conclusions from the demonstrative evidence that weigh in favor of the defendants.

Quicknotes

MEDICAL MALPRACTICE Conduct on the part of a doctor falling below that demonstrated by other doctors of ordinary skill and competency under the circumstances, resulting in damages.

NEGLIGENCE Conduct falling below the standard of care that a reasonable person would demonstrate under similar conditions.

Helling v. Carey

Blind patient (P) v. Opthalmologists (D)

Wash. Sup. Ct., 83 Wash. 2d 514, 519 P.2d 981 (1974).

NATURE OF CASE: Appeal of denial of damages for medical malpractice.

FACT SUMMARY: Ophthalmologists Carey (D) and Laughlin (D) did not test Helling (P) for glaucoma until five years after she first complained of eye irritation.

RULE OF LAW

Reasonable medical care, which is the level of care that insulates a doctor from liability for medical malpractice, may require more than merely following the prevailing professional standard of care.

FACTS: In 1959, Helling (P) consulted ophthalmologists Carey (D) and Laughlin (D) for nearsightedness, and they fitted her with contact lenses. From 1963 to 1968, Helling (P) had 10 consultations with Carey (D) and Laughlin (D) concerning eye irritation. They believed the irritations were related solely to the contact lenses. During Helling's (P) tenth visit, Carey (D) and Laughlin (D) performed a "pressure test" and discovered glaucoma. By this point Helling (P), then 32 years old, was nearly blind. Helling (P) sued Carey (D) and Laughlin (D) for malpractice, alleging that had her glaucoma been detected earlier she would have retained more of her sight. Expert testimony established that the pressure test is simple, harmless, and inexpensive and that absent the test glaucoma is often undetectable. The experts agreed, though, that unless complaints and symptoms indicated that glaucoma should be suspected, prevailing ophthalmology standards did not require routine pressure tests for patients under 40 because the incidence of glaucoma in that group is just one in 25,000. The jury found Carey (D) and Laughlin (D) not liable. Helling (P) appealed, claiming she should have been allowed to argue to the jury that the prevailing standard of care for ophthalmology was inadequate to protect her from glaucoma and, thus, not reasonable care. The appeals court affirmed, and Helling (P) appealed.

ISSUE: Can reasonable medical care require more than following the prevailing professional standard of care?

HOLDING AND DECISION: (Hunter, J.) Yes. Reasonable medical care, which is the level of care that insulates a doctor from liability for negligence, may require more than merely following the prevailing professional standard of care. "What usually is done may be evidence of what ought to be done, but what ought to be done is fixed by a standard of reasonable prudence, whether it usually is complied with or not." These are precautions so imperative that even universal disregard will not excuse their omission. The pressure test is simple and harmless and is essential for the early detection of glaucoma when it can be arrested to avoid the disease's debilitating effects. The precaution of giving this test to patients under 40 is so imperative that, irrespective of its disregard by the ophthalmology profession, it is the duty of courts to say that giving the test is necessary. Considering Helling's (P) persistent complaints of eye irritation over a five-year period, reasonable prudence required ophthalmologists Carey (D) and Laughlin (D) to perform a pressure test. In failing to do so they were negligent, and this conduct proximately caused Helling's (P) blindness. Reversed.

ANALYSIS

Helling states the minority rule. It is among a very few cases rejecting the prevailing professional standard of care, also known as "customary practice," as the level of care required to avoid medical malpractice liability. These cases have involved easily understandable medical procedures (like the pressure test for glaucoma), where the trier of fact can competently weigh the risks of using the procedure versus the risks of not using it. The majority of jurisdictions have refused to replace customary medical practice with the case-by-case judicial balancing exhibited in *Helling*.

Quicknotes

DUTY OF CARE A principle of negligence requiring an individual to act in such a manner as to avoid injury to a person to whom he or she owes an obligatory duty.

Strasel v. Seven Hills OB-GYN Associates, Inc.

Patient (P) v. Healthcare provider (D)

Ohio Ct. App., 170 Ohio App. 3d 98, 866 N.E.2d 48 (2007).

NATURE OF CASE: Appeal of denial of prejudgment interest on a jury's award of damages.

FACT SUMMARY: A woman was misdiagnosed as not pregnant, and underwent a dilatation and curettage (D&C) at her doctor's suggestion. Several weeks later, it was discovered she was pregnant, and that the D&C might have caused serious harm to the fetus. Fearing for her unborn baby's health, the woman suffered severe depression and stress and sued the doctor and hospital.

RULE OF LAW

A woman who delivers a healthy baby can recover for negligent infliction of emotional distress based upon her fear for her baby's well-being, if the baby had been placed in real danger by the alleged negligence of the defendants.

FACTS: Christina Strasel (P), who was obese, went to Seven Hills OB-GYN Associates (D) for an initial pregnancy appointment. A sonogram showed a sac in her uterus, but the sonographer could not detect a heartbeat or a fetal pole. The sonographer's report stated that she suspected a blighted ovum, which is a condition in which an empty placental sac develops in the uterus without a fetus, but that because of Strasel's (P) obesity, her ability to see was limited. The sonographer recommended a follow-up sonogram. Strasel's (P) medical file was given to Dr. Xavier G. Ortiz (D), who diagnosed Strasel (P) with a blighted ovum. He did not examine Strasel (P), but scheduled a dilatation and curettage (D&C) procedure for Strasel (P). Several weeks after the procedure, Strasel (P) still believed she was pregnant, and made an appointment at Seven Hills (D). After a positive blood test, she was given another sonogram, and the sonographer told Strasel (P) that she was 13 weeks pregnant. Ortiz (D) then told Strasel (P) that he had misdiagnosed her viable pregnancy as a blighted ovum, and that her baby might suffer problems as a result of the D&C. Strasel (P) subsequently learned that the possible problems were severe. She worried constantly about her unborn baby throughout her pregnancy, withdrew from her other children, and separated from her husband. Even after she gave birth to a healthy baby girl, she continued to worry about the possibility of neurological diseases that hadn't yet presented themselves. She was diagnosed as having a major depressive disorder and post-traumatic stress disorder as a result of the D&C and the uncertainty of how it would affect her child. Strasel (P) and her husband then filed suit for malpractice and negligent infliction of emotional distress, and requested punitive damages. At arbitration, she was awarded $210,000, but Ortiz (D) and Seven Hills (D) appealed the arbitration award. A jury then returned a verdict of $372,000 in Strasel's (P) favor, but against Strasel's (P) husband. Strasel (P) then filed a motion for prejudgment interest, which the trial court denied.

ISSUE: Can a woman who delivers a healthy baby recover for negligent infliction of emotional distress based upon her fear for her baby's well-being, if the baby had been placed in real danger by the alleged negligence of the defendants?

HOLDING AND DECISION: (Per curiam) Yes. A woman who delivers a healthy baby can recover for negligent infliction of emotional distress based upon her fear for her baby's well-being, if the baby had been placed in real danger by the alleged negligence of the defendants. Strasel's (P) baby was subjected to real physical peril by the D&C regardless of whether the peril led to actual injury, so this is not a case in which the peril was non-existent. Strasel's (P) emotional distress resulted from the very real risk of injury to a seven-week-old fetus that was subjected to a procedure tantamount to an abortion.

ANALYSIS

Note that damages cannot be recovered for psychological harm and emotional injuries that arise from fear of a "non-existent peril." The fact that Strasel (P) delivered a healthy baby does not mean that the "peril" was non-existent; it means only that there was no actual injury resulting from the negligence. The peril existed—it was the threat of actual and physical bodily harm to the fetus—and it was caused by the negligence. Because Strasel's (P) emotional distress was caused by the peril, it too was caused by the negligence.

Quicknotes

ARBITRATION An alternative resolution process where a dispute is heard and decided by a neutral third party, rather than through legal proceedings.

DAMAGES Monetary compensation that may be awarded by the court to a party who has sustained injury or loss to his person, property or rights due to another party's unlawful act, omission or negligence.

NEGLIGENT INFLICTION OF EMOTIONAL DISTRESS Violation of the duty of care owed to another that occurs when an

Continued on next page.

individual creates a foreseeable risk of injury to the other person, causing that person emotional distress.

PUNITIVE DAMAGES Damages exceeding the actual injury suffered for the purposes of punishment of the defendant, deterrence of the wrongful behavior or comfort to the plaintiff.

Wickline v. State

Patient (P) v. Health care provider (D)

Cal. Ct. App., 192 Cal. App. 3d 1630 (1986).

NATURE OF CASE: Appeal of jury damages award in a suit for negligent discontinuance of Medi-Cal eligibility.

FACT SUMMARY: Because Medi-Cal (D) rejected further hospitalization costs, Wickline (P) was discharged sooner than her doctor believed appropriate, and she suffered a blood clot in her leg, requiring amputation.

RULE OF LAW

Since a patient's health care payor is not responsible for discharge determinations, liability will not attach to the payor for a negligent discharge.

FACTS: Wickline (P) suffered an arterial blockage in her leg. After multiple surgeries with complications, her doctor, Dr. Polonsky, determined that she should remain hospitalized for eight extra days. The doctor requested a Medi-Cal (D) approval for the extra days, but only four extra days were approved. Dr. Polonsky did not challenge this finding, though an appeal route existed. After the four days, Wickline (P) was discharged. Several physicians agreed that the discharge was reasonable given the current standard of medical practice. However, complications with Wickline's (P) leg at home eventually required amputation. Wickline (P) filed suit against Medi-Cal (D) for negligently interfering with her doctor's discretion. The jury found for Wickline (P), and Medi-Cal (D) appealed.

ISSUE: Does a patient's health care payor bear the primary responsibility for allowing a patient to be discharged from a hospital, thus incurring liability for a negligent discharge?

HOLDING AND DECISION: (Rowen, J.) No. Since a patient's health care payor is not responsible for discharge determinations, liability will not attach to the payor for a negligent discharge. A patient's physician is in a far better position to determine medically necessary procedures than is Medi-Cal (D). When an appeal route exists and is not used, then the physician cannot shift responsibility to the payor. In this case, Dr. Polonsky admitted that it was his primary responsibility to care for Wickline (P). He felt that four more days of hospitalization were needed, but he did not challenge the initial Medi-Cal (D) finding. Medi-Cal (D) based its decision on a limited set of facts that Dr. Polonsky could have questioned. Medi-Cal (D) is not liable for Wickline's (P) injuries. Reversed.

ANALYSIS

The decision in this case has been substantially narrowed in subsequent cases. Outside entities that deny care can be liable for negligently reviewing medical records. Apparently there is a growing concern that cost-containment procedures are interfering with physicians' decisions.

Quicknotes

MEDICAID A welfare program for the poor administered by the state.

NEGLIGENCE Conduct falling below the standard of care that a reasonable person would demonstrate under similar conditions.

Chumbler v. McClure

Patient (P) v. Physician (D)

505 F.2d 489 (6th Cir. 1974).

NATURE OF CASE: Appeal of a directed verdict in a medical malpractice suit.

FACT SUMMARY: Dr. McClure (D) was the only neurosurgeon of nine in the city prescribing a female hormone, with known side effects, for cerebral vascular insufficiency.

RULE OF LAW

Where multiple schools of thought exist on the proper treatment for an ailment, it is not malpractice to deviate from the majority in a particular community so long as responsible medical authority supports the treatment.

FACTS: Chumbler (P) was diagnosed with cerebral vascular insufficiency. Dr. McClure (D) prescribed him a female hormone to treat the problem; the hormone had known side effects, which included enlargement of breast tissue and loss of libido. Dr. McClure (D) was the only neurosurgeon of nine in Nashville who used the hormone for this condition. The medical community at large was divided on the use of the hormone. Chumbler (P) filed suit for malpractice, and the court directed a verdict for Dr. McClure (D). Chumbler (P) appealed.

ISSUE: Where multiple schools of thought exist on the proper treatment for an ailment, is it malpractice to deviate from the majority's preferred treatment in a particular community?

HOLDING AND DECISION: [Judge not stated in casebook excerpt.] No. Where multiple schools of thought exist on the proper treatment for an ailment, it is not malpractice to deviate from the majority in a particular community so long as responsible medical authority supports the treatment. The test for malpractice and community standards is not determined by plebiscite. A doctor may be in the minority in a community but be supported by sound research and a substantial number of physicians throughout the country. In this case, Dr. McClure (D) was alone in Nashville in using the female hormone to treat Chumbler's (P) type of disorder. However, the medical community at large was divided on the issue. Dr. McClure's (D) decision was based upon responsible medical authority; the choice of treatment was reasonable. Affirmed.

ANALYSIS

When the medical community does not have a definitive treatment for a disorder, it is hard to find liability for any rational approach, even if it is in the extreme minority. Many respected medical methods began as minority treatments, proving themselves over time. A physician's determination must be accorded respect consistent with the best information available at the time; otherwise physicians could never escape liability when they applied a pioneering treatment.

Quicknotes

DIRECTED VERDICT A verdict ordered by the court in a jury trial.

PLEBISCITE A proposed regulation that is submitted for decision by the voting public in order to effectuate a change that is beyond the authority of the legislature.

Henderson v. Heyer-Schulte Corp.

Patient (P) v. Physician (D)

Tex. Ct. Civ. App., 600 S.W.2d 844 (1980).

NATURE OF CASE: Appeal from denial of damages for medical malpractice.

FACT SUMMARY: Rothenberg (D), defending a suit for malpractice following a surgical procedure he performed, contended that the fact that he had utilized a method used by numerous other doctors shielded him from liability for his choice of methods.

RULE OF LAW

The fact that a surgeon elects to employ a surgical method widely used by doctors will not in itself shield him from liability for his choice of methods.

FACTS: Henderson (P) underwent a breast augmentation surgical procedure, which was performed by her physician, Rothenberg (D). She suffered numerous complications that required various corrective procedures. She later sued Rothenberg (D), claiming, among other things, that he had elected to use an improper surgical technique. Rothenberg (D) contended, and the judge so instructed the jury, that his choice of techniques would be legitimate if he used a procedure recognized in the medical community. [The jury returned a defense verdict, and Henderson (P) appealed.]

ISSUE: Will the fact that a surgeon elects to employ a surgical method widely used by other doctors in itself shield him from liability for his choice of methods?

HOLDING AND DECISION: [Judge not stated in casebook excerpt.] No. The fact that a surgeon elects to employ a surgical method used by doctors will not in itself shield him from liability for his choice of methods. The key to standard of care in choice of methods is not the acceptance of a technique by other doctors but, rather, whether the use of such a technique is reasonable and prudent. Recognition of the technique by other doctors bears on this issue but is not determinative. Since the trial court omitted the reasonable and prudent requirement, its instruction was in error. [The court went on to hold the error harmless and affirmed.]

ANALYSIS

The defense employed by Rothenberg (D) is what has been termed "the two schools of thought" doctrine. As the name implies, the doctrine holds that when two alternate and/or competing schools of thought exist on an issue in medicine, it is not negligent for a physician to choose either. The defense has met with varied levels of acceptance among the jurisdictions.

Quicknotes

DUTY OF CARE A principle of negligence requiring an individual to act in such a manner as to avoid injury to a person to whom he or she owes an obligatory duty.

MALPRACTICE A failure to perform one's professional duties during the course of a client relationship, either intentionally or negligently, or the poor or improper discharge of one's professional obligations.

NEGLIGENCE Conduct falling below the standard of care that a reasonable person would demonstrate under similar conditions.

Brook v. St. John's Hickey Memorial Hospital

Patient (P) v. Radiologist (D)

Ind. Sup. Ct., 269 Ind. 270, 380 N.E.2d 72 (1978).

NATURE OF CASE: Appeal of reversal of defense verdict in malpractice action.

FACT SUMMARY: Fischer (D), a radiologist, elected to inject a contrast medium into Brook's (P) calves, an unusual place to do so, on the basis of prior experience and literature he had read.

RULE OF LAW

A physician does not conduct an experiment on a patient by undertaking an unusual procedure if the physician has a reasonable basis for doing so.

FACTS: Brook (P), a two-year-old, had a urological problem which required certain X-ray studies involving injection of a contrast dye. The standard location of injection was the buttocks. However, Fischer (D), the radiologist performing the procedure, had seen literature to the effect that injecting the substance into their buttocks and thighs could be harmful to young patients. He wanted to inject in the buttocks but could not find a vein. He then injected into the calves. Subsequent to this, Brook (P) developed an Achilles tendon condition which required therapy. Brook (P) sued Fischer (D) for malpractice. The trial court rejected Brook's (P) proffered instruction that injection in a site other than that recommended by the medical community constituted improper experimentation on her. A jury rendered a defense verdict. The court of appeals reversed, holding that the instruction should have been given. The Indiana Supreme Court granted review.

ISSUE: Does a physician conduct an experiment on a patient by undertaking an unusual procedure if the physician has a reasonable basis for doing so?

HOLDING AND DECISION: (Hunter, J.) No. A physician does not conduct an experiment on a patient by undertaking an unusual procedure if the physician has a reasonable basis for doing so. Matters of judgment should not be confused with experimentation. The everyday practice of medicine sometimes presents unusual situations requiring therapeutic innovation. Such innovation, if done on reasonable grounds, is not tantamount to experimentation. Here, Fischer (D), based on literature he had read, declined to effect the injection in the usual manner. This was not an experiment, as he based his decision on legitimate information. Consequently, the trial court here was right in excluding Brook's (P) instructions. Reversed.

ANALYSIS

Generally speaking, conducting experimental procedures on patients is forbidden outside the clinical trial situation. As drugs and medical devices require FDA approval, discerning what is experimental and what is not is relatively easy. Other types of treatments can be more difficult to classify.

Quicknotes

FOOD AND DRUG ADMINISTRATION A federal agency responsible for establishing safety and quality standards for foods, drugs, and cosmetics.

NEGLIGENCE Conduct falling below the standard of care that a reasonable person would demonstrate under similar conditions.

Richardson v. Miller

Patient (P) v. Doctors (D)

Tenn. Ct. App., 44 S.W.3d 1 (2000).

NATURE OF CASE: Appeal of order excluding evidence.

FACT SUMMARY: A doctor used an infusion pump to administer a drug to stop a pregnant woman's premature labor. The use as prescribed was off-label and was not included in the drug's reference in the Physician's Desk Reference (PDR). The woman suffered a heart attack, and after giving birth to a healthy baby, sued the doctor and supplier of the infusion pump for malpractice.

RULE OF LAW

A prescription drug's labeling or parallel PDR reference is admissible with regard to the standard of care for using and administering the drug, so long as other expert evidence regarding the standard of care is also introduced.

FACTS: Cynthia Richardson (P) sought prenatal care from Dr. James Miller (D). When Richardson (P) complained that she experienced periods of palpitations, rapid heartbeats, and shortness of breath, Miller (D) referred her to a cardiologist. The cardiologist determined that she required no additional medical care. Richardson (P) visited Miller (D) for her last prenatal office visit when she was 35 weeks pregnant. The next day, she was admitted to the hospital in labor. Miller (D) gave her medication to stop her contractions by relaxing her uterine muscles, a process known as tocolysis. When the contractions did not stop, Miller (D) ordered the drug terbutaline sulfate. Terbutaline had been approved by the FDA only for treating bronchial asthma, but was also being widely used "off-label" as a tocolytic agent because it relaxes smooth muscles, including the muscles of the uterus. After a day of taking terbutaline orally, Richardson (P) awoke with chest pain. Miller (D) examined her and discovered that her chest pains subsided, but that she was still in labor. He suggested using an infusion pump to subcutaneously infuse smaller, timed doses of terbutaline into Richardson's (P) system, and she agreed. Tokos Medical Corporation (D) was contacted to procure a pump, and a nurse employed by Tokos (D) showed Richardson (P) and the hospital nursing staff instructions on using the pump. After taking the drug for three days, her labor abated, but on that day, she had a heart attack. Her baby was born that night. She recuperated for several days and was discharged. She then filed suit. Just before trial, Miller (D) moved to prevent the Richardsons (P) from introducing or using any information from both terbutaline's drug package insert and the PDR indicating that the drug had not been approved by the federal Food and Drug Administration for use in stopping premature labor. The trial court granted the motion. The Richardsons (P) did not claim that Miller (D) was negligent for initially attempting to use orally administered terbutaline to slow Richardson's (P) labor, an off-label use of the drug; rather, they claimed that Miller (D) breached the standard of care by continuing tocolysis using terbutaline after Richardson (P) began experiencing chest pain while taking the drug orally and by choosing to administer it subcutaneously using an infusion pump. The jury returned a verdict in favor of Miller (D) and Tokos (D).

ISSUE: Is a prescription drug's labeling or parallel PDR reference admissible with regard to the standard of care for using and administering the drug, so long as other expert evidence regarding the standard of care is also introduced?

HOLDING AND DECISION: (Koch, Jr., J.) Yes. A prescription drug's labeling or parallel PDR reference is admissible with regard to the standard of care for using and administering the drug, so long as other expert evidence regarding the standard of care is also introduced. In this case, the Richardsons (P) intended to call expert witnesses on the issue of the applicable standard of care, in addition to presenting evidence about terbutaline's Food and Drug Administration-approved labeling or the parallel PDR reference. Their testimony, when coupled with evidence that Miller (D) should not have continued Richardson (P) on terbutaline after she began experiencing chest pain would have been sufficient to require Miller (D) to explain why he continued administering terbutaline after Richardson (P) began experiencing severe chest pain, as well as the basis for his decision to use an infusion pump and how the proper dosage was determined. Reversed and remanded.

ANALYSIS

The ruling in this case is straightforward enough: a drug's labeling, off-label uses, and PDR reference are admissible to show the standard of care for using and administering the drug, but only if other evidence is also offered to show the standard of care. The opinion is particularly useful for its description of the Food and Drug Administration's process for approving drugs, and for its primer on the drug industry lexicon. Note also that off-label uses of drugs are not necessarily negligent—and in fact, they are common in the practice of medicine.

Quicknotes

MALPRACTICE A failure to perform one's professional duties during the course of a client relationship, either

Continued on next page.

intentionally or negligently, or the poor or improper discharge of one's professional obligations.

NEGLIGENCE Conduct falling below the standard of care that a reasonable person would demonstrate under similar conditions.

Hardi v. Mezzanotte

Physician (D) v. Patient (P)

D.C. Ct. App., 818 A.2d 974 (2003).

NATURE OF CASE: Appeal from a bench trial judgment in favor of plaintiff.

FACT SUMMARY: Dr. Hardi (D) appeals the judgment rendered in favor of Mezzanotte (P) in relation to a missed diagnosis which resulted in an unnecessary hysterectomy and the severe complications associated with a preventable case of peritonitis.

RULE OF LAW

Under this jurisdiction's discovery rule, a cause of action for medical malpractice does not accrue until the plaintiff discovers, or reasonably should have discovered, all of the essential elements of the action.

FACTS: In 1990, Mezzanotte (P) was treated by Dr. John O'Connor for diverticulitis [a condition where unnatural "pouches" or diverticulum form in the intestine and subsequently become infected. Diverticulitis is customarily treated with a course of antibiotics when the condition is in its uncomplicated form.] In January 1994, Mezzanotte (P) had a recurrence of symptoms and sought treatment from Dr. Hardi (D). Dr. Hardi (D), a Board-certified gastroenterologist, took Mezzanotte's (P) history, noted her previous treatment with antibiotics for diverticulitis and conducted a physical exam. Dr. Hardi (D) detected an abdominal mass, which could have been either gastrointestinal or gynecological in nature, but he failed to perform a differential diagnosis or initiate treatment of any kind. Instead, he referred Mezzanotte (P) to Dr. Match, a gynecologist. On February 8, 1994, Mezzanotte (P) saw Dr. Match per Dr. Hardi's (D) recommendation. Dr. Match, despite having received contradicting results from laboratory and ultrasound tests, concluded that Mezzanotte (P) had ovarian cancer and scheduled a complete hysterectomy. Dr. Match shared his diagnosis with Dr. Hardi (D), and despite the lack of evidence to support the diagnosis of uterine cancer, Dr. Hardi (D) "cleared" the need for the hysterectomy. While awaiting the surgery, Dr. Hardi (D) attempted to perform a sigmoidoscopy and ordered a barium enema study of Mezzanotte's (P) colon to rule out any other gastrointestinal disease. All of these studies had to be aborted because a significant obstruction of Mezzanotte's (P) colon was detected. Colon obstruction is a symptom consistent with worsening diverticulitis. On March 2, 1994, after the attempts at performing these final diagnostic procedures failed, Mezzanotte's (P) condition deteriorated and she was admitted to the hospital as an emergency patient. On March 8, 1994, Dr. Match performed the hysterectomy and it was discovered then that her undiagnosed diverticulitis had progressed to the point where the diverticulum in the intestinal wall had ruptured spreading the infection throughout her abdomen, i.e., peritonitis. This life-threatening infection caused multiple complications requiring Mezzanotte (P) to undergo four additional abdominal surgeries including a colostomy, or diversion of her bowels, and the repairs to multiple abdominal hernias caused by the weakening of her abdominal wall. Mezzanotte (P) spent a total of eighty-three days in the hospital and at a nursing home recovering. Mezzanotte (P) filed suit on March 6, 1997. Dr. Hardi (D) argued that the claim was time-barred by the state's three-year statute of limitations and that the last day any alleged misdiagnosis could have occurred was on March 2, 1994, when he last provided her with medical care prior to the hysterectomy. The trial judge, however, applied the discovery rule and extended the statute of limitations to three years after the date of her surgery on March 8, 1994, the day when Mezzanotte (P) could reasonably have discovered the misdiagnosis. This appeal ensued.

ISSUE: Under this jurisdiction's discovery rule, does a cause of action for medical malpractice accrue when the plaintiff discovers, or reasonably should have discovered, all of the essential elements of the action?

HOLDING AND DECISION: [Judge not stated in casebook excerpt.] Yes. Under this jurisdiction's discovery rule, a cause of action for medical malpractice does not accrue until the plaintiff discovers, or reasonably should have discovered, all of the essential elements of the action. These elements include the duty owed, the breach of the duty, causation and damages. Mezzanotte (P), as with any other patient, is clearly disadvantaged by the disparity in knowledge between the professional practitioners and their clientele. Mezzanotte (P) could not have been expected to be instantly aware of the negligence that was occurring in association with her misdiagnosis and treatment. It was only when the first abdominal surgery was performed that she learned of the actual cause of her illness and that it could have been treated earlier and prevented significant health complications and injury. On March 8, 1994, Mezzanotte (P) should have reasonably discovered all of the essential elements of her malpractice action. Her claim was filed on March 6, 1997, within the three-year statute following discovery. The judgment of the trial court is affirmed.

ANALYSIS

As a product of "tort reform" many states have enacted very short statutes of limitation for medical malpractice actions when compared to the limitations periods for general

Continued on next page.

negligence cases. This provides the defense with a strong affirmative defense because it often takes significant time to discover that medical malpractice occurred and it is frequently discovered by another practitioner in the course of providing services to correct the injury sustained from the prior practitioner's negligent acts. Recognizing that there can be lag time in discovering that malpractice has occurred, some jurisdictions have adopted compromise provisions such as "discovery rules" that allow a victim time to learn of the malpractice, especially considering that medical practitioners have superior knowledge as to whether the standard of care was breached. Most states adopting discovery rules, however, have also capped those rules with statutes of repose bringing finality to all claims at a set number of years, regardless if it took a longer period of time in which to discover the injury.

Quicknotes

CAUSATION The aggregate effect of preceding events that bring about a tortious result; the causal connection between the actions of a tortfeasor and the injury that follows.

CAUSE OF ACTION A fact or set of facts the occurrence of which entitles a party to seek judicial relief.

DUTY OF CARE A principle of negligence requiring an individual to act in such a manner as to avoid injury to a person to whom he or she owes an obligatory duty.

MALPRACTICE A failure to perform one's professional duties during the course of a client relationship, either intentionally or negligently, or the poor or improper discharge of one's professional obligations.

STATUTE OF LIMITATIONS A law prescribing the period in which a legal action may be commenced.

Ostrowski v. Azzara

Diabetic (P) v. Podiatrist (D)

N.J. Sup. Ct., 111 N.J. 429, 545 A.2d 148 (1988).

NATURE OF CASE: Appeal from denial of damages in malpractice action.

FACT SUMMARY: A jury found that Ostrowski's (P) health habits had been the principal cause of her medical complications following treatment by Azzara (D) and, consequently, denied her damages in a malpractice action.

RULE OF LAW

That a patient's health habits are the principal cause of posttreatment complications is not a basis for denying damages for malpractice.

FACTS: Ostrowski (P) was an insulin-dependent diabetic with a history of heavy smoking. She at one point presented herself to Azzara (D), a podiatrist, with a toenail inflammation. Azzara (D) performed a surgical incision on the toenail. As a result of poor circulation from the diabetes, Ostrowski's (P) toe failed to heal, and gangrene began to set in. Ostrowski (P) underwent two bypass operations and a vein transplant in an effort to save her foot. During this period of time, she continued to smoke, in contravention to Azzara's (D) advice. Ostrowski (P) sued for malpractice. The jury found the surgical procedure to have been inappropriate for Ostrowski's (P) condition but held Ostrowski (P) primarily responsible due to her smoking. The jury returned a defense verdict, and Ostrowski (P) appealed.

ISSUE: Is the fact that a patient's health habits are the primary cause of posttreatment complications a basis for denying damages for malpractice?

HOLDING AND DECISION: (O'Hern, J.) No. That a patient's health habits are the principal cause of posttreatment complications is not a basis for denying damages for malpractice. Resolution of this issue involves a subtle interplay between the concepts of avoidable consequences, comparative negligence, particularly susceptible victims, aggravation of preexisting conditions, and proximate cause. Avoidable consequences concerns the plantiff's carelessness after the defendant's legal wrong. Comparative negligence is a threshold matter. If the plaintiff is more responsible than the defendant for injury, then recovery is barred. "Particularly susceptible victim" is merely a restatement of the maxim that a defendant takes a plaintiff as he finds him. Aggravation of preexisting condition is a mitigation of the previous doctrine. A defendant who aggravates a preexisting condition will be responsible only to the extent of the aggravation, not the prior condition itself. Proximate cause serves as a foundation to the allocation of risk via the tort system and sometimes focuses on foreseeability of a particular risk. Applying these concepts to the present matter, Ostrowski (P) was not responsible for her initial injury, so comparative negligence should not have been found against her. Ostrowski (P) was more susceptible to surgical complication than most patients, but that is how Azzara (D) found her, and so she must take her. On the other hand, to the extent Ostrowski (P) would have deteriorated absent Azzara's (D) malpractice, Azzara (D) is not liable therefor. Finally, to the extent Ostrowski (P) could have avoided her problems by not smoking, as she was ordered to do, she may not recover. This matter must be remanded for a reconsideration of damages in light of these principles. Reversed and remanded for new trial.

ANALYSIS

Contributory or comparative negligence is not commonly applied against a patient, outside of something obvious, like a self-inflicted injury. More generally applied has been failure to mitigate damages. Its analysis was somewhat circuitous, but that is essentially the doctrine employed by the court here.

Quicknotes

COMPARATIVE NEGLIGENCE Doctrine whereby the court in assessing the appropriate measure of damages compares the relative fault of the parties and reduces the amount of damages to be collected by the plaintiff in proportion to his degree of fault.

PROXIMATE CAUSE The natural sequence of events without which an injury would not have been sustained.

Robins v. Garg

Patient's estate (P) v. Doctor (D)

Mich. Ct. App., 276 Mich. App. 351, 741 N.W.2d 49 (2007).

NATURE OF CASE: Appeal of summary judgment.

FACT SUMMARY: A woman with asthma and myocardial infarction died, and her estate sued her doctor.

RULE OF LAW

Expert testimony that contradicts a medical examiner's conclusion constitutes a genuine issue of material fact in a medical malpractice case, making summary judgment inappropriate.

FACTS: Dr. Tilak Garg (D) was a general practitioner who treated Ilene Robins (P) between 1986 and 1998. Garg (D) noted that Robins (P) was at risk for heart disease because she had a family history of heart disease, high cholesterol, and a history of smoking. He checked her cholesterol in 1986, but did not refer her to a cardiologist. In 1998, he again checked her cholesterol, and it was still high. He prescribed medication, but she didn't take it. He did not order or perform any other testing. In 2001, she came to Garg's (D) office with chest and back pain. He and his assistant took her to the EKG room, and he told the assistant to call an ambulance. Before it arrived, however, she died. A medical examiner determined the cause of death to be asthma with a contributing cause of myocardial infarction, but one of the plaintiff's witnesses provided expert testimony that the cause of death was a myocardial infarction.

ISSUE: Does expert testimony that contradicts a medical examiner's conclusion constitute a genuine issue of material fact in a medical malpractice case, making summary judgment inappropriate?

HOLDING AND DECISION: [Judge not stated in casebook excerpt.] Yes. Expert testimony that contradicts a medical examiner's conclusion constitutes a genuine issue of material fact in a medical malpractice case, making summary judgment inappropriate. The medical examiner's findings of fact were not subject to contradiction, but his interpretation of the facts was. Robins's (P) expert created a question of fact regarding whether plaintiff's heart condition caused her death. Questions of fact are appropriate for a jury, and summary judgment for Garg (D) was inappropriate. Reversed and remanded.

ANALYSIS

This is a clear case of how causation can be a central focus in a medical malpractice case. Often, a patient suffers from multiple health issues that can make the issue of causation extremely complicated.

Quicknotes

CAUSATION The aggregate effect of preceding events that bring about a tortious result; the causal connection between the actions of a tortfeasor and the injury that follows.

MEDICAL MALPRACTICE Conduct on the part of a doctor falling below that demonstrated by other doctors of ordinary skill and competency under the circumstances, resulting in damages.

SUMMARY JUDGMENT Judgment rendered by a court in response to a motion made by one of the parties, claiming that the lack of a question of material fact in respect to an issue warrants disposition of the issue without consideration by the jury.

Herskovits v. Group Health Cooperative of Puget Sound

Representative of decedent (P) v. Health care provider (D)

Wash. Sup. Ct., 99 Wash. 2d 609, 664 P.2d 474 (1983).

NATURE OF CASE: Appeal from summary judgment dismissing wrongful death/malpractice action.

FACT SUMMARY: A trial court dismissed Herskovits's (P) malpractice action when she failed to show that her decedent would probably have survived absent the alleged malpractice.

RULE OF LAW

A plaintiff in a wrongful death/malpractice action need not prove that the decedent more likely than not would have survived absent the alleged malpractice.

FACTS: Herskovits's (P) decedent presented himself to Group Health Cooperative of Puget Sound (D) complaining of coughs and chest pain. Group Health (D) failed to diagnose lung cancer, which was diagnosed by another facility one year later. The decedent's lung was removed, but he died 20 months later. Herskovits (P) sued Group Health (D) for negligent failure to diagnose. Group Health (D) moved for summary judgment, contending that the decedent suffered from a probability of dying even if it had promptly diagnosed the cancer. At best, the decedent had a 39% chance of recovery; the hospital's (D) alleged negligence reduced it to 25%. The trial court granted summary judgment, and Herskovits (P) appealed.

ISSUE: Must a plaintiff in a wrongful death/malpractice action prove that the decedent more likely than not would have survived absent the alleged malpractice?

HOLDING AND DECISION: (Dore, J.) No. A plaintiff in a wrongful death/malpractice action need not prove that the decedent more likely than not would have survived absent the alleged malpractice. To hold otherwise would have the practical effect of shielding medical providers from liability anytime a decedent did not have a greater than 50% chance of living, no matter how egregious its negligence. This is not a proper result. Analytically, the issue boils down to proximate cause, a jury question. Using this case as an example, the question is whether a diminution in chances of survival from 39% to 25% could be considered a substantial factor in bringing about injury. This, as noted before, is a jury question, and not properly resolvable at the summary judgment level. The trial court was therefore in error in so granting. Reversed.

CONCURRENCE: (Pearson, J.) All that is required to be shown is that a substantial reduction in chance of survival was caused by the alleged malpractice.

DISSENT: (Brachtenbach, J.) The basic question is whether the doctor's malpractice caused the patient's death. When the patient probably would have died anyway, this cannot be so.

ANALYSIS

The opinion was concerned with liability only. However, damages recoverable would be an issue in the context of this case. One possible measure of damages would be to make them commensurate with the lessening of the decedent's chance of survival due to the malpractice. In this case, Herskovits (P) would get 14% of full recovery under the measure.

Quicknotes

PROXIMATE CAUSE The natural sequence of events without which an injury would not have been sustained.

SUMMARY JUDGMENT Judgment rendered by a court in response to a motion by one of the parties, claiming that the lack of a question of material fact in respect to an issue warrants disposition of the issue without consideration by the jury.

CHAPTER 6

Liability of Health Care Institutions

Quick Reference Rules of Law

14. Physician Incentive Systems. (1) An HMO's committee meeting minutes are not discoverable if they are privileged under state law. (2) In a negligence claim alleging deviations from the applicable standard of care, documents concerning compensation and bonuses paid to a doctor by an HMO are not discoverable to show an incentive to refuse to refer for expensive tests. (Brannan v. Northwest Permanente, P.C.) *75*

Grimm v. Summit County Children Services Board

Patient (P) v. Healthcare system (D)

2006 WL 1329689 (Ohio App. 2006).

NATURE OF CASE: Negligence claim against hospital.

FACT SUMMARY: Shenna Grimm (P) claimed that the failure of Summa Health System (D) to immediately report suspected child abuse by her stepfather caused her damage.

RULE OF LAW

Nurses' failure to report suspected child abuse as shown by the patient's chart, in which the nurses noted events that were consistent with a history of sexual abuse, may be imputed to the employer under the doctrine of respondeat superior.

FACTS: Shenna Grimm (P) claimed that the failure of Summa Health System (D) to immediately report suspected child abuse by her stepfather caused her damage. [Her stepfather, who was the father of her child, was present in the delivery room when she gave birth, was seen in the hospital room when she was naked, and was present when she was breastfeeding.]

ISSUE: May nurses' failure to report suspected child abuse as shown by the patient's chart, in which the nurses noted events that were consistent with a history of sexual abuse, be imputed to the employer under the doctrine of respondeat superior?

HOLDING AND DECISION: [Judge not stated in casebook excerpt.] Yes. Nurses' failure to report suspected child abuse as shown by the patient's chart, in which the nurses noted events that were consistent with a history of sexual abuse, may be imputed to the employer under the doctrine of respondeat superior. In addition, whether any Summa (D) employee knew or suspected child abuse is a matter within the common knowledge and experience of lay jurors, and expert testimony is not required to find breach of the duty to report, proximate cause, and damages. Testimony of hospital staff and the content of the medical records reflect that Summa (D) employees had suspicions that Grimm (P) was or could be an abused child, and that they failed to make a timely report to Children Services Board. The suspicion triggered the duty to report, and failure to adhere to that duty imposed negligence per se. Moreover, an employee's negligence per se can be imputed to an employer through the doctrine of respondeat superior.

ANALYSIS

Note that in this case, the establishment of employee negligence was made through the doctrine of negligence per se—the doctrine that violation of a statute that sets forth specific duties constitutes negligence per se. Negligence per se can, in turn, be imputed to the employer through respondeat superior.

Quicknotes

NEGLIGENCE Conduct falling below the standard of care that a reasonable person would demonstrate under similar conditions.

NEGLIGENCE PER SE Conduct amounting to negligence as a matter of law because it is either so contrary to ordinary prudence or is in violation of statute.

RESPONDEAT SUPERIOR Rule that the principal is responsible for tortious acts committed by its agents in the scope of their agency or authority.

Scott v. SSM Healthcare St. Louis

Hospital (D) v. Patient (P)

Mo. Ct. App., 70 S.W.3d 560 (2002).

NATURE OF CASE: Appeal of denial of judgment notwithstanding the verdict.

FACT SUMMARY: Matthew Scott (P) suffered serious injuries as a result of a sinus infection that spread into his brain. He and his mother sued the hospital (D), the emergency room physician (D), and the radiologist (D).

RULE OF LAW

The fact that a physician retains independent medical judgment does not preclude a court from finding the existence of an employer-employee or principal-agent relationship between the hospital and physician.

FACTS: Matthew Scott (P) suffered serious injuries as a result of a sinus infection that spread into his brain. First, however, he was involved in a car accident and was taken to the hospital (D) where he was treated for minor injuries and released to his father. Two days later, he returned to the emergency room complaining of a severe headache. Dr. Doumit (D) ordered a CT scan of his head. Dr. Richard Koch (D), a radiologist and partner at Ragiologic Imaging Consultants (RIC), read the CT film and found the scan to be normal. Matthew was diagnosed with a mild concussion and sent home. When his headache had not subsided by the next day, his parents called the hospital (D) three times and informed Doumit (D) that Matthew was lethargic, nauseous, and vomiting. Doumit (D) told them these were signs of minor concussion and that if he did not improve in a few days, they should bring him back. The next day, he collapsed, losing all use of the right side of his body. A spinal tap and CT scan revealed an infection at the top of his brain. A number of surgeries were performed, and he was in a coma for several weeks. He recovered to a degree, but sustained serious permanent injuries, including a significant degree of paralysis on the right side of his body. He and his mother sued the hospital (D), Doumit (D) and Koch (D).

ISSUE: Does the fact that a physician retains independent medical judgment preclude a court from finding the existence of an employer-employee or principal-agent relationship between the hospital and physician?

HOLDING AND DECISION: [Judge not stated in casebook excerpt.] No. The fact that a physician retains independent medical judgment does not preclude a court from finding the existence of an employer-employee or principal-agent relationship between the hospital and physician. First, a jury question is presented when the evidence is sufficiently conflicting that reasonable minds could differ as to whether agency existed. There is no dispute that Doumit (D) was on staff, and therefore was an agent of the hospital (D). Koch (D), however, worked for RIC, which was a partnership and signatory to a contract with the hospital (D). The hospital (D) did not pay Koch (D), assign his hours, or bill for his services. But on the other hand, with respect to Koch (D), the hospital (D) set the medical standards, established qualifications, set prices, set liability insurance requirements, maintained a right to terminate, and provided office space, among other things. And the fact that the hospital (D) doesn't have the right to stand over Koch's (D) shoulder and dictate how to treat patients does not negate the existence of a factual issue regarding the existence of an agency relationship.

ANALYSIS

Questions about the status of a physician with respect to her relationship to a hospital are often left to a jury, because the relationship is complicated. Doctors need to be autonomous to do their work, and so have considerably more independence than employees in other industries. The fact that they are "agents" of the hospital can therefore be less than obvious.

Burless v. West Virginia University Hospitals, Inc.

Patients (P) v. Hospital (D)

W. Va. Sup. Ct., 215 W. Va. 765, 601 S.E.2d 85 (2004).

NATURE OF CASE: Appeal of order granting summary judgment to hospital.

FACT SUMMARY: Two women who brought lawsuits against West Virginia University Hospital, alleging they were injured by negligent treatment received at the hospital. The trial court did not allow the women to present evidence to support their claims that the physicians who treated them appeared to be hospital employees, even though they were actually independent contractors.

RULE OF LAW

Where a physician charged with negligence is an independent contractor, the hospital at which he works nevertheless may be found vicariously liable for his negligence.

FACTS: Jaclyn Burless (P) found out in July 1998. In November 1998 she went to West Virginia University Hospital (WVUH) for an ultrasound. At that time, Burless (P) signed a consent form that stated that the faculty physicians and resident physicians who provide treatment in the hospital are not employees of the hospital. When she ultimately delivered at WVUH in late February 1999, complications arose and her daughter, Alexis Price, experienced seizures and suffered a stroke. Burless (P) alleged that the doctors and hospital were negligent in failing to monitor her labor and delivery, and that the negligence caused severe and permanent mental, neurological, and psychological injuries to her daughter. Her lawsuit said WVUH was vicariously liable based upon a theory of apparent agency between WVUH and the physicians who provided the allegedly negligent care. Melony Pritt's (P) case [consolidated by the court for review purposes] arose out of a visit to the emergency department at WVUH in June 1998. She was diagnosed at that time as nine weeks pregnant, with a cyst on her left ovary. When she returned later in her pregnancy to have the cyst removed, she signed an informed consent for a laparotomy and left ovarian cystectomy. The surgery was complicated by a rupture of the cyst that was not properly contained or treated with antibiotics. Although discharged on that date, she returned two days later with a massive abdominal infection that resulted in premature labor and delivery of her son. According to Pritt (P), her son suffered severe permanent mental, neurological, and psychological injuries. Pritt (P) then sued WVUH, claiming that injuries to herself and her son resulted from the negligence of the physicians in recommending and performing an elective laproscopic cystectomy procedure. In both cases, a state circuit court found that WVUH could not be liable, because the women had signed consent forms and the hospital had not through its actions or its conduct, held the physicians out to be its employees.

ISSUE: Where a physician charged with negligence is an independent contractor, may the hospital at which he works nevertheless be found vicariously liable for his negligence?

HOLDING AND DECISION: (Davis, J.) Yes. Where a physician charged with negligence is an independent contractor, the hospital at which he works nevertheless may be found vicariously liable for his negligence. There is no evidence that the physicians actually worked for the hospital, and the hospital therefore cannot be found liable under the doctrine of respondeat superior, but it can be held liable under a theory of apparent agency. Under West Virginia law, regardless of any contractual arrangements with independent contractors, the hospital is liable to the injured patient for acts of malpractice committed in its emergency room, so long as the requisite proximate cause and damages are present. That same rule should apply outside of the emergency room setting. The public's confidence in the modern hospital's portrayal of itself as a full service provider of health care appears to be at the foundation of the national trend toward adopting a rule of apparent agency to find hospitals liable, under the appropriate circumstances, for the negligence of physicians providing services within its walls. In addition, the hospital did not unequivocally inform Pritt (P) and Burless (P) that the physicians treating them were not employees of the hospital. The disclaimer language used by WVUH, which indicated that faculty physicians and resident physicians who provide treatment in the hospital are independent contractors, was not sufficient to support a grant of summary judgment in the hospital's favor.

ANALYSIS

Remember that in order to show that the physician is an employee of the hospital, evidence of control must be present, in accordance with the tests for respondeat superior. Courts turn to apparent agency tests where there might be vicarious liability for the negligence of independent contractors.

Quicknotes

MEDICAL MALPRACTICE Conduct on the part of a doctor falling below that demonstrated by other doctors of ordinary

Continued on next page.

skill and competency under the circumstances, resulting in damages.

NEGLIGENCE Conduct falling below the standard of care that a reasonable person would demonstrate under similar conditions.

RESPONDEAT SUPERIOR Rule that the principal is responsible for tortious acts committed by its agents in the scope of their agency or authority.

SUMMARY JUDGMENT Judgment rendered by a court in response to a motion made by one of the parties, claiming that the lack of a question of material fact in respect to an issue warrants disposition of the issue without consideration by the jury.

Washington v. Washington Hospital Center

Patient (P) v. Hospital (D)

D.C. Ct. App., 579 A.2d 177 (1990).

NATURE OF CASE: Appeal of award of damages for negligence.

FACT SUMMARY: Washington Hospital Center (WHC) (D) was found negligent for not providing an end-tidal carbon monoxide monitor during surgery on Thompson (P).

RULE OF LAW

To establish the applicable standard of care in a medical malpractice action, a party must provide expert testimony sufficient to avoid jury findings based on speculation or conjecture.

FACTS: During Thompson's (P) 1986 abortion and tubal ligation surgery at Washington Hospital Center (WHC) (D), the anesthesiologist improperly inserted an endotracheal tube. Before the error was discovered, Thompson (P) suffered brain injuries that put her in a permanent vegetative state. Part of Thompson's (P) suit alleged that WHC (D) was negligent for not providing an end-tidal carbon monoxide monitor, which would have warned the doctors that Thompson (P) was not getting enough oxygen to her brain. Thompson's (P) expert, Dr. Steen, testified that he believed that by 1986 monitors were required in operating rooms, that they were available at his hospital, and that he had read publications that "recommended" monitors and described their use as an "emerging" practice. Evidence showed that at least four other hospitals used monitors by 1986. WHC's (D) expert testified that WHC (D) used monitors and that many hospitals were in the process of installing them. A requisition form for monitors submitted by WHC's (D) Department of Anesthesiology chairman stated that if monitors were not provided, WHC (D) would "fail to meet the national standard of care." The jury found WHC (D) negligent and awarded Thompson (P) damages. The trial judge denied WHC's (D) judgment N.O.V. motion. WHC (D) appealed, arguing that Dr. Steen failed to demonstrate an adequate basis for his opinion that a monitor should have been provided because he gave no testimony regarding the number of hospitals having monitors and cited no written standards or authorities stating that monitors were mandatory.

ISSUE: To establish the applicable standard of care in a medical malpractice action, must a party provide expert testimony sufficient to avoid jury findings based on speculation or conjecture?

HOLDING AND DECISION: (Farrell, J.) Yes. To establish the applicable standard of care in a medical malpractice action, a party must provide expert testimony sufficient to avoid jury findings based on speculation or conjecture. In a negligence action based on medical malpractice, the patient must establish: (1) the applicable standard of care, (2) a deviation from that standard, and (3) that the deviation caused the injury. Expert testimony is required except where proof is so obvious as to lie within the ken of the average lay juror. The standard of care is the course of action a reasonably prudent institution or professional with the same specialty would have taken under similar circumstances. The standard of care is national, not local. The standard of care may require more than mandatory procedures and precautions. Based on the testimony in this case, a reasonable jury could have found that the standard of care required WHC (D) to provide a monitor. Affirmed.

ANALYSIS

Courts rarely have applied negligence per se for statutory violations in medical malpractice cases against health care institutions. In some jurisdictions, evidence of violation of specific statutes or accreditation standards, supported by expert testimony, may create a permissive inference of violation of the standard of care. This inference allows a plaintiff to get his case to the jury, which may accept or reject the inference of negligence.

Quicknotes

JUDGMENT N.O.V. A judgment entered by the trial judge reversing a jury verdict if the jury's determination has no basis in law or fact.

NEGLIGENCE PER SE Conduct amounting to negligence as a matter of law because it is either so contrary to ordinary prudence or it is in violation of statute.

Muse v. Charter Hospital of Winston-Salem, Inc.

Decedent's parents (P) v. Hospital (D)

N.C. Ct. App., 117 N.C. App. 468, 452 S.E.2d 589 (1995).

NATURE OF CASE: Appeal of an award of damages in a wrongful death action.

FACT SUMMARY: Muse was discharged from Charter Hospital of Winston-Salem, Inc. (D), against his doctor's wishes because his insurance had expired.

RULE OF LAW

Hospitals have a duty not to institute policies or practices that require patients to be discharged because their insurance has expired and against the medical judgment of a doctor.

FACTS: Joe Muse, a sixteen-year-old, was hospitalized in June 1986, for treatment related to his depression. Joe had suicidal thoughts and impulses. Joe's insurance coverage was due to expire on July 12, 1986. As that date approached, Joe's doctor, Barnhill, decided that a blood test was necessary to determine a proper drug dosage. The blood test was scheduled for July 13. Barnhill requested that Charter Hospital of Winston-Salem, Inc. (D) allow Joe to stay a few extra days and Joe's parents, the Muses (P), agreed to pay for these days. Joe was discharged on July 14 although his blood results had not yet come back. Subsequently, on July 31, Joe committed suicide. The Muses (P) filed suit against Charter Hospital (D) for negligence in that it had a policy of discharging patients when their insurance expired despite the medical judgment of the patient's doctors. A jury awarded the Muses (P) $1 million in compensatory and $2 million in punitive damages. Charter Hospital (D) appealed, claiming that hospitals could not be liable for this type of action.

ISSUE: Do hospitals have a duty not to institute policies or practices that require patients to be discharged because their insurance has expired and against the medical judgment of a doctor?

HOLDING AND DECISION: (Lewis, J.) Yes. Hospitals have a duty not to institute policies or practices that require patients to be discharged because their insurance has expired and against the medical judgment of a doctor. It has been recognized that hospitals have a duty of care to their patients and must obey the instructions of a doctor. Hospitals must also make a reasonable effort to monitor and oversee the treatment prescribed. Therefore, it is clear that hospitals also have the duty not to discharge patients for insurance reasons if it interferes with the medical judgment of the patient's doctors. The evidence presented at trial shows that Charter Hospital (D) had a policy of discharging patients when their insurance expired. The record also shows that Dr. Barnhill made it evident to Charter Hospital (D) that he believed Joe should not be discharged. The compensatory damages are affirmed. The punitive damages are reversed for other reasons. No error in part, reversed in part, and remanded.

ANALYSIS

The court also ruled that the jury was justified in finding that Charter Hospital's (D) conduct was willful and recklessly indifferent. This case goes further than other decisions in defining a hospital's duty. The decision seems based on the notion that health care is a different type of service that mandates different types of duties.

Quicknotes

DUTY OF CARE A principle of negligence requiring an individual to act in such a manner as to avoid injury to a person to whom he or she owes an obligatory duty.

RECKLESSNESS The conscious disregard of substantial and justifiable risk.

Darling v. Charleston Community Memorial Hospital

Patient (P) v. Hospital (D)

Ill. Sup. Ct., 33 Ill. 2d 326, 211 N.E.2d 253 (1965).

NATURE OF CASE: Appeal from award of damages for medical malpractice.

FACT SUMMARY: Darling (P) sought to hold Charleston Community Memorial Hospital (D) liable for the alleged negligence of its staff.

RULE OF LAW

A hospital may be liable for the negligence of its staff.

FACTS: When Darling (P) broke his leg, he was taken to the emergency room at Charleston Community Memorial Hospital (D). The attending physician, Alexander (D), set the break and put the leg in a cast. The next day, Darling's (P) toes turned dark and cold. The cast was removed, but much of the tissue in the leg had become necrotic as a result of the constriction caused by the cast. The lower leg eventually had to be amputated. Darling (P) sued Alexander (D) and Charleston (D). After settling with Alexander (D), Darling (P) tried the case against the Charleston (D). The jury returned a verdict of $150,000. This was affirmed by the court of appeals, and the Supreme Court granted review on the issue of whether a hospital could be held liable for the negligence of its staff.

ISSUE: May a hospital be liable for the negligence of its staff?

HOLDING AND DECISION: [Judge not stated in casebook excerpt.] Yes. A hospital may be liable for the negligence of its staff. The notion that a hospital only provides facilities and does not purport to act through its staff physicians and nurses does not reflect reality. Modern hospitals do much more than provide facilities. They employ a large staff of doctors, nurses, administrators, and other workers, and do not hesitate to collect fees for services performed at the hospital. A person availing himself of a hospital reasonably expects the hospital as an entity to treat him. Consequently, no legitimate basis for not holding a hospital vicariously responsible for the torts of its staff exists. Here, the jury found both Alexander (D) negligent in the procedures he utilized, and the nursing staff negligent in their follow-ups. This was amply supported by the evidence. Affirmed.

ANALYSIS

Traditionally, doctors have been viewed as independent contractors by their hospitals. Under the common-law "independent contractor" rule, one employing a contractor as opposed to an employee will not be vicariously responsible therefor. Just as the rule has been weakened in recent times in society in general, so it has in medicine.

Quicknotes

INDEPENDENT CONTRACTOR A party undertaking a particular assignment for another who retains control over the manner in which it is executed.

Thompson v. Nason Hosp.

Patient (P) v. Hospital (D)

Pa. Sup. Ct., 527 Pa. 330, 591 A.2d 703 (1991).

NATURE OF CASE: Appeal from judgment for plaintiff and allocatur.

FACT SUMMARY: Nason Hospital (D) was held liable for negligent medical services.

RULE OF LAW

For a hospital to be charged with negligence, it is necessary to show that the hospital had actual or constructive knowledge of the defect or procedures that caused the harm, and the hospital's negligence must have been a substantial factor in bringing about the harm.

FACTS: When Mrs. Thompson (P) was admitted to Nason Hospital (D) after an automobile accident, she was in intensive care for three days. The fourth day she developed complete paralysis of the left side, from which she never recovered. Thompson (P) sued Nason (D), alleging that her injuries were the direct and proximate result of the negligence of Nason (D) acting through its agents, servants, and employees in failing to adequately examine and treat her. The court adopted a theory of corporate liability with respect to Nason (D) and found it liable. Nason (D) appealed.

ISSUE: For a hospital to be charged with negligence, is it necessary to show that the hospital had actual or constructive knowledge of the defect or procedures that caused the harm, and must the hospital's negligence have been a substantial factor in bringing about the harm?

HOLDING AND DECISION: (Zappala, J.) Yes. For a hospital to be charged with negligence, it is necessary to show that the hospital had actual or constructive knowledge of the defect or procedures that caused the harm, and the hospital's negligence must have been a substantial factor in bringing about the harm. There was a material issue of fact with respect to the hospital's (D) duty to monitor the medical services provided Thompson (P). There was a failure to report changes in the patient's condition that was not in accord with standard medical practice. Affirmed.

ANALYSIS

The court here adopted the doctrine of corporate negligence or corporate liability as a theory of hospital liability. A hospital is liable if it fails to uphold the proper standard of care. Such corporate liability is an emerging modern trend.

Quicknotes

AGENCY A fiduciary relationship whereby authority is granted to an agent to act on behalf of the principal in order to effectuate the principal's objective.

CONSTRUCTIVE KNOWLEDGE Knowledge that is imputed to an individual as a result of its being either in the public record or discoverable through the exercise of reasonable care.

CORPORATE LIABILITY The imposition of liability on a corporation's directors, officers, and shareholders if the corporation is established solely in order to perpetrate fraud or if other unlawful activity is conducted in the corporation's name.

NEGLIGENCE Conduct falling below the standard of care that a reasonable person would demonstrate under similar conditions.

STANDARD OF CARE A uniform degree of behavior against which a person's conduct can be measured when determining liability in negligence cases.

Carter v. Hucks-Folliss

Patients (P) v. Hospital (D)

N.C. Ct. App., 131 N.C. App. 145, 505 S.E.2d 177 (1998).

NATURE OF CASE: Appeal from summary judgment.

FACT SUMMARY: A man suffered permanent nervous system damage after undergoing surgery by a physician who was not Board certified. He sued the hospital.

RULE OF LAW

A hospital owes a duty of care to its patients to ascertain that a physician is qualified to perform surgery before granting that physician the privilege of conducting surgery in that hospital.

FACTS: Dr. Anthony Hucks-Folliss performed neck surgery on Tommy Carter (P) at Moore Regional Hospital (D). Hucks-Folliss was a neurosurgeon, and was on Moore's (D) staff for over twenty years. He was never certified by the American Board of Neurological Surgery, and failed the certification examination three times. Credentialing and re-credentialing at Moore (D) was required to comply with standards set by the Joint Commission on Accreditation of Healthcare Organizations (JCAHO), which stated that Board certification was an "excellent benchmark and to be considered when delineating clinical privileges." Hucks-Folliss specifically stated on his re-credentialing applications that he was not Board certified. Two witnesses testified for Carter (P) that Moore (D) seemed not to have considered that Hucks-Folliss was not Board certified during the re-credentialing process.

ISSUE: Does a hospital owe a duty of care to its patients to ascertain that a physician is qualified to perform surgery before granting that physician the privilege of conducting surgery in that hospital?

HOLDING AND DECISION: (Greene, J.) Yes. A hospital owes a duty of care to its patients to ascertain that a physician is qualified to perform surgery before granting that physician the privilege of conducting surgery in that hospital. Failure to comply with the standards of JCAHO is some evidence of negligence, because Moore (D) agreed to be bound by its standards. Moore (D) argued that it did, in fact, "consider" that Hucks-Folliss was not Board certified, but the evidence still presents a genuine issue of material fact that precludes summary judgment. Reversed and remanded.

ANALYSIS

In this case, it is the hospital's failure to comply with the recommendations of the JCAHO that provides some evidence of negligence. The court essentially adopts the JCAHO's standards as the negligence standard. On remand, the prudent attorney for the hospital will challenge that holding, because in fact, many working physicians are not board certified—rightly or wrongly.

Quicknotes

DUTY OF CARE Duty that an officer or director owes to the corporation, by virtue of his fiduciary relationship, to act for the benefit of the corporation.

NEGLIGENCE Conduct falling below the standard of care that a reasonable person would demonstrate under similar conditions.

SUMMARY JUDGMENT Judgment rendered by a court in response to a motion made by one of the parties, claiming that the lack of a question of material fact in respect to an issue warrants disposition of the issue without consideration by the jury.

Larson v. Wasemiller

Patients (P) v. Hospital (D)

Minn. Sup. Ct., 738 N.W.2d 300 (2007).

NATURE OF CASE: Appeal of dismissal of medical malpractice case.

FACT SUMMARY: A woman alleging negligent post-surgery care by two doctors sought to also sue the hospital, on the theory it negligently credentialed one of the doctors. The appeals court ruled that Minnesota law precluded such a cause of action against the hospital.

RULE OF LAW

A hospital may be held liable for negligent credentialing decisions.

FACTS: Mary Larson (P) filed a lawsuit against Dr. James Wasemiller (D) and Dr. Paul Wasemiller (D), claiming they provided negligent post-surgery care. Larson (P) also brought a negligent credentialing claim against St. Francis Medical Center (D), asserting the hospital should have known that James Wasemiller (D) posed an unreasonable danger of harm to patients undergoing bariatric surgery. The trial court denied the hospital's motion to dismiss, recognizing a common-law cause of action for negligent credentialing or privileging. The trial court also concluded that Minnesota's peer-review statute did not grant immunity or limit liability of a hospital or other review organization. The appeals court ruling found the confidentiality provisions in Minnesota's peer-review statute (Minn. Stat. § 145.63–.64) did not indicate any legislative intent to create or recognize a cause of action for negligent credentialing or privileging, saying it was up to the state's supreme court or Legislature to establish a new cause of action. The appeals court also held that while nothing in Minnesota's peer-review statute provides immunity from a negligent credentialing or privileging cause of action, Minn. Stat. § 145.63 limits liability to unwarranted peer-review actions, given the facts available to the hospital or reviewing organization. The appeals court also held that Minn. Stat. § 145.64 prevents any disclosure of what would appear to be information necessary to an intelligent inquiry into whether a review committee acted with a reasonable belief that its action was warranted by known facts.

ISSUE: May a hospital be held liable for negligent credentialing decisions?

HOLDING AND DECISION: (Hanson, J.) Yes. A hospital may be held liable for negligent credentialing decisions. In Minnesota, negligent credentialing claims brought to enforce a state's requirements that hospitals exercise reasonable care in granting physician privileges are not barred by the state's peer-review statute. Minnesota law does not preclude recognition of the existing common-law duty that hospitals have to ensure they exercise reasonable care in their credentialing decisions. Although the confidentiality provision of Minnesota's peer review statute may make the proof of a common-law negligent-credentialing claim more complicated, it does not preclude such a claim. The policy considerations underlying the tort of negligent credentialing outweigh the policy considerations reflected in the peer review statute because the latter policy considerations are adequately addressed by the preclusion of access to the confidential peer review materials. Reversed and remanded

CONCURRENCE: (Barry, J.) While the statute clearly contemplates a cause of action against a review organization for negligent credentialing, negligent credentialing litigation may not improve health care. The peer review statute may not be fulfilling the intended purpose. The legislature should act on this.

ANALYSIS

The court notes that there is an issue about whether a patient must first prove negligence on the part of a physician before a hospital can be liable for negligently credentialing the physician, but does not find this to be a barrier to the patient's cause of action, stating that "these are questions of trial management [that are] best left to the trial judge and that cannot be effectively addressed in the context." But remember to apply this principle to similar fact patterns on exams. Also note that this case follows the majority view that a hospital can be negligent for a credentialing decision.

Quicknotes

IMMUNITY Exemption from a legal obligation.

MEDICAL MALPRACTICE Conduct on the part of a doctor falling below that demonstrated by other doctors of ordinary skill and competency under the circumstances, resulting in damages.

MOTION TO DISMISS Motion to terminate an action based on the adequacy of the pleadings, improper service or venue, etc.

NEGLIGENCE Conduct falling below the standard of care that a reasonable person would demonstrate under similar conditions.

Kadlec Medical Center v. Lakeview Anesthesia Associates

Medical center (P) v. Medical center (D)

2005 WL 1309153 (E.D. La. 2005).

NATURE OF CASE: Motion for summary judgment.

FACT SUMMARY: A medical center provided incomplete information about a former staff member, who had been fired for drug abuse, to another medical center that was considering hiring him.

RULE OF LAW

A medical center is liable if, motivated by pecuniary interests, it fails to exercise reasonable care in communicating to another medical center an accurate performance evaluation of a former staff doctor who had been disciplined.

FACTS: Dr. Robert Lee Berry, an anesthesiologist, was fired by LRMC (D), a Louisiana medical center, and Louisiana Anesthesia Associates on suspicion of using Demerol. He applied for a position at Kadlec Medical Center (P), and during the application process, Kadlec (P) asked LRMC (D) for evidence of competence and a candid evaluation of Berry's training and performance. LRMC (D) sent a brief letter indicating the dates of Berry's employment with LRMC (D). Kadlec (P) hired Berry, and a year later, a patient suffered extensive brain damage and went into a coma during a tubal ligation surgery at which Berry was the anesthesiologist. It was alleged that he was impaired by drugs during the surgery. Kadlec (P) settled with the patient's family, and then sued LRMC (D) for intentional misrepresentation, negligent misrepresentation, strict responsibility misrepresentation, and negligence due to omission of material facts.

ISSUE: Is a medical center liable if, motivated by pecuniary interests, it fails to exercise reasonable care in communicating to another medical center an accurate performance evaluation of a former staff doctor who had been disciplined?

HOLDING AND DECISION: [Judge not stated in casebook excerpt.] Yes. A medical center is liable if, motivated by pecuniary interests, it fails to exercise reasonable care in communicating to another medical center an accurate performance evaluation of a former staff doctor who had been disciplined. LRMC (D) omitted the information at issue because it feared liability to Berry for defamation and other causes of action based on disclosure. It also had a pecuniary interest in responding to credentialing inquiries, since a failure to respond would have created difficulty in recruiting and retaining physicians.

ANALYSIS

It is fairly common for companies to set policy allowing managers to verify only dates of service and salary when asked for a reference by another company. Clearly, the rule is different in the health care field, and not without good reason.

Quicknotes

INTENTIONAL MISREPRESENTATION A statement or conduct by one party to another that constitutes a false representation of fact.

NEGLIGENCE Conduct falling below the standard of care that a reasonable person would demonstrate under similar conditions.

NEGLIGENT MISREPRESENTATION A misrepresentation that is made pursuant to a business relationship, in violation of an obligation owed, upon which the plaintiff relies to his detriment.

PECUNIARY INTEREST A monetary interest.

SUMMARY JUDGMENT Judgment rendered by a court in response to a motion made by one of the parties, claiming that the lack of a question of material fact in respect to an issue warrants disposition of the issue without consideration by the jury.

Petrovich v. Share Health Plan of Illinois, Inc.

Patient (P) v. Physician and HMO (D)

Ill. Sup. Ct., 188 Ill.2d 17, 719 N.E.2d 756 (1999).

NATURE OF CASE: Appeal from reversal of summary judgment for defendant in medical malpractice action.

FACT SUMMARY: Petrovich (P) claimed that Share Health Plan (D), a health maintenance organization (HMO), was vicariously liable for the negligence of its independent contractor physicians.

RULE OF LAW

Vicarious liability may be imposed for the actions of independent contractors where either the doctrine of apparent authority or of implied authority creates an agency relationship.

FACTS: Petrovich (P) visited physicians at her health maintenance organization (HMO) (D) repeatedly before they discovered she had cancer. Petrovich (P) later underwent surgery and alleged the physicians had been negligent in failing to diagnose her cancer in a timely manner. Petrovich (P) sued the physicians and the HMO (D) for medical malpractice. The trial court awarded summary judgment to Share (D), but the appellate court reversed. Share (D) appealed.

ISSUE: Can vicarious liability be imposed for the actions of independent contractors where either the doctrine of apparent authority or of implied authority creates an agency relationship?

HOLDING AND DECISION: (Bilandic, J.) Yes. Vicarious liability may be imposed for the actions of independent contractors where either the doctrine of apparent authority or of implied authority creates an agency relationship. Where an HMO holds itself out as being the health care provider without informing its patients that the physicians are independent contractors, and if the patient justifiably relies upon the HMO's conduct, looking to it for the provision of health care as opposed to an individual physician, then an apparent agency relationship is said to exist. Apparent agency is a question of fact, and if established the HMO can be held vicariously liable for the actions of its independent contractor physicians. In terms of whether or not an apparent agency relationship exists in this case, the evidence demonstrates that Share (D) represented to its employees in their employee handbook that the HMO provided their health care. The handbook referred to the physicians as being the HMO's staff, and the employees were never informed that the physicians were independent contractors. Share (D) also restricted their members' choice of physicians forcing them to reasonably rely on the HMO, not an individual physician, for the provision of their health care. Implied authority arises in situations where the facts and circumstances demonstrate that the defendant exerted sufficient control over the alleged agent to effectively negate the person's status as an independent contractor. The hallmark for determining the existence of implied authority is evaluating how much control over the work the alleged agent actually retains and exercises. In this case, Share's (D) capitation method of reimbursing its physicians controls what the physician can and cannot order in terms of medical treatment. Share (D) in fact, penalizes the physicians financially if they deviate from the range of care and treatment modalities that the HMO has approved. Petrovich (P) presented adequate evidence to support claims under both apparent and implied authority doctrines, and the circuit court's award of summary judgment to Share (D) was in error. The court of appeals decision to reverse the circuit court's judgment and remand the case for further proceedings is affirmed.

ANALYSIS

The court found that Petrovich (P) was entitled to a trial. The HMO (D) could be held vicariously liable under either of two theories. It could be vicariously liable under the doctrine of apparent authority or implied authority.

Quicknotes

APPARENT AUTHORITY The authority granted to an agent to act on behalf of the principal in order to effectuate the principal's objective, which is not expressly granted but which is inferred from the principal's conduct.

IMPLIED AUTHORITY Inferred power granted to an agent to act on behalf of the principal in order to effectuate the principal's objective.

INDEPENDENT CONTRACTOR A party undertaking a particular assignment for another who retains control over the manner in which it is executed.

NEGLIGENCE Conduct falling below the standard of care that a reasonable person would demonstrate under similar conditions.

VICARIOUS LIABILITY The imputed liability of one party for the unlawful acts of another.

Pagarigan v. Aetna U.S. Healthcare of California, Inc.

Patient's family (P) v. HMO (D)

Cal. Ct. App., 2005 WL 2742807 (2005).

NATURE OF CASE: Appeal of dismissal for failure to state a claim upon which relief could be granted.

FACT SUMMARY: The family of a woman who died because of alleged neglect by her healthcare provider sued, among others, the HMO. The lower court dismissed the claims.

RULE OF LAW

A health maintenance organization that contracts out its coverage decisions and medical care responsibilities to health care providers and other intermediaries can be held liable for malpractice committed by those contracting parties.

FACTS: California Civil Code § 3428(d) imposes a general duty of care on health insurance plans, like Aetna U.S. Healthcare of California, Inc. (D), when arranging health care services for their enrollees. Johnnie Pagarigan was a member of Aetna's HMO plan when she suffered a stroke and thereafter required nursing home care. Aetna (D) contracted with a management organization, which had contracted with two medical groups who, in turn, contracted with Magnolia Gardens nursing home to provide care for Pagarigan. After Pagarigan developed a large pressure sore and a severe infection during her stay at Magnolia Gardens, the nursing home delayed several months before sending Pagarigan to a hospital for treatment. By that time, it was too late to cure her condition, and Pagarigan died. Pagarigan's surviving children then filed a lawsuit against the nursing home, the treating physician, all intermediary health management firms, and Aetna (D).

ISSUE: Can a health maintenance organization that contracts out its coverage decisions and medical care responsibilities to health care providers and other intermediaries be held liable for malpractice committed by those contracting parties?

HOLDING AND DECISION: [Judge not stated in casebook excerpt.] Yes. A health maintenance organization that contracts out its coverage decisions and medical care responsibilities to health care providers and other intermediaries can be held liable for malpractice committed by those contracting parties. Aetna (D) has a duty of care when choosing providers who will supply health services to its enrollees and a duty to avoid executing contracts with terms that may require or encourage below-standard care. Aetna (D) may be liable if it knowingly entered into an agreement with a provider or a managed care intermediary it knew or should have known was incapable of providing its enrollee, Pagarigan, with medically necessary care, either because the contractor was improperly administered and inadequately funded and staffed, or because the contracting agreement provided the contractor with insufficient funds to give proper care. Similarly, a plan breaches its duty of ordinary care in arranging services for its enrollees if the plan negotiates a per capita payment so low the plan knows or should know it will require the provider to furnish substandard services and/or deny medically necessary services in order to survive. Plans like Aetna's (D) employ no doctors or hospitals. Instead, through a "capitation" arrangement, the HMO agrees to pay a contractor a specified amount each year for every enrollee in the HMO plan. The Pagarigans (P) are granted leave to amend their complaint to state a cause of action against Aetna (D) for negligence and wrongful death, but the lower court's dismissal of seven other claims against the HMO is affirmed.

ANALYSIS

While holding that an HMO can be liable vicariously for the negligence of contracting parties, the court does not indicate the standard by which the HMO's liability should be measured. The HMO owes a duty to avoid contracting with deficient providers or negotiating contract terms encouraging denials of service, but the limits of that duty are unclear.

Quicknotes

CAUSE OF ACTION A fact or set of facts the occurrence of which entitles a party to seek judicial relief.

MALPRACTICE A failure to perform one's professional duties during the course of a client relationship, either intentionally or negligently, or the poor or improper discharge of one's professional obligations.

NEGLIGENCE Conduct falling below the standard of care that a reasonable person would demonstrate under similar conditions.

Shannon v. McNulty

Patient (P) v. Hospital (D)

Pa. Super. Ct., 718 A.2d 828 (1998).

NATURE OF CASE: Appeal from denial of a motion to remove a compulsory nonsuit.

FACT SUMMARY: The Shannons (P) alleged that their physician, Dr. McNulty (D), and their HMO, HealthAmerica (D), were vicariously liable for the premature delivery and subsequent death of their son.

RULE OF LAW

When a benefits provider such as an HMO interjects itself into the rendering of medical decisions affecting a subscriber's care, it must do so in a medically reasonable manner.

FACTS: When Mrs. Shannon (P) suffered abdominal and back pain during her first pregnancy, she repeatedly called her physician, Dr. McNulty (D), and her HMO's (D) emergency phone line for advice. McNulty (D) was impatient with her and did not want to see her again, and the triage nurses told her to call her physician. She later went into preterm labor and delivered a baby who died due to his severe prematurity. Mrs. Shannon (P) sued for negligence under either a corporate or vicarious liability theory, but the trial court granted McNulty's (D) motion for a compulsory nonsuit. The Shannons (P) filed timely post-trial motions seeking to have the nonsuit removed. After denial of such motions, this appeal followed.

ISSUE: When a benefits provider, such as an HMO, interjects itself into the rendering of medical decisions affecting a subscriber's care, must it do so in a medically reasonable manner?

HOLDING AND DECISION: (Melvin, J.) Yes. When a benefits provider such as an HMO interjects itself into the rendering of medical decisions affecting a subscriber's care, it must do so in a medically reasonable manner. The corporate liability applicable to hospitals may be extended to HMOs as care providers with a substantial role in the total health care of patients. Here, HealthAmerica (D) provided a phone service for emergent care staffed by triage nurses. Hence, it was under a duty to oversee that the dispensing of such advice by those nurses would be performed in a medically reasonable manner. HMOs may therefore be held corporately liable for a breach of duties which causes harm to its subscribers. Reversed and remanded.

ANALYSIS

The court in this case cited to the case of *Thompson v. Nason Hospital*, 527 Pa. 330 (Pa. 1991). Pennsylvania first adopted the theory of corporate liability as it relates to hospitals in that case. An injured party does not have to rely on and establish the negligence of a third party when a hospital is liable under the corporate negligence theory.

Quicknotes

STANDARD OF CARE A uniform degree of behavior against which a person's conduct can be measured when determining liability in negligence cases.

Brannan v. Northwest Permanente, P.C.

Patient's family (P) v. Health care provider (D)

2006 WL 2794881 (W.D. Wash. 2006).

NATURE OF CASE: Motion to compel production of documents in malpractice litigation.

FACT SUMMARY: The estate of Barbara Brannan (P) sought from Kaiser Foundation Health Plan of the Northwest and Northwest Permanente PC (D) records of meetings of one of the HMO's committees, as well as documents held by one of Barbara's physicians concerning compensation and bonuses paid him by the HMO.

RULE OF LAW

(1) An HMO's committee meeting minutes are not discoverable if they are privileged under state law. (2) In a negligence claim alleging deviations from the applicable standard of care, documents concerning compensation and bonuses paid to a doctor by an HMO are not discoverable to show an incentive to refuse to refer for expensive tests.

FACTS: The estate of Barbara Brannan (P) sought from Kaiser Foundation Health Plan of the Northwest and Northwest Permanente PC (D) records of meetings of the HMO's regional formulary and therapeutics committee. The estate (P) also sought documents held by one of Barbara's physicians concerning compensation and bonuses paid him by the HMO. Brannan's representative claimed information on bonuses would show an incentive to refuse to refer for expensive tests, which the estate claimed contributed to Brannan's injuries.

ISSUE: (1) Are an HMO's committee meeting minutes discoverable if they are privileged under state law? (2) In a negligence claim alleging deviations from the applicable standard of care, are documents concerning compensation and bonuses paid to a doctor by an HMO discoverable to show an incentive to refuse to refer for expensive tests?

HOLDING AND DECISION: [Judge not stated in casebook excerpt.] (1) No. An HMO's committee meeting minutes are not discoverable if they are privileged under state law. In this case, the Ore. Rev. Stat. § 41.675 peer review and quality assurance provisions cover the meeting minutes, which are therefore privileged. The argument that the privilege only applied in the context of disciplinary actions is unpersuasive. The statute applies to "peer review" bodies, including governing bodies or committees, medical staff committees of a health care facility, and providers of medical services in connection with bona fide medical research, quality assurance, utilization review, credentialing, education, training, or supervision. Medical staff should be allowed to speak frankly about what drugs to include in the institution's formulary and the therapeutic value of prescribing certain drugs for specific conditions without concern or fear that the discussions will be used in litigation. The value of keeping a formulary and therapeutic committee's discussions confidential ultimately is for the good of the patients in allowing drugs to be either added or withdrawn for good therapeutic reasons as well as for the protection of the institution in having full and frank discussions about the uses of available drugs. (2) No. In a negligence claim alleging deviations from the applicable standard of care, documents concerning compensation and bonuses paid to a doctor by an HMO are not discoverable to show an incentive to refuse to refer for expensive tests. Even if true, such information is irrelevant to negligence claims alleging deviations from the applicable standard of care. While HMOs frequently have an incentive system in place discouraging staff physicians from making referrals and ordering diagnostic tests, the alleged motive of the physician in this case alleged is not relevant in a medical malpractice claim where the fundamental issue is whether the defendant breached the standard of care and caused injury to the plaintiff, regardless of what the defendant's state of mind was.

ANALYSIS

This is a straightforward case, but raises important issues to consider. Whatever the contractual agreements between physicians and HMOs—however they deviate from the goal of providing quality health care—they are not relevant to a negligence claim, which deals specifically with deviation from a standard of care, without contemplation of motive. In addition, whenever you are faced with a motion to compel documents, the privilege issue should always be raised.

Quicknotes

MALPRACTICE A failure to perform one's professional duties during the course of a client relationship, either intentionally or negligently, or the poor or improper discharge of one's professional obligations.

NEGLIGENCE Conduct falling below the standard of care that a reasonable person would demonstrate under similar conditions.

Note: There are no principal cases in Chapter 7 of the casebook.

CHAPTER 8

Access to Health Care

Quick Reference Rules of Law

Ricks v. Budge

Patient (P) v. Physician (D)

Utah Sup. Ct., 91 Utah 307, 64 P.2d 208 (1937).

NATURE OF CASE: Appeal of directed verdict denying award of damages for medical malpractice.

FACT SUMMARY: Dr. Budge (D) ceased treating Ricks (P) due to an unpaid account.

RULE OF LAW

A physician may not unilaterally cease treating a patient due to lack of payment.

FACTS: From March 11 to March 15 [the year was not stated] Ricks (P) was treated by Dr. Budge (D) for an infected hand. He was released on March 15. On March 17, he again presented himself, being symptomatic. Dr. D. C. Budge (D) sent him to a hospital, where S. M. Budge (D) was on staff. Dr. S. M. Budge (D) refused to treat Ricks (P), as his account was past due. Ricks (P) went to another facility, where he was treated. Eventually, part of his hand had to be amputated. Ricks (P) sued the Budges (D) for malpractice. The trial court directed a verdict in favor of the Budges (D), and Ricks (P) appealed.

ISSUE: May a physician unilaterally cease treating a patient due to lack of payment?

HOLDING AND DECISION: (Hanson, J.) No. A physician may not unilaterally cease treating a patient due to lack of payment. A physician, upon undertaking to treat a patient, must continue to care for the patient until such time as care is no longer required. A physician can withdraw from care of a patient, but he must give the patient sufficient notice as to allow him to find alternative care. Here, the evidence was sufficient to go to a jury as to whether the Budges (D) had continued their care of Ricks (P) and then ceased to provide services without allowing him sufficient time to seek alternate care. Reversed.

DISSENT IN PART: (Folland, J.) There was evidence that the Budges (D) abandoned Ricks (P) but insufficient evidence for a jury to conclude that Ricks (P) was damaged thereby.

ANALYSIS

Many states have ethical or legal rules regarding the duty of physicians to care for those who cannot pay for services. The nature of the duty, as well as its source, varies. Clashing as they do with economic reality, these rules are usually more notable for being an aspiration than a practice.

Quicknotes

DAMAGES Monetary compensation that may be awarded by the court to a party who has sustained injury or loss to his or her person, property or rights due to another party's unlawful act, omission or negligence.

MEDICAL MALPRACTICE Conduct on the part of a doctor falling below that demonstrated by other doctors of ordinary skill and competency under the circumstances, resulting in damages to patients.

Childs v. Weis

Patient (P) v. Physician (D)

Tex. Ct. Civ. App., 440 S.W.2d 104 (1969).

NATURE OF CASE: Appeal of dismissal of malpractice action.

FACT SUMMARY: Dr. Weis (D), upon being told that Childs (P) was beginning labor, did not treat her but rather referred her to her regular physician.

RULE OF LAW
A physician who does not undertake to treat a patient cannot be liable for malpractice.

FACTS: Childs (P), seven months pregnant, was away from her residence in the city of Dallas. When she began having labor pains, she went to an emergency room. A nurse telephoned Dr. Weis (D), who suggested Childs (P) call her regular doctor. The nurse apparently misrelayed the message, telling her to go to her doctor in Dallas. The baby was born in transit and did not survive. Childs (P) sued Weis (D) for malpractice. The trial court granted summary judgment, dismissing the action, and Childs (P) appealed.

ISSUE: Can a physician who does not undertake to treat a patient be liable for malpractice?

HOLDING AND DECISION: (Williams, J.) No. A physician who does not undertake to treat a patient cannot be liable for malpractice. The relation of physician and patient is dependent upon contract. A physician is not to be held liable for refusing to respond to the call of a person even urgently in need of medical services. Absent such agreement, no liability can accrue. Here, Weis (D) at no time agreed to treat Childs (P), as he referred her to her own doctor. While it is true that the nurse to some extent misconveyed Weis's (D) suggestion, this in no way affected Weis's (D) position. Affirmed.

ANALYSIS

It is nearly universal that a physician is under no duty to help one even greatly in need of medical care. To encourage doctors to provide assistance in emergencies, some states have enacted "Good Samaritan" laws, relieving doctors who treat accident or emergency victims of civil liability absent recklessness. The idea of imposing an affirmative duty to help has been debated, but the issue raises numerous moral and constitutional questions.

Quicknotes

GOOD SAMARITAN LAW A statute relieving a bystander from tort liability for the attempted rescue of another.

MALPRACTICE A failure to perform one's professional duties during the course of a client relationship, either intentionally or negligently, or the poor or improper discharge of one's professional obligations.

Williams v. U.S.

Administratrix (P) v. Federal government (D)

242 F.3d 169 (4th Cir. 2001).

NATURE OF CASE: Appeal from dismissal for lack of subject matter jurisdiction.

FACT SUMMARY: Williams (P), adminstratrix for the decedent, brought suit against the United States (D) for refusal to render emergency medical treatment to the decedent resulting in his death.

RULE OF LAW

Neither a physician, nor a private hospital, has a duty to render medical services to every person requesting them.

FACTS: Berlie White, decedent, presented to Cherokee Indian Hospital (CIH) suffering from respiratory distress. CIH, the nearest hospital he could reach at the time, was an Indian hospital operated on the Cherokee Reservation by the United States Public Health Service. CIH was operated under the federal Indian Health Care Improvement Act (IHCI Act), which prohibits treatment of non-Indians, except for discretionary treatment in emergency situations. The federal employees at CIH refused to treat Mr. White, and refused to refill his oxygen tank. He was referred to another hospital ten miles away. Upon arrival at that hospital, he was in extreme distress and he died from complications of oxygen deprivation the following day. Williams (P), the adminstratrix of Mr. White's estate, brought suit under various theories alleging the breach of a duty to provide emergency treatment on a non-discriminatory basis. The district court dismissed and this appeal followed.

ISSUE: Does either a physician, or a private hospital, have a duty to render medical services to every person requesting them?

HOLDING AND DECISION: (Niemeyer, J.) No. Neither a physician, nor a private hospital, has a duty to render medical services to every person requesting them. Williams (P) raises four theories in an attempt to establish a duty on the part of health care providers to provide emergency services. Williams (P) argues: (1) North Carolina General Statutes (NCGS) § 58-65-85 prohibits non-profit hospitals from discriminating on the basis of race, color and natural origin; (2) NCGS § 131A-8 requires all health care facilities receiving state funding to be operated to serve and benefit the public in a non-discriminatory manner; (3) the Patients' Bill of Rights, § 3C.4103, promulgated pursuant to NCGS § 131E-75 requires that care be provided; and (4) the common-law duty for public utilities whereby, once a public institution has held itself out as providing a service, it cannot arbitrarily refuse to provide that service to a member of the public. The problem with Williams's (P) theories is that none of the alleged "duties" created by statute authorize any mechanism for their enforcement, and the common-law public utility doctrine has no application toward health care providers in private settings. At best the IHCI Act provided for discretionary treatment, which the federal employees declined to render. While the circumstances of this case are morally repugnant, the scope of the law is much "narrower than the reach of moral command." The Court affirms the dismissal by the district court.

ANALYSIS

The casebook author uses this case as an illustration of there being no general duty to provide medical treatment, nor the presence of a law to prevent discrimination in allocating treatment. It should be noted that the procedural posture of this case hinged on the application of the Federal Torts Claim Act (FTCA) in association with the Emergency Medical Treatment and Active Labor Act (EMTALA). The federal government has sovereign immunity from suit even when violating its own Acts unless, as provided in the FTCA, the liability would exist if the government were acting as a private person in accordance with the law on private parties in the locality where the alleged tort occurred. Consequently, since Williams (P) was unable to establish any private duty to provide medical treatment in North Carolina, the United States (D) was immune from suit. Even though there is, for the most part, no affirmative duty to provide health care, once a decision is made to offer services and a physician-patient relationship is formed, then traditional medical malpractice negligence law is applicable. Also consider that had this been a private hospital receiving federal funds, then EMTALA would have required, at minimum, stabilization of Mr. White prior to being transferred to another facility, and the private hospital would not have immunity from suit.

Quicknotes

EMTALA Requires hospitals that accept Medicare payments and have emergency departments to furnish emergency medical screening and treatment.

Baber v. Hospital Corporation of America

Decedent's brother (P) v. Hospital (D)

977 F.2d 872 (4th Cir. 1992).

NATURE OF CASE: Appeal from summary judgment in an action based on violations of the Emergency Medical Treatment and Active Labor Act (EMTALA).

FACT SUMMARY: When Baber's (P) sister died after being treated in Raleigh General Hospital's (RGH) (D) emergency room, where she fell and struck her head while having a convulsion, Baber (P) brought this suit, alleging violations of the requirements of EMTALA.

RULE OF LAW

A hospital must provide a medical screening examination that is appropriate and within the capability of the hospital's emergency department when determining the existence of an emergency medical condition.

FACTS: Baber's (P) sister sought treatment at Raleigh General Hospital's (RGH) (D) emergency room for agitation caused by her mental illness. Even after medication was administered, she remained agitated. While pacing around the emergency department, she convulsed and fell, striking her head on a table. Ms. Baber became calmer and drowsy after the resulting wound was sutured but still experienced some agitation and disorientation. Concluding that her behavior was due to her chronic mental illness, the treating physician transferred her to a hospital with a psychiatric ward, where she had another seizure. A CT scan revealed a fractured skull. Ms. Baber was transferred back to RGH (D), became comatose, and died. Baber (P) brought this suit, alleging several violations of EMTALA due to RGH's (D) failure to provide an appropriate medical screening for his sister. The district court granted summary judgment for RGH (D). Baber (P) appealed.

ISSUE: Must a hospital provide a medical screening examination that is appropriate and within the capability of the hospital's emergency department when determining the existence of an emergency medical condition?

HOLDING AND DECISION: (Williams, J.) Yes. A hospital must provide a medical screening examination that is appropriate and within the capability of the hospital's emergency department when determining the existence of an emergency medical condition. The goal of the screening examination is to determine whether a patient with acute or severe symptoms has a life-threatening or serious medical condition. While EMTALA requires a hospital emergency department to apply its standard uniformly, it does not guarantee that the emergency personnel will correctly diagnose a patient's condition as a result of this screening. While Ms. Baber did exhibit some of the signs and symptoms of patients with severe head injuries, the treating physician believed her condition was stable prior to transfer and that she was not suffering from an emergency medical situation. He, therefore, determined that a CT scan or x-rays were not indicated at that time. Although his assessment and judgment may have been erroneous, the screening examination was not so substandard as to amount to no examination. Affirmed.

ANALYSIS

Baber (P) also alleged that RGH (D) inappropriately transferred his sister to the psychiatric hospital. In order to recover for violations of EMTALA's transfer provisions, a plaintiff must prove that (1) the patient had an emergency medical condition; (2) the hospital knew of the condition; (3) the patient was not stabilized before transfer; and (4) the hospital did not follow appropriate transfer procedures. Here, Baber (P) did not present any evidence beyond his own belief that his sister had an emergency condition or that the hospital knew about it.

Quicknotes

EMTALA Requires hospitals that receive Medicare payment and have emergency departments to furnish emergency medical screening and treatment.

Bragdon v. Abbott

Dentist (D) v. Patient (P)

524 U.S. 624 (1998).

NATURE OF CASE: Review of summary judgment for plaintiff in case alleging violation of the Americans with Disabilities Act of 1990 (ADA).

FACT SUMMARY: Abbott (P) alleged that her dentist, Bragdon (D), discriminated against her in violation of the ADA when he refused to treat her in his office.

RULE OF LAW

The existence or nonexistence of a significant health or safety risk must be determined from the standpoint of the person who refuses treatment or accommodation, and the risk assessment must be based on medical or other objective evidence.

FACTS: Abbott (P), who was infected with human immunodeficiency virus (HIV), disclosed her infection when she visited Bragdon (D), a dentist. When Bragdon (D) informed Abbott (P) of his policy against filling cavities of HIV-infected patients, he offered to perform the work at a hospital with no added fee for his services, though Abbott (P) would be responsible for the cost of using the hospital's facilities. Abbott (P) sued under § 302 of the ADA, alleging discrimination on the basis of her disability. The district court ruled in favor of Abbott (P), holding that her HIV infection was a disability under the ADA, even though her infection had not yet progressed to the symptomatic stage. The court of appeals agreed that treating Abbott (P) in the dental office would not have posed a direct threat to the health and safety of others. Bragdon (D) appealed. The Supreme Court granted certiorari.

ISSUE: Must the existence or nonexistence of a significant health or safety risk be determined from the standpoint of the person who refuses the treatment or accommodation, and must the risk assessment be based on medical or other objective evidence?

HOLDING AND DECISION: (Kennedy, J.) Yes. The existence or nonexistence of a significant health or safety risk must be determined from the standpoint of the person who refuses treatment or accommodation, and the risk assessment must be based on medical or other objective evidence. No individual is required to participate in or benefit from the services in any place of public accommodation when such individual poses a direct threat to the health or safety of others. Bragdon (D) failed to present any objective medical evidence showing that treating Abbott (P) in a hospital would be safer or more efficient in preventing HIV-transmission than treatment in a well-equipped dental office. This court is concerned, however, that the court of appeals mistakenly relied on the 1993 CDC Dentistry Guidelines, and the 1991 American Dental Association Policy on HIV. This evidence is not definitive. As of September 1994, the CDC had identified seven dental workers with possible occupational transmission of HIV. It is not clear on this record, however, whether this information was available to Bragdon (D). If not, the seven cases might have provided some support for his position. The proper course is to give the court of appeals the opportunity to determine whether our analysis of some of the studies cited by the parties would change its conclusion that Bragdon (D) presented neither objective evidence nor a triable issue of fact on the question of risk. Reversed and remanded.

CONCURRENCE: (Stevens, J.) Bragdon (D) has not sustained his burden of adducing evidence sufficient to raise a triable issue of fact on the significance of the risk posed by treating Abbott (P) in his office. I join the court's opinion even though I would prefer an outright affirmance.

CONCURRENCE AND DISSENT: (Rehnquist, C.J.) Bragdon (D) has presented more than enough evidence to avoid summary judgment on the direct threat question. Given the severity of the risk here and the absence of protocol for eliminating this risk, it seems likely that he can establish that it was objectively reasonable for him to conclude that treating Abbott (P) in his office posed a direct threat to his safety.

CONCURRENCE AND DISSENT: (O'Connor, J.) The court of appeals failed to properly determine whether Abbott's (P) condition posed a direct threat, and remand is necessary on that issue.

ANALYSIS

Before this case, the CDC guidelines were relied on as an authoritative source on level of risk and necessary precautions. The rule from this case has also been applied to cases alleging employment discrimination. The ADA's direct threat provision codified the holding from *School Board of Nassau County v. Arline*, 480 U.S. 273 (1987).

Quicknotes

REHABILITATION ACT OF 1973 Prohibits discrimination against handicapped individuals.

Howe v. Hull

Personal representative (P) v. Physician (D)

874 F. Supp. 779 (N.D. Ohio 1994).

NATURE OF CASE: Hearing on a motion for summary judgment.

FACT SUMMARY: Howe (P), personal representative for decedent, Mr. Charon (Charon), brought suit against Dr. Hull (D) alleging discrimination associated with the transfer of decedent to another hospital.

RULE OF LAW

The statutory exception to the common-law no-duty rule created in the Americans with Disabilities Act applies even if the person's disability was only one reason of many for the discrimination.

FACTS: Charon and Howe (P) were traveling through Ohio at the time Charon began taking a new prescription antibiotic called "floxin." Apparently Charon had an allergic reaction to the medication and experienced fever, headache, nausea, joint pain, and redness of the skin. Charon sought treatment in the emergency room of Fremont Memorial Hospital (FMH) and received an initial diagnosis of toxic epidermal necrolysis (TEN), a serious, rare and frequently lethal skin condition. The physician who first examined Charon was planning to admit him to FMH, but when the supervising physician discovered that Charon was infected with the human immunodeficiency virus (HIV) he ordered that Charon be transferred to the Medical College of Ohio (MCO). Testimony revealed that when MCO was called and asked to accept transfer of Charon that there was no discussion of a diagnosis of TEN. The only discussion concerning Charon's transfer was his status of being HIV positive. Prior to being transferred, the examining physician essentially admitted that the transfer was based upon discrimination. Dr. Hull (D), the physician in charge of admissions that day, had told the examining physician that, "if you get an AIDS patient in the hospital, you will never get him out." Once Charon arrived at MCO he was diagnosed with a simple allergic reaction, and was treated and released from the hospital. Charon's personal representative, Howe (P), brought a discrimination action against Hull (D) alleging violations of the Americans with Disabilities Act (ADA) and the Federal Rehabilitation Act of 1973 (FRA). Hull (D) moved for summary judgment and this hearing ensued.

ISSUE: Does the statutory exception to the common-law no-duty rule created in the Americans with Disabilities Act apply if the person's disability was only one reason of many for the discrimination?

HOLDING AND DECISION: (Potter, J.) Yes. The statutory exception to the common-law no-duty rule created in the Americans with Disabilities Act applies even if the person's disability was only one reason of many for the discrimination. There are three elements to establish a prima facie case of discrimination under the ADA: (1) the plaintiff must have a disability, (2) there must be discrimination against the plaintiff by the defendant, and (3) the discrimination must be based upon the disability. In contrast, a prima facie case of discrimination under the FRA requires: (1) the plaintiff to have a disability, (2) the plaintiff must have been otherwise qualified to participate in the program that was denied, (3) the discrimination must have been based solely upon the disability, and (4) the program must have received federal funding. There are two distinctions in the requirements for these two provisions. First, the FRA requires that the services or program that were denied were receiving federal funding. Second, the FRA requires that the discrimination be solely based upon the disability, whereas the ADA does not. Under the facts of this case, a fact-finder could reasonably believe that the diagnosis of TEN, a rare disease process, was pretextual and that the only reason Charon was transferred was because of his HIV status. There is sufficient evidence to establish a prima facie case for both the ADA and FRA claims to survive a motion for summary judgment and as such the motion is denied.

ANALYSIS

In this case, the examining physician, Dr. Reardon, essentially admitted to Charon that the transfer was related to his HIV status. Dr. Reardon told Charon, "I'm sure you've dealt with this before . . ." Howe (P) asked, "What's that, discrimination?" Dr. Reardon replied, "You have to understand, this is a small community, and the admitting doctor does not feel comfortable admitting [Charon]." In other cases, it may be much more difficult to prove that discrimination was involved in the medical decision due to the complexity of a patient's condition. Thus, in cases where a disease process involves multiple body systems the court may find itself in a position of deference to the practitioners providing a defense, even if that provider's motives are questionable. Also, Titles II and III of the ADA, covering access to professional offices of health care providers and access to government programs, contain an exception when an individual with a disability poses a direct threat to the health or safety of others. A direct threat is defined as a significant risk to the health or safety of others that cannot be eliminated or satisfactorily mitigated by reasonable modifications to the covered entity's procedures. Current case

Continued on next page.

law indicates that the "direct threat" defense for denying treatment on the basis of HIV infection would have to be evaluated on a case-by-case basis, but this again creates a legal defense contingent on medical expertise that may trump a strict legal decision.

Quicknotes

AMERICANS WITH DISABILITIES ACT Prohibits discrimination in employment, housing, transportation and other services on the basis of an individual's physical or mental disabilities.

PRIMA FACIE An action in which the plaintiff introduces sufficient evidence to submit an issue to the judge or jury for determination.

CHAPTER 9

Private Health Insurance and Managed Care: State Regulation and Liability

Quick Reference Rules of Law

1. **Contract Liability of Private Insurers and Managed Care Organizations.** If an insurance provider attempts to exclude a new procedure from coverage as experimental under an exclusion clause, the terms of the clause will be construed as liberally as possible in favor of the insured to maximize coverage. (Lubeznik v. Healthchicago, Inc.) *86*

2. **Attempts to Increase Access to Insurance Through Regulation.** Insurance pool contributions are a valid exercise of the legislature's power to regulate, and an enactment intended to regulate rather than generate revenue is not a tax. (Colonial Life Insurance Company of America v. Curiale) *87*

Lubeznik v. Healthchicago, Inc.

Cancer patient (P) v. Health maintenance organization (D)

Ill. App. Ct., 268 Ill. App. 3d 953, 644 N.E.2d 777 (1994).

NATURE OF CASE: Appeal of an injunction requiring precertification for certain medical treatments.

FACT SUMMARY: Lubeznik (P) sought precertification from her insurance company for bone marrow transplants to treat her advanced ovarian cancer.

RULE OF LAW

If an insurance provider attempts to exclude a new procedure from coverage as experimental under an exclusion clause, the terms of the clause will be construed as liberally as possible in favor of the insured to maximize coverage.

FACTS: Bonnie Lubeznik (P) suffered from Stage III ovarian cancer. All conventional therapies had failed to arrest the cancer. A specialist, Dr. Stiff, determined that an autologous bone marrow transplant combined with high-dose chemotherapy would provide the best chance for Lubeznik (P). In twenty-one other cases, Dr. Stiff had a seventy-five percent success rate of complete remission. Dr. Stiff sought precertification of payment from Healthchicago, Inc. (D). Healthchicago (D) denied the request under an exclusion clause for experimental procedures. However, Healthchicago (D) had not sought a determination from expert medical boards as to whether the procedure was still considered experimental. Lubeznik (P) filed suit, seeking an injunction ordering precertification. Her injunction was granted. Healthchicago (D) appealed.

ISSUE: If an insurance provider attempts to exclude a new procedure from coverage as experimental under an exclusion clause, will the terms of the clause be construed as liberally as possible in favor of the insured to maximize coverage?

HOLDING AND DECISION: (Johnson, J.) Yes. If an insurance provider attempts to exclude a new procedure from coverage as experimental under an exclusion clause, the terms of the clause will be construed as liberally as possible in favor of the insured to maximize coverage. The disparity in bargaining power and expertise between insured and insurer justifies the law's presumption that all clauses are to be construed as favorably as possible to the insured. In this case, Lubeznik's (P) only viable chance for treatment was the bone marrow donation procedure. Healthchicago (D) was predisposed to find the procedure experimental given that it did not contact the appropriate medical boards for an expert opinion. The failure to comply with its own clause renders Healthchicago's (D) position unsupportable. Affirmed.

ANALYSIS

Courts have consistently been skeptical of insurance provision contracts. The complex nature of such agreements makes fair bargaining almost impossible. While insurance providers argue that they have to control risk exposure, courts generally feel that where doubt exists, the insurer must bear the burden since it drafted the provisions in question.

Quicknotes

INJUNCTION A remedy imposed by the court ordering a party to cease the conduct of a specific activity.

PRECERTIFY Agree in advance to pay for the treatment.

Colonial Life Insurance Company of America v. Curiale

Insurance company (P) v. State insurance superintendent (D)

N.Y. Sup. Ct. App. Div., 205 A.D.2d 58, 617 N.Y.S.2d 377 (1994).

NATURE OF CASE: Appeal from dismissal of part and allowance of part of suit challenging insurance regulations.

FACT SUMMARY: Colonial Life Insurance Company of America (P) challenged new regulations establishing a pool system to share the costs of insurance.

RULE OF LAW

Insurance pool contributions are a valid exercise of the legislature's power to regulate, and an enactment intended to regulate rather than generate revenue is not a tax.

FACTS: Colonial Life Insurance Company of America (P) was a commercial insurance company that issued small group health insurance policies. When the Superintendent of Insurance (D) promulgated regulations requiring community rating and open enrollment for insurance policies issued in New York, Colonial (P) sought to have the new provisions invalidated. The court granted the petition in part and both parties appealed.

ISSUE: Are insurance pool contributions a valid exercise of the legislature's power to regulate, and is an enactment intended to regulate rather than generate revenue not a tax?

HOLDING AND DECISION: (Peters, J.) Yes. Insurance pool contributions are a valid exercise of the legislature's power to regulate, and an enactment intended to regulate rather than generate revenue is not a tax. The lower court properly rejected the contention that the pooling contributions contributed a gift of state money to a private organization. The Superintendent exceeded his statutory authority by promulgating a rule that changed the minimum participation requirements. Affirmed.

ANALYSIS

The laws required community rating and open enrollment. These laws made it necessary to establish an insurance risk pool. Individuals were not included in small group pooling requirements.

CHAPTER 10

Regulation of Insurance and Managed Care: The Federal Role

Quick Reference Rules of Law

Rush Prudential HMO, Inc., v. Debra C. Moran, et al.

HMO (D) v. HMO beneficiary (P)

536 U.S. 355 (2002).

NATURE OF CASE: Appeal from the reversal of a state court judgment enforcing a health maintenance organization (HMO) act.

FACT SUMMARY: On remand from federal court, a state court ordered Rush Prudential HMO, Inc. (D) to comply with a state statute providing a right to independent medical review for its beneficiary, Debra C. Moran (P). Rush (D) continued to deny Moran's (P) claim and the court of appeals reversed.

RULE OF LAW

A state HMO Act is a law directed toward the insurance industry and as such is saved from ERISA preemption.

FACTS: Debra C. Moran (P) is a beneficiary of an employee welfare benefit plan provided by Rush Prudential HMO, Inc. (D) and sponsored by her husband's employer. In 1996, Moran (P) began to have pain and numbness in her right shoulder. Moran's (P) primary care physician, Dr. LaMarre, unsuccessfully administered conservative treatments. In October 1997, Dr. LaMarre recommended that Rush (D) approve surgery by an unaffiliated specialist, Dr. Terzis, who had developed an unconventional treatment for Moran's (P) condition. Rush (D) denied the request, despite Dr. LaMarre's assurances that Moran (P) would be best served by this treatment. Rush (D) proposed that Moran (P) undergo standard surgery by a Rush-affiliated physician. In January 1998, Moran (P) made a written demand for an independent medical review of her claim. Rush (D) failed to provide an independent review, and Moran (P) filed a state court action demanding compliance with a state HMO Act providing a right to independent medical review of certain denials of benefits. Rush (D) removed the claim to federal court, arguing that a cause of action was completely preempted under the Employment Retirement Income Security Act (ERISA). While her suit was pending, Moran (P) had the surgery by Dr. Terzis at her own expense and submitted a $94,841.27 reimbursement claim to Rush (D). Rush (D) commenced a new inquiry to determine coverage. The federal court remanded the case to a state court, which enforced the state statute. The doctor selected for the independent review found the treatment to be medically necessary, but Rush (D) continued to deny Moran's (P) claim for coverage. The Seventh Circuit Court of Appeals reversed.

ISSUE: Is a state HMO statute providing a right to independent medical review of certain denials of benefits preempted by the Employment Retirement Income Security Act?

HOLDING AND DECISION: (Souter, J.) No. A state HMO statute providing a right to independent medical review of certain denials of benefits is not preempted by ERISA. The ERISA statute preempts state laws that relate to employee benefit plans. Moran (P) is a beneficiary of an employee benefit plan. However, the ERISA statute has a savings clause stating that it is not meant to relieve any person from any law of any state which regulates insurance, banking, or securities. Rush's (D) argument that HMOs are not insurers falls short. HMOs have taken over much of the business formerly performed by traditional indemnity insurers, and they are almost universally regulated as insurers under state law. The HMO Act in question here is directed toward the insurance industry and thus is saved from ERISA preemption. Affirmed.

DISSENT: (Thomas, J.) Section 502, the civil enforcement provision of ERISA, provides the exclusive procedure for benefit claims governed by ERISA. State laws creating additional remedial schemes are completely preempted by the broad language of section 514(a) providing that ERISA "shall supersede any and all State Laws insofar as they . . . relate to any employee benefit plan." The Court today breaks from precedent, and from congressional intent, to allow Moran (P) to exercise an additional state statutory remedy provided by section 4-10 of the Illinois HMO Act allowing her benefit claim to be determined by an arbitration-like procedure. While such an independent HMO benefit review provision sounds appealing, it undermines the ability of the HMO to control health care costs and the ability of employers to provide basic coverage to all of its employees.

ANALYSIS

The ERISA statute, as drafted, leaves much doubt as to its interpretation and a myriad issues for the courts to determine.

Quicknotes

EMPLOYEE RETIREMENT INCOME SECURITY ACT OF 1974 (ERISA) Federal law of employee benefits which establishes minimum standards to protect employees from breach of benefit promises made by employers.

INDEMNITY The duty of a party to compensate another for damages sustained.

PREEMPTION Doctrine holding that matters of national interest take precedence over matters of local interest; the federal law takes precedence over state law.

Retail Industry Leaders Association v. Fielder

State (D) v. Trade association (P)

475 F.3d 180 (4th Cir. 2007).

NATURE OF CASE: Appeal of district court finding of federal preemption of a state law.

FACT SUMMARY: The Maryland fair share law requires for-profit employers with 10,000 or more Maryland employees to spend at least 8 percent of their total payroll on employees' health insurance costs or pay the amount their spending falls short to the state of Maryland. The U.S. District Court for the District of Maryland ruled that the Employment Retirement Income Security Act of 1974 (ERISA) preempted the Fair Share Act.

RULE OF LAW

The Employment Retirement Income Security Act preempts Maryland's Fair Share Health Care Fund Act, which mandates employee health care coverage by certain large employers.

FACTS: The Maryland fair share law requires for-profit employers with 10,000 or more Maryland employees to spend at least 8 percent of their total payroll on employees' health insurance costs or pay the amount their spending falls short to the state of Maryland. Although Maryland currently has four employers with 10,000 or more workers, only Wal-Mart, which employs approximately 16,000 in Maryland, would currently be subject to enforcement under the law's minimum spending requirements. The Retail Industry Leaders Association (RILA) (P) filed a lawsuit against James D. Fielder, Jr. (D), the Maryland Secretary of Labor, Licensing, and Regulation, seeking an injunction barring the enforcement of the fair share law. The U.S. District Court for the District of Maryland ruled in favor of RILA (P), agreeing with RILA (P) that the Fair Share Act was preempted by ERISA.

ISSUE: Does the Employment Retirement Income Security Act preempt Maryland's Fair Share Health Care Fund Act, which mandates employee health care coverage by certain large employers?

HOLDING AND DECISION: (Niemeyer, J.) Yes. The Employment Retirement Income Security Act of 1974 preempts Maryland's Fair Share Health Care Fund Act, which mandates employee health care coverage by certain large employers. Because the Fair Share Act effectively mandates that employers structure their employee health care plans to provide a certain level of benefits, the Act has an obvious connection with employee benefit plans and is therefore preempted by ERISA. Several other states and local governments have adopted or are considering health care spending mandates that would clash with fair share laws, and if permitted to stand, these laws would force Wal-Mart to tailor its health care benefit plans to each specific State, and even to specific cities and counties. This is precisely the regulatory mess that Congress sought to avoid by enacting ERISA's preemption provision. The only rational choice employers have under the fair share law is to structure their ERISA health plans so as to meet the state law's minimum spending threshold. Moreover, the Act gives employers the irresistible incentive to provide their employees with a greater level of health benefits rather than paying a fee to the state. The effect of this provision will force employers to structure their recordkeeping and health care benefit spending to comply with the Fair Share Act. Functioning in that manner, the Act would disrupt employers' uniform administration of employee benefit plans on a nationwide basis. In addition, the choices given in the Fair Share Act, on which the Secretary (D) relies to argue that the Act is not a mandate on employers, are not meaningful alternatives by which an employer can increase its health care spending to comply with the Fair Share Act without affecting its ERISA plans. Affirmed.

DISSENT: (Michael, J.) The fair share law is not preempted by ERISA because the state law does not force a covered employer to make a choice that impacts an employee benefit plan. The Act does not compel an employer to establish or maintain an ERISA plan in order to comply with its provisions. ERISA plan expenditures are considered in the calculation of an employer's total level of health insurance spending, but this factor does not create an impermissible connection with an ERISA plan.

ANALYSIS

Other state health care funding programs may stall in the wake of this decision, as states will be reluctant to do what Maryland has done for fear of inviting the same judicial response. But because the Maryland law targeted only one employer and because its sponsors clearly indicated their objective was to mandate Wal-Mart to expand its health coverage, the decision may not affect state health care access programs imposing a tax on a broad segment of employers. And the court's opinion seems to leave open the question of lower taxes; it does not directly address a tax-financed program that allows an employer a dollar-for-dollar credit for any employee health coverage it offers, for example, which some states favor.

Continued on next page.

Quicknotes

EMPLOYEE RETIREMENT INCOME SECURITY ACT OF 1974 (ERISA) Federal law of employee benefits which establishes minimum standards to protect employees from breach of benefit promises made by employers.

INJUNCTION A court order requiring a person to do, or prohibiting that person from doing, a specific act.

PREEMPTION Doctrine holding that matters of national interest take precedence over matters of local interest; the federal law takes precedence over state law.

Pegram v. Herdrich

Physician (D) v. Patient (P)

530 U.S. 211 (2000).

NATURE OF CASE: Review of medical malpractice action.

FACT SUMMARY: The appellate court found that the health maintenance organization (HMO) acted as a fiduciary when its physicians made medical decisions and could be held liable for breach of fiduciary duties.

RULE OF LAW

Treatment decisions made by an HMO, acting through its physicians, are not fiduciary acts within the meaning of the Employee Retirement Income Security Act of 1974 (ERISA).

FACTS: Pegram (D), the HMO treating plan physician, examined Herdrich (P) but failed to immediately order an ultrasound. When Pegram (D) ultimately ordered the ultrasound, Herdrich (P) had to go to a distant facility owned by the HMO. Because of the delay, Herdrich's (P) appendix ruptured, causing peritonitis. Herdrich (P) sued Pegram (D) and the HMO (D) in state court for medical malpractice and later added two counts charging state law fraud. The HMO (D) and Pegram (D) asserted that ERISA preempted the new counts and removed the case to federal court where they then sought summary judgment on the state law fraud counts. The court dismissed one count, but allowed Herdrich (P) to amend the one remaining. Herdrich (P) then alleged that provision of medical services under the terms of the HMO (D), rewarding physicians for limiting medical care, entailed an inherent or anticipatory breach of an ERISA fiduciary duty. The district court granted the HMO's (D) motion to dismiss the ERISA count for failure to state a claim upon which relief may be granted. The Seventh Circuit Court of Appeals reversed. The U.S. Supreme Court granted certiorari.

ISSUE: Are treatment decisions made by an HMO, acting through its physicians, fiduciary acts within the meaning of ERISA?

HOLDING AND DECISION: (Souter, J.) No. Treatment decisions made by an HMO, acting through its physicians, are not fiduciary acts within the meaning of ERISA. Since courts are not in a position to differentiate among the various types of HMOs and their organizational structures, all decisions by HMOs acting through their owner or employee physicians are to be judged by the same standards and subject to the same claims. Congress did not intend any HMO to be treated as a fiduciary to the extent that it makes mixed eligibility decisions acting through its physicians. The congressional policy of allowing HMO organizations would be threatened by ERISA fiduciary claims portending wholesale attacks on existing HMOs solely because of their structure, untethered to claims of concrete harm. For all practical purposes, every such claim of fiduciary breach by an HMO physician would boil down to a malpractice claim. Reversed.

ANALYSIS

The court here found that in most cases, the eligibility decision and the treatment decision were inextricably mixed. Such mixed decisions include physicians' recommendations of tests, decisions about referrals and consultations with other physicians or facilities, proper standards of care, etc. Decisions involving medical judgment were found not to be related to ERISA.

Quicknotes

EMPLOYEE RETIREMENT INCOME SECURITY ACT OF 1974 (ERISA) Federal law of employee benefits which establishes minimum standards to protect employees from breach of benefit promises made by employers.

MEDICAL MALPRACTICE Conduct on the part of a doctor falling below that demonstrated by other doctors of ordinary skill and competency under the circumstances, resulting in damages to patients.

NEGLIGENCE Conduct falling below the standard of care that a reasonable person would demonstrate under similar conditions.

Aetna Health Inc. v. Davila

HMOs (D) v. Participants (P)

542 U.S. 200 (2004).

NATURE OF CASE: Appeal by health maintenance organizations (HMOs) of Fifth Circuit decision to the Supreme Court.

FACT SUMMARY: Two participants (P) filed state law claims against their HMOs (D) for failure to administer proper care. The HMOs (D) argued that their claims were preempted by the Employment Retirement Income Security Act of 1974 (ERISA). The U.S. Court of Appeals found in favor of the participants (P), and the HMOs (D) appealed.

RULE OF LAW

If an individual brings suit complaining of a denial of coverage for medical care, where the individual is entitled to such coverage only because of the terms of an ERISA-regulated employee benefit plan, and where no legal duty (state or federal) independent of ERISA or the plan terms is violated, the suit falls within the scope of ERISA § 502(a)(1)(B).

FACTS: Ruby R. Calad (P) and Juan Davila (P) were among four HMO subscribers who sued their HMOs (D) for violating Texas law by denying or delaying their receipt of health benefits. Calad (P), who was a beneficiary of a health plan offered by CIGNA HealthCare of Texas Inc. (D), had a hysterectomy, and CIGNA (D) authorized coverage for only a one-day hospital stay despite the recommendation of Calad's (P) doctor that she stay in the hospital longer. After Calad (P) suffered complications that caused her to return to the hospital a few days after her release, she sued CIGNA (D) in a Texas state court under the Texas Health Care Liability Act (THCLA). CIGNA (D) removed the case to federal court as preempted by ERISA, and the federal court dismissed Calad's (P) claims as preempted by ERISA. Davila (P) was insured through Aetna Health Inc. (D). His doctor prescribed the drug Vioxx for Davila's (P) arthritis pain, but Aetna (D) required that Davila (P) enter its "step program," under which Davila (P) would try a less expensive drug before trying Vioxx. Three weeks after he started taking the less expensive drug, Davila (P) was rushed to the emergency room where he was diagnosed with a bleeding ulcer. Davila (P) sued Aetna (D), claiming it violated the THCLA. The Texas federal court found his claim also was preempted by ERISA. The U.S. Court of Appeals for the Fifth Circuit consolidated their cases and found that the HMOs (D) were not acting as plan fiduciaries when they denied medical treatment, and that ERISA § 502(a)(2) did not completely preempt the THCLA claims. Section 502(a)(2) allows plan participants or beneficiaries to sue for "appropriate relief" for fiduciary breach. The Fifth Circuit relied on the U.S. Supreme Court's decision in *Pegram v. Herdrich*, 530 U.S. 211 (2000), in which the high court found that mixed eligibility and treatment decisions made by HMOs are not subject to ERISA § 502(a)(2) because such decisions are not fiduciary acts. Aetna (D) and CIGNA (D) filed separate petitions asking the high court to review the Fifth Circuit's ruling.

ISSUE: If an individual brings suit complaining of a denial of coverage for medical care, where the individual is entitled to such coverage only because of the terms of an ERISA-regulated employee benefit plan, and where no legal duty (state or federal) independent of ERISA or the plan terms is violated, does the suit fall within the scope of ERISA § 502(a)(1)(B)?

HOLDING AND DECISION: (Thomas, J.) Yes. If an individual brings suit complaining of a denial of coverage for medical care, where the individual is entitled to such coverage only because of the terms of an ERISA-regulated employee benefit plan, and where no legal duty (state or federal) independent of ERISA or the plan terms is violated, the suit falls within the scope of ERISA § 502(a)(1)(B). Section 502(a)(1)(B) provides that a civil action may be brought by a plan participant or beneficiary to recover benefits due under the terms of his or her plan, to enforce his or her rights under the plan terms, and to clarify his or her rights to future plan benefits. The state law claims asserted by Davila (P) and Calad (P) fell within the scope of ERISA § 502(a)(1)(B) because Davila (P) and Calad's (P) only relationship with or connection to Aetna (D) and CIGNA (D) was through ERISA-governed benefit plans. Several other considerations support the conclusion that ERISA preempts the state law claims. First, the duties imposed on HMOs (D) by the THCLA did not arise independently of ERISA or the plans' terms. The THCLA imposed on HMOs (D) a duty to "exercise ordinary care when making health care treatment decisions." But the THCLA provides that HMOs and other managed care entities are not liable under the state law if the relevant health plans do not provide for coverage for particular medical procedures. Because interpretation of the terms of Davila (P) and Calad's (P) benefit plans formed an essential part of their THCLA claims, their claims were preempted by ERISA. Second, the Fifth Circuit's conclusion that Davila (P) and Calad (P) asserted "tort claims for tort damages," which would not be preempted by ERISA, rather than "contract claim for contract damages," which would be preempted by ERISA, is rejected. Distinguishing between preempted and non-preempted claims based on

Continued on next page.

the particular label would elevate form over substance and allow parties to avoid the preemptive scope of ERISA simply by relabeling their claims. Third, the Fifth Circuit's determination that, under earlier Supreme Court decisions, a state law is not preempted by ERISA unless it "duplicates" the elements of a claim available under ERISA is rejected, as is Davila (P) and Calad's (P) argument that the THCLA was a law that regulated insurance and was therefore saved from ERISA preemption. Congress's intent to make the ERISA civil enforcement mechanism exclusive would be undermined if state causes of action that supplement the ERISA § 502(a) remedies were permitted, even if the elements of the state cause of action did not exactly duplicate the elements of an ERISA claim. Fourth, Davila (P) and Calad (P), as well as several federal courts, have read *Pegram* too broadly. In *Pegram*, the Supreme Court found that ERISA's fiduciary duty requirements do not attach to treatment decisions and mixed eligibility and treatment decisions made by HMOs. In this case, benefit determinations are "part and parcel" of the ordinary fiduciary responsibilities connected to administration of a plan. The fact that a benefits determination mixes with medical judgments does not alter this result. *Pegram* only makes sense when the underlying negligence that plausibly constitutes medical malpractice is caused by a party who is either a treating physician or a physician's employer. Here, Aetna (D) and CIGNA (D) are neither respondents' treating physicians nor the employers of respondents' treating physicians. The HMO's (D) coverage decisions are pure eligible decisions, and *Pegram* does not apply.

CONCURRENCE: (Ginsburg, J.) Congress should revisit ERISA to ensure that the federal statute provides "make whole" relief. A series of the Court's decisions has created many situations in which persons adversely affected by ERISA-proscribed wrongdoing cannot gain make-whole relief.

ANALYSIS

Immediately after this case was decided, members of Congress concerned with health plans' treatment of beneficiaries reacted. Rep. John D. Dingell (D-Mich.), ranking member of the House Energy and Commerce Committee, announced he and other Democrats would immediately re-introduce the Patients' Bill of Rights. Dingell released a statement saying that a patients' rights law is needed to "establish minimum federal law protections to permit patients injured by health plans to seek redress under state laws that provide additional health care protections for patients." Sen. John Edwards (D-N.C.) said in a statement that the court ruled "managed care insurance programs cannot be held responsible in state courts," underscoring the need for a national patient protection law. The decision "casts a legal cloud over similar provisions of patient protection laws in North Carolina and other states and leaves millions of working people with "nowhere to go when HMO bureaucrats overrule their doctors' decisions." And Rep. Charles Norwood (R-Ga.) said in a statement that the ruling was a "blow to patients' rights" and that "[w]ith this decision, Americans in a dozen states have lost their right to hold their HMO accountable and Americans in the rest of the country have had the door closed on them."

Quicknotes

CONTRACT DAMAGES Monetary compensation awarded by the court to a party as the result of a breach of contract by another party.

EMPLOYEE RETIREMENT INCOME SECURITY ACT OF 1974 (ERISA) Federal law of employee benefits which establishes minimum standards to protect employees from breach of benefit promises made by employers.

FIDUCIARY Person holding a legal obligation to act for the benefit of another.

MEDICAL MALPRACTICE Conduct on the part of a doctor falling below that demonstrated by other doctors of ordinary skill and competency under the circumstances, resulting in damages.

NEGLIGENCE Conduct falling below the standard of care that a reasonable person would demonstrate under similar conditions.

PREEMPTION Doctrine holding that matters of national interest take precedence over matters of local interest; the federal law takes precedence over state law.

TORT DAMAGES Monetary compensation awarded by the court to a party injured as the result of the tortious act of another.

Doe v. Group Hospitalization & Medical Services

Physician (P) v. Health maintenance organization (D)

3 F.3d 80 (4th Cir. 1993).

NATURE OF CASE: Appeal from summary judgment for defendant in Employment Retirement Insurance Security Act action.

FACT SUMMARY: Doe (P) alleged that Blue Cross (D) had improperly denied him benefits.

RULE OF LAW

When a fiduciary exercises discretion in interpreting a disputed term of the contract where one interpretation will further the financial interests of the fiduciary, the court will not act as deferentially as would otherwise be appropriate.

FACTS: When Doe (P) was diagnosed with a rare form of cancer, his physician recommended treatment that included a bone marrow transplant. His health insurance carrier, Blue Cross (D), denied benefits, relying on language in the contract excluding benefits for bone marrow transplants. Doe (P) sued Blue Cross (D) under section 502 of the Employee Retirement Insurance Security Act (ERISA), claiming Blue Cross (D) had improperly denied benefits based solely upon improperly adopted amendments to the group insurance contract. The district court entered judgment for Blue Cross (D), and Doe (P) appealed, claiming that Blue Cross (D) operated under a conflict of interest when it denied the benefits.

ISSUE: When a fiduciary exercises discretion in interpreting a disputed term of the contract where one interpretation will further the financial interests of the fiduciary, will the court act as deferentially as would otherwise be appropriate?

HOLDING AND DECISION: (Niemeyer, J.) No. When a fiduciary exercises discretion in interpreting a disputed term of the contract where one interpretation will further the financial interests of the fiduciary, the court will not act as deferentially as would otherwise be appropriate. To the extent Blue Cross (D) has discretion to avoid paying claims, it thereby promoted the potential for its own profits. Although health care benefits provided in an employee benefit plan are not vested benefits, and may be modified or withdrawn by the employer at any time, the employer's decision will be entitled to less deference when a substantial conflict of interest occurs. In this case, the contract will be construed for the beneficiaries, and the coverage provided elsewhere in the group insurance contract, and not otherwise explicitly excluded, will be enforced. Affirmed in part, reversed in part, and remanded.

ANALYSIS

The court here found that cancer-treating procedure was covered by the contract. The exclusion of the ancillary bone marrow transplant procedure could not be construed to withdraw coverage explicitly granted elsewhere in the contract. Also, ambiguity must be construed against the drafting party.

Quicknotes

AMBIGUOUS Vague; unclear; capable of more than one meaning.

CONTRACT An agreement pursuant to which a party agrees to act, or to forbear from acting, in exchange for performance on the part of the other party.

EMPLOYEE RETIREMENT INCOME SECURITY ACT OF 1974 (ERISA) Federal law of employee benefits which establishes minimum standards to protect employees from breach of benefit promises made by employers.

FIDUCIARY Person holding a legal obligation to act for the benefit of another.

Winslow v. IDS Life Insurance Co.

Applicant (P) v. Insurance company (D)

29 F. Supp. 2d 557 (D. Minn. 1998).

NATURE OF CASE: Motion for summary judgment in suit alleging discrimination.

FACT SUMMARY: Winslow (P) alleged that IDS Life Insurance Company (D) discriminated against her on the basis of a disability, in violation of the Americans with Disabilities Act (ADA), and state law.

RULE OF LAW

It is a violation of the ADA for an insurance company to categorically deny long-term disability coverage to individuals who are mentally disabled.

FACTS: Winslow (P) indicated on her application for insurance with IDS Life Insurance Company (D) that she had been treated for mental illness within the past year and was currently taking medication. When she received notice of the denial of her long-term disability insurance application, she sued, alleging violation of the ADA. Winslow (P) claimed that IDS (D) regarded her as disabled and treated her as having a physical or mental impairment that substantially limited one or more of the major life functions. IDS (D) asserted that even if she could show that IDS (D) regarded her as likely to suffer a substantially limiting impairment in the future, she had failed to show that IDS (D) regarded her as disabled at the time it denied her application for the insurance, as required by the statutory language of the ADA, which contains no future tense.

ISSUE: Is it a violation of the ADA for an insurance company to categorically deny long-term disability coverage to individuals who are mentally disabled?

HOLDING AND DECISION: (Davis, J.) Yes. It is a violation of the ADA for an insurance company to categorically deny long-term disability coverage to individuals who are mentally disabled. When IDS (D) denied Winslow's (P) application based on her depression and anxiety, IDS (D) implicitly considered her to be impaired, and likely unable to perform either a class of jobs or a broad range of jobs in various classes in the future. Based on the Department of Justice interpretation of Title III of the ADA, and the reasoning adopted by a growing number of district courts, this court finds that Title III of the ADA is applicable to insurance policies and not limited to access to actual physical structures. The McCarran-Ferguson Act does not invalidate, impair, or supersede the relevant Minnesota statutes and does not bar Winslow's (P) ADA claims. As IDS's (D) policy of denying long-term disability insurance to those treated for mental conditions within the past year denies said individuals access to insurance coverage, the policy is founded on a disability-based discrimination violative of the ADA. Motion denied.

ANALYSIS

The court in this case denied defendant's motion for summary judgment. A genuine issue of material fact was found to exist as to whether IDS's (D) long-term disability insurance eligibility criteria conformed to sound actuarial principles, or other substantial data, as required by state law. The court also found that IDS (D) violated Minnesota's Human Rights Act, but concluded that punitive damages were not available because there was no willful indifference in IDS's (D) conduct toward Winslow (P).

Quicknotes

ACT 15 U.S.C. § 1012 et seq. Bars application of federal statutes which conflict with state insurance laws.

ADA 42 U.S.C. § 12101 et seq. Prohibits discrimination on the basis of a disability.

PUNITIVE DAMAGES Damages exceeding the actual injury suffered for the purposes of punishment, deterrence and comfort to plaintiff.

CHAPTER 11

Public Health Care Financing Programs

Quick Reference Rules of Law

Bellevue Hospital Center v. Leavitt

Hospitals (P) v. Government (D)

443 F.3d 163 (2d Cir. 2006).

NATURE OF CASE: Appeal of district court judgment.

FACT SUMMARY: The Bellevue Hospital Center (P) filed an action challenging the Department of Health and Human Services' method for calculating Medicare reimbursements. Because the statutory scheme requires hospitals' cost to be averaged, hospitals with dissimilar costs would inevitably be lumped together.

RULE OF LAW

(1) The Medicare statute authorizes the use of "metropolitan statistical areas" (MSAs) as a proxy for "geographic area" as specified in the statute.
(2) Expansion of the New York City MSAs to include New Jersey hospitals, where wages are somewhat lower, is not arbitrary or capricious even though it causes the average wage level in the MSA to drop.
(3) Health and Human Services' implementation of adjustments regarding hiring decisions at hospitals was arbitrary and capricious.

FACTS: The Bellevue Hospital Center (P) filed an action challenging the Department of Health and Human Services' method for calculating Medicare reimbursements. Bellevue (P) argued that the new metropolitan statistical areas (MSAs) for New York City, which included New Jersey hospitals, an area where wages are somewhat lower, led Bellevue (P) to conclude that it would receive $812 million less in reimbursements over the next 10 years than they would have under their former wage adjustment. The U.S. District Court for the Southern District of New York found that the term "geographic areas" in the Medicare statute was ambiguous, and that the use of MSAs to fill the gap was reasonable. Because the statutory scheme requires hospitals' costs to be averaged, hospitals with dissimilar costs would inevitably be lumped together.

ISSUE:
(1) Does the Medicare statute authorize the use of "metropolitan statistical areas" (MSAs) as a proxy for "geographic area" as specified in the statute?
(2) Is expansion of the New York City MSAs to include New Jersey hospitals, where wages are somewhat lower, arbitrary or capricious even though it causes the average wage level in the MSA to drop?
(3) Was Health and Human Services' implementation of adjustments regarding hiring decisions at hospitals arbitrary or capricious?

HOLDING AND DECISION: (Katzmann, J.)
(1) Yes. The Medicare statute authorizes the use of "metropolitan statistical areas" (MSAs) as a proxy for "geographic area" as specified in the statute. The use of MSAs to fill the gap left by the ambiguous term "geographic areas" is reasonable. Health and Human Services' Centers for Medicare & Medicaid Services (CMS) has used MSAs to fill the statutory gap for more than two decades without any action from Congress expressing disapproval, which demands deference at this point.
(2) No. Expansion of the New York City MSAs to include New Jersey hospitals, where wages are somewhat lower, is not arbitrary or capricious even though it causes the average wage level in the MSA to drop. It is rational and permissible for an agency to adopt an already existing measure, such as MSAs, that uses objective criteria rather than assuming the task of creating its own measure in the face of a sharply divided regulated industry that has not proposed any clearly superior alternatives. Under these circumstances, the agency's continued use of MSAs was not arbitrary and capricious.
(3) Yes. Health and Human Services' implementation of adjustments regarding hiring decisions at hospitals was arbitrary and capricious. Application of the adjustment must be implemented in full by Sept. 30, 2006, which is three years after CMS's initial deadline for data collection. Had CMS complied with Congress's dictate, it would have been required to complete its second round of data collection by that date.

ANALYSIS

The issues surrounding the Medicare system are voluminous, and care must be taken when analyzing a particular set of facts to ascertain exactly what the issues are, in order to also decipher which agency is responsible for resolving the issue. Failure to follow procedures set by the various agencies associated with the Medicare system can impact a plaintiff's case.

Quicknotes

ARBITRARY AND CAPRICIOUS STANDARD Standard imposed in reviewing the decision of an agency or court when the decision may have been made in disregard of the facts or law.

Shalala v. Illinois Council on Long Term Care, Inc.

Secretary of Health and Human Services (D) v. Nursing homes (P)

529 U.S. 1 (2000).

NATURE OF CASE: Appeal from dismissal of complaint challenging Medicare-related regulations.

FACT SUMMARY: The district court found that regulations must be first challenged through government agency procedures and not in federal court.

RULE OF LAW

A legal claim challenging Medicare regulations must be channelled first to the government agency promulgating the regulations.

FACTS: When Illinois Council on Long Term Care (P), an association of nursing homes, sued the Secretary of Health and Human Services (D) in federal court, the district court dismissed for lack of jurisdiction. The court of appeals reversed, holding that only reviews of amount determinations are barred. Shalala (D) appealed.

ISSUE: Must a legal claim challenging Medicare regulations be channelled first to the government agency promulgating the regulations?

HOLDING AND DECISION: (Breyer, J.) Yes. A legal claim challenging Medicare regulations must be channelled first to the government agency promulgating the regulations. Congress, in both the Social Security Act and the Medicare Act, insisted upon an initial presentation of the matter to the agency. This method was thought to produce speedier, as well as better, review overall. Reversed.

ANALYSIS

This decision was arrived at by a five-to-four vote. Three justices wrote dissenting opinions. The dissenters would have permitted federal question jurisdiction over challenges to the validity of the secretary's instructions and regulations.

Quicknotes

AGENCY A fiduciary relationship whereby authority is granted to an agent to act on behalf of the principal in order to effectuate the principal's objective.

FEDERAL QUESTION JURISDICTION The authority of the federal courts to hear and determine in the first instance matters pertaining to the federal Constitution, federal law, or treaties of the United States.

SOCIAL SECURITY ACT Federal law creating the Social Security Administration, which is charged with the administration of a national program wherein contributions from employers and employees are held until the worker retires or is disabled, at which time they are paid out.

Lankford v. Sherman

Disabled Medicare recipients (P) v. State Social Services (D)

451 F.3d 496 (8th Cir. 2006).

NATURE OF CASE: Appeal of denial of preliminary injunction.

FACT SUMMARY: Seven disabled Medicaid recipients and 10 public-interest advocacy groups were denied a preliminary injunction by a federal district court seeking to prohibit Missouri's director of social services from enforcing a state regulation that reduces the provision of durable medical equipment (DME) for most of the state's categorically needy Medicaid beneficiaries.

RULE OF LAW

A state regulation is preempted by the U.S. Constitution's Supremacy Clause if it fails to meet federal requirements that the state treat Medicaid recipients using reasonable, nondiscriminatory standards.

FACTS: Seven disabled Medicaid recipients and 10 public-interest advocacy groups (P) filed suit contesting an emergency regulation that eliminates Medicaid coverage for most durable medical equipment (DME) for the categorically needy who are aged or disabled, like the individual plaintiffs, but maintains full DME coverage for blind recipients. The plaintiffs claimed the new regulation precludes them from Medicaid coverage for orthotics, parenteral nutrition, catheters, augmentative communication devices, hospital beds, bed rails, lifts, wheelchair batteries, and repair items. They argued that the state cannot legally provide additional DME benefits to blind recipients without providing similar benefits to all adult recipients. After the emergency regulation was implemented, the Centers for Medicare & Medicaid Services (CMS) denied Missouri a waiver to provide additional benefits to the blind. In response, the state deleted the portion of its plan that used federal funding to pay for additional DME benefits for blind recipients. Instead, Missouri now uses only state funds to provide additional DME services for the blind.

ISSUE: Is a state regulation preempted by the U.S. Constitution's Supremacy Clause if it fails to meet federal requirements that the state treat Medicaid recipients using reasonable, nondiscriminatory standards?

HOLDING AND DECISION: (Benton, J.) Yes. A state regulation is preempted by the U.S. Constitution's Supremacy Clause if it fails to meet federal requirements that the state treat Medicaid recipients using reasonable, nondiscriminatory standards. As currently funded, Missouri's plan does not violate the federal comparability requirement. While a state plan must comply with all federal statutory and regulatory requirements, a state may give additional medical assistance under its own legislation, independent of federal reimbursement. But despite its discretion to determine the optional services in its Medicaid plan, a state's failure to provide Medicaid coverage for non-experimental, medically necessary services within a covered Medicaid category is both per se unreasonable and inconsistent with the stated goals of Medicaid. Under CMS policy, which is entitled to "considerable deference," a plan without a meaningful procedure for requesting non-covered items is inconsistent with the reasonable-standards requirement and the objectives of Medicaid. Under Missouri's Medicaid plan, a recipient denied DME benefits can seek qualification for home health care, which requires that the recipient be confined to the home, or they can seek an exception for non-covered items through an exceptions procedure. Missouri's home health plan does not comply with CMS's policy restricting home health care to "homebound" recipients. Therefore, it does not afford a meaningful opportunity to obtain non-covered DME items. Similarly, the exceptions process does not provide a reasonable opportunity to obtain noncovered items. The regulation allows no exception for items that are restricted under state law—and the DME regulation specifically restricts all non-covered DME items. Because the DME regulation restricts available DME, and plaintiffs have no other procedure to obtain it, the regulation appears unreasonable under directives from both CMS and this court.

ANALYSIS

Medicaid is a welfare program for the poor, and its status is always in flux, because there are some who believe that it should be run as an entitlement program at the state level. Similar controversy has not attended the Medicare program, which was created at roughly the same time as the Medicaid program. Medicare was, however, the primary program.

Quicknotes

PREEMPTION Doctrine holding that matters of national interest take precedence over matters of local interest; the federal law takes precedence over state law.

PRELIMINARY INJUNCTION A judicial mandate issued to require or restrain a party from certain conduct; used to preserve a trial's subject matter or to prevent threatened injury.

SUPREMACY CLAUSE Article VI, ¶ 2 of the U.S. Constitution, which provides that federal action must prevail over inconsistent state action.

Westside Mothers v. Haveman

Patients (P) v. Administrative officer (D)

289 F.3d 852 (6th Cir. 2002).

NATURE OF CASE: Appeal from ruling of district court to dismiss for lack of jurisdiction.

FACT SUMMARY: Westside Mothers (Mothers) (P) brought suit against James Haveman (D), the director of the Michigan Department of Community Health, alleging the state of Michigan failed to provide medical services required by the Medicaid program.

RULE OF LAW

(1) Medicaid is not a contract between the states that participate and the federal government.
(2) Sovereign immunity does not bar a § 1983 action against a state official for noncompliance with Medicaid regulations.
(3) A plaintiff does have a private right of action under § 1983 to enforce rights provided under Medicaid.

FACTS: The Medicaid program provides federal subsidies to participating states to reimburse poor persons for the cost of certain medical care. Participating states must comply with the requirements imposed by the Act, as well as with regulations promulgated by the Secretary of Health and Human Services (HHS). One such requirement is the provision of "early and periodic screening, diagnostic, and treatment services" for eligible persons under 21 years of age. See § 1396d(a)(4)(B). These services include periodic physical exams, immunization, laboratory tests, eye exams, eyeglasses, dental exams and teeth maintenance, hearing exams and treatment of hearing disorders, and health education. The Secretary of HHS has the authority to withhold funding to states in noncompliance with any of Medicaid's requirements. Westside Mothers (Mothers) (P) alleged that James Haveman (D) refused to provide, or require participating HMOs to provide, the above named services and sought declaratory and injunctive relief under 42 U.S.C. § 1983. Section 1983 creates a cause of action against state action that deprives an individual of any "rights, privileges, or immunities secured by the Constitution and laws" of the United States. The district court dismissed finding that: (1) the Medicaid Act was only a contract between the state and federal government, and not the supreme law of the land; (2) the state of Michigan was the real defendant and sovereign immunity barred the suit; and (3) § 1983 does not create a private cause of action for the enforcement of Medicaid provisions. Mothers (P) appealed.

ISSUE:

(1) Is Medicaid a contract between the states that participate and the federal government?
(2) Does sovereign immunity bar a § 1983 action against a state official for noncompliance with Medicaid regulations?
(3) Does a plaintiff have a private right of action under § 983 to enforce rights provided under Medicaid?

HOLDING AND DECISION: (Merritt, J.)

(1) No. Medicaid is not a contract between the states that participate and the federal government. The Supreme Court has already spoken to this issue and has held that the Medicaid Act, and its accompanying regulations, are federal laws and are not contractual provisions. See *Pennhurst State School and Hosp. v. Halderman*, 451 U.S. 1 (1981). Federal-state cooperative programs that are enacted under the federal spending power, as is Medicaid, fall within the Supremacy Clause and are the supreme law of the land.
(2) No. Sovereign immunity does not bar a § 1983 action against a state official for noncompliance with Medicaid regulations. Under the legal fiction developed in *Ex Parte Young*, 209 U.S. 123 (1908), a suit alleging violation of the constitution or a federal law by a state official is not barred by sovereign immunity. The injunctive relief requested seeks an order for the state official to comply with the law. The suit does not seek enforcement of any discretionary functions of a state officer, nor does it seek enforcement of a contractual provision. Moreover, the Medicaid Act's allowance for the Secretary of HHS to withholding funding to states in noncompliance with the Act is not expressly the exclusive remedy under the Act.
(3) Yes. A plaintiff does have a private right of action under § 1983 to enforce rights provided under Medicaid. The Supreme Court has recognized a private right for suit pursuant to § 1983 and has outlined a framework for evaluating such claims. See *Blessing v. Freestone*, 520 U.S. 329 (1997). Applying this framework, the court finds that the regulations at issue were clearly designed to benefit the plaintiffs, the provisions are binding upon the state of Michigan, and these provisions are not vague or ambiguous so as to defeat judicial enforcement. Plaintiffs have pleaded a proper cause of action pursuant to § 1983 and the district's court dismissal is reversed.

ANALYSIS

While it might seem axiomatic that federal statutes such as Medicaid create substantive and enforceable rights, a

Continued on next page.

cause of action under a federal statute generally must be express and not implicit in the statute. The specific nature of the requirements embodied in the Medicaid Act and their accompanying regulations outline the rights, but the enforcement mechanism is not always as clear. Had the statute indicated that only the Secretary of the HHS could bring suit, the plaintiffs in this case would have been foreclosed from bringing the action. However, because the statute did not eliminate an individual remedy, and because the legal fiction of *Ex parte Young* was available to create a proper defendant, the suit was allowed to proceed.

Quicknotes

EX PARTE A proceeding commenced by one party without providing any opposing parties with notice or which is uncontested by an adverse party.

FOURTEENTH AMENDMENT 42 U.S.C. § 1983 Defamation by state officials in connection with a discharge implies a violation of a liberty interest protected by the due process requirements of the U.S. Constitution.

INJUNCTIVE RELIEF A court order issued as a remedy, requiring a person to do, or prohibiting that person from doing, a specific act.

MEDICAID A welfare program for the poor administered by the state.

PRIVATE RIGHT OF ACTION A fact or set of facts the occurrence of which entitles a party to seek judicial relief.

CHAPTER 12

Professional Relationships in Health Care Enterprises

Quick Reference Rules of Law

Sokol v. Akron General Medical Center

Physician (P) v. Hospital (D)

173 F.3d 1026 (6th Cir. 1999).

NATURE OF CASE: Appeal from dismissal of motion for injunction.

FACT SUMMARY: Sokol (P) claimed that Akron General Hospital (D) had abused its discretion in limiting his hospital privileges.

RULE OF LAW

The board of trustees of a private hospital has broad discretion in determining who shall be permitted to have staff privileges.

FACTS: Sokol (P) was a cardiac surgeon at Akron General Hospital (D). When informed that Sokol's (P) patients had an excessively high mortality rate, Akron General (D) gave him notice that his privileges were being curtailed. The Hearing Committee recommended that Sokol's (P) privileges be restored. The Medical Council rejected this recommendation and reaffirmed its original decision. Sokol (P) then asked the district court for injunctive relief. The magistrate judge found that the Medical Council's decision to take action against Sokol (P) based on his mortality rate was arbitrary. On appeal, Sokol (P) alleged that the adverse decision was arbitrary, capricious, and unreasonable.

ISSUE: Does the board of trustees of a private hospital have broad discretion in determining who shall be permitted to have staff privileges?

HOLDING AND DECISION: (Norris, J.) Yes. The board of trustees of a private hospital has broad discretion in determining who shall be permitted to have staff privileges. However, the hospital must provide procedural due process in adopting and applying reasonable, nondiscriminatory criteria. The board of trustees will not have abused its discretion so long as its decision was supported by any evidence. Reversed.

DISSENT: (Merritt, J.) The heart surgeon (P) was treated unfairly by the Hospital (D). The committee completely exonerated him and there was no evidence of any mistakes made by Sokol (P).

ANALYSIS

This case is an example of new outcome measures being used in hospitals. It is somewhat controversial for hospitals to use mortality rates and to reveal them to the public. The court just examined the fairness of the procedures used by the hospital.

Quicknotes

ARBITRATION An agreement to have a dispute heard and decided by a neutral third party, rather than through legal proceedings.

DUE PROCESS CLAUSE Clauses found in the Fifth and Fourteenth Amendments to the United States Constitution providing that no person shall be deprived of "life, liberty, or property, without due process of law."

Mateo-Woodburn v. Fresno Community Hospital

Anesthesiologists (P) v. Hospital (D)

Cal. Ct. App., 221 Cal. App. 3d 1169 (1990).

NATURE OF CASE: Appeal of order dismissing action challenging hospital staffing system.

FACT SUMMARY: A hospital's system of regulating anesthesiologists was challenged as violating the physicians' rights.

RULE OF LAW

A hospital may regulate departmental staffing through an exclusive arrangement with one or more doctors.

FACTS: Prior to 1985, Fresno Community Hospital (FCH) (D) had an "open" system of staffing for its anesthesiologists, meaning that the various doctors worked out their schedules among themselves. FCH (D) became concerned that the system utilized by the thirteen staff anesthesiologists resulted in inefficient resource utilization and, in some cases, substandard patient care. To alleviate this problem, FCH (D) signed an exclusive contract with Dr. Hass, P.C. (D), giving Hass (D) the right to regulate the hours of any physician with whom it might wish to subcontract. Six of the anesthesiologists (P) refused to sign the subcontract offered by Hass (D), believing that it infringed on their professional freedom. A trial court entered a preliminary injunction against the contract but, after a hearing, dissolved the injunction and dismissed. An appeal was taken.

ISSUE: May a hospital regulate departmental staffing through an exclusive arrangement with one or more doctors?

HOLDING AND DECISION: (Brown, J.) Yes. A hospital may regulate departmental staffing through an exclusive arrangement with one or more doctors. A hospital may make a decision to enter into an exclusive contract for the provision of a set of medical services. As long as the decision was rationally based on a legitimate concern with the providing of medical services, such a decision is not subject to judicial review. Here, FCH (D) was concerned with inadequate provision of anesthesia services by its unregulated anesthesiologists. The contract with Dr. Hass, P.C. (D), was a response to this legitimate concern and had no basis for judicial review. Affirmed.

ANALYSIS

Explosions in costs are a major issue in medicine today. Many see the contracting of services as an answer to this problem. Others, however, see this as anticompetitive and, therefore, antithetical to minimizing costs.

Quicknotes

INJUNCTION A court order requiring a person to do, or prohibiting that person from doing, a specific act.

JUDICIAL REVIEW The authority of the courts to review decisions, actions or omissions committed by another agency or branch of government.

Mahan v. Avera St. Luke's

Physician (P) v. Medical center (D)

S.D. Sup. Ct., 621 N.W.2d 150 (2001).

NATURE OF CASE: Appeal from finding of breach of contract.

FACT SUMMARY: The circuit court found that Avera St. Luke's (ASL) (D) did not have the right to initiate actions that affected the privileges of medical staff such as Dr. Mahan (P) when they had previously delegated this authority.

RULE OF LAW

The medical staff bylaws of a hospital do not trump the Board of Directors' ability to make administrative decisions.

FACTS: Avera St. Luke's (ASL) (D) is part of a regional health care system sponsored by the Sisters of the Presentation of the Blessed Virgin Mary of Aberdeen, South Dakota. Since 1901, the Presentation Sisters have provided quality health services to the Aberdeen community. In mid-1996, ASL's (D) neurosurgeon left Aberdeen. During the process of recruiting his replacement, ASL (D) learned that most neurosurgeon applicants would not be interested in coming to Aberdeen if there was already an orthopedic surgeon practicing in the area. ASL (D) successfully recruited a neurosurgeon in December of 1996. Around this time, ASL (D) learned that OSS (P), a group of Aberdeen orthopedic surgeons, had decided to build a day surgery center that would directly compete with ASL (D). During the first seven months that OSS's (P) surgery center was open, ASL (D) suffered a 1,000-hour loss of operating room usage. In response, ASL (D) closed ASL's (D) medical staff with respect to physicians requesting privileges for spine surgery and closed its medical staff to applicants for orthopedic surgery privileges. In the summer of 1998, OSS (P) recruited Dr. Mahan (P), a spine-fellowship-trained orthopedic surgeon engaged in the practice of orthopedic surgery. Mahan (P) applied for staff privileges at ASL (D) but was denied. Mahan (P) and OSS (P) commenced this action against ASL (D), challenging the Board's decision to close the staff. The circuit court determined that ASL (D) breached the Staff Bylaws because it delegated power regarding medical staff issues by closing the staff without first consulting the staff. ASL (D) appealed.

ISSUE: Does a delegation of authority in medical staff bylaws concerning staff privileges trump a hospital board's authority to make business decisions relating to staff privileges?

HOLDING AND DECISION: (Gilbertson, J.) No. The medical staff bylaws of a hospital do not trump the Board of Directors' ability to make administrative decisions. This is not a case concerning issues delegated to the expertise of medical staff concerning appointments and privileges. Rather, it was an adminisitrative decision by ASL's (D) Board to close ASL's (D) staff for certain procedures to ensure ASL's (D) economic survival. Allowing the medical staff to pass on valid business decisions by the Board as to any issue that incidentally affects the medical staff would render the Board ineffectual. Hospitals have a duty of responsibility with regards to hiring competent physicians. To impose this duty and leave hospital boards powerless to make any decisions regarding medical staff as the lower court suggests would lead to illogical results. Reversed.

ANALYSIS

Despite the arguments made in *Mahan* that hospital boards should not just act as a rubber stamp in approving physicians for staff privileges that are approved or recommended by staff, this is how most hospitals actually function.

Quicknotes

DUTY OF CARE A principle of negligence requiring an individual to act in such a manner as to avoid injury to a person to whom he or she owes an obligatory duty.

Potvin v. Metropolitan Life Ins. Co.

Physician (P) v. Managed care organization (D)

Cal. Sup. Ct., 22 Cal. 4th 1060, 997 P.2d 1153 (2000).

NATURE OF CASE: Appeal from summary judgment for defendant.

FACT SUMMARY: Potvin (P) sued Metropolitan Life Ins. Co. (MetLife) (D) when his name was removed from the list of preferred provider physicians.

RULE OF LAW

When an insurer which possesses power so substantial that removal from its preferred provider list significantly impairs the ability of an ordinary, competent physician to practice medicine or a medical specialty in a particular geographic area, thereby affecting an important, substantial economic interest, decides to remove a doctor from its preferred provider list, the insurer must comply with the common-law right to fair procedure.

FACTS: Potvin (P), an obstetrician and gynecologist, had practiced medicine for over 35 years when he contracted with Metropolitan Life Ins. Co. (MetLife) (D) to be placed on its list of preferred providers. MetLife (D) later terminated Potvin's (P) preferred provider status without cause. When Potvin (P) insisted on an explanation, he was told that he did not meet their standard for malpractice history because he had been sued four times for malpractice. After MetLife (D) refused to respond to Potvin's (P) request for a hearing, Potvin (P) filed a complaint alleging violation of the common law right to fair procedure. The district court granted MetLife's (D) motion for summary judgment, but the appellate court reversed. MetLife (D) appealed to the state supreme court for review.

ISSUE: When an insurer which possesses power so substantial that removal from its preferred provider list significantly impairs the ability of an ordinary, competent physician to practice medicine or a medical specialty in a particular geographic area, thereby affecting an important, substantial economic interest, decides to remove a doctor from its preferred provider list, must the insurer comply with the common-law right to fair procedure?

HOLDING AND DECISION: (Kennard, J.) Yes. When an insurer which possesses power so substantial that removal from its preferred provider list significantly impairs the ability of an ordinary, competent physician to practice medicine or a medical specialty in a particular geographic area, thereby affecting an important, substantial economic interest, decides to remove a doctor from its preferred provider list, the insurer must comply with the common-law right to fair procedure. Potvin (P) alleged that the adverse effects of removal from MetLife's (D) preferred provider lists included rejection by physician groups and devastation of his practice. The "without cause" termination clause in the contract was unenforceable to the extent it purported to limit an otherwise existing right to fair procedure under the common law. Affirmed.

DISSENT: (Brown, J.) The standard announced today is unworkable because it will be unpredictable. The standard purports to draw distinctions based on an insurer's share of the market in a particular geographic area, which would lead to uncertain results. The "without cause" termination provision should be enforced because there was no showing of bad faith.

ANALYSIS

The dissent argued that the court was concerned with maintaining the physician's guaranteed minimum income. MetLife (D) would not include physicians who had more than two malpractice lawsuits on its preferred provider lists. The American Medical Association and the California Medical Association were amici curiae for Potvin (P) in this matter.

Quicknotes

AMICUS CURIAE A third party, not implicated in the suit, which seeks to file a brief containing information for the court's consideration in conformity with its position.

COMMON LAW A body of law developed through the judicial decisions of the courts as opposed to the legislative process.

FIDUCIARY Person holding a legal obligation to act for the benefit of another.

FUNDAMENTAL RIGHT A liberty that is either expressly or impliedly provided for in the United States Constitution, the deprivation or burdening of which is subject to a heightened standard of review.

Wright v. Shriners Hospital for Crippled Children

Terminated nurse (P) v. Hospital (D)

Mass. Sup. Jud. Ct., 412 Mass. 469, 589 N.E.2d 1241 (1992).

NATURE OF CASE: Appeal of an award of damages for wrongful termination.

FACT SUMMARY: Wright (P), a nurse, was fired from Shriners Hospital for Crippled Children (D) for criticizing hospital practices.

RULE OF LAW

A public policy exception to the rule of at-will employment does not exist for nurses who make internal criticism of hospital practices.

FACTS: Wright (P) worked as a nurse at Shriners Hospital for Crippled Children (D). She was an at-will employee who received excellent evaluations throughout her employment. After receiving a complaint about the hospital (D), the national Shriners organization sent a survey team to the Hospital (D). Wright (P) told the team about problems between the medical and nursing staffs. The administrator of Shriners Hospital (D) was upset with Wright's (P) criticism and terminated her employment. Wright (P) filed suit for wrongful termination, claiming that she was fired in violation of public policy. A jury awarded Wright (P) $100,000, and Shriners Hospital (D) appealed.

ISSUE: Does a public policy exception to the rule of at-will employment exist for nurses who make internal criticism of hospital practices?

HOLDING AND DECISION: (O'Connor, J.) No. A public policy exception to the rule of at-will employment does not exist for nurses who make internal criticisms of hospital practices. Generally, employment at will is terminable by either the employee or the employer without notice for almost any reason. There is an exception to this rule when employment is terminated contrary to a well-defined public policy, such as refusing to break the law. The trial court found that it was in the public interest for health care providers to report on substantial patient care issues. This was based on various laws that require health care providers to inform public authorities about dangers to patients. However, these statutes are not really applicable to Wright's (P) situation. There is no state law that deals with a requirement to make internal criticism of hospital policies and practices. While there may a private ethical code supporting such action, there is no well-defined public policy sufficient to modify the general at-will employment rule. Accordingly, the judgment for Wright (P) is reversed and remanded.

DISSENT: (Liacos, C.J.) Given the public interest in good patient care, there must be a public policy to encourage hospital employees to identify problems with care. Otherwise, employers could deter such reporting by threatening their jobs.

ANALYSIS

This decision represents the majority view on the scope of the public policy exception. It appears that the case would have come out differently had Wright (P) reported problems to an outside public agency. However, even Wright (P) admitted that the problems at the Hospital (D) did not rise to the level of patient abuse or neglect.

Quicknotes

AT-WILL EMPLOYMENT The rule that an employment relationship is subject to termination at any time, or for any cause, by an employee or an employer in the absence of a specific agreement otherwise.

Oakwood Healthcare, Inc.

Union (P) v. Employer (D)

348 NLRB No. 37 (2006).

NATURE OF CASE: Resolution by the National Labor Relations Board of labor dispute between a union and an employer.

FACT SUMMARY: A union (P) argued that all charge nurses at Oakwood Heritage Hospital (D) should be included in the bargaining unit, but Oakwood (D) argued that some of them were supervisors, and therefore should be excluded from the bargaining unit.

RULE OF LAW

Registered nurses who serve as charge nurses on a permanent basis, and in that capacity regularly assign other personnel to specific patients and exercise independent judgment in doing so—as opposed to those who undertake charge nurse duties on a rotating basis, are supervisors for purposes of the National Labor Relations Act.

FACTS: The 257-bed Oakwood Heritage Hospital (D) has approximately 181 RNs who provide direct care to patients in 10 units. The RNs report to a nursing manager, clinical managers, clinical supervisors, and assistant clinical supervisors, all of whom are indisputably supervisors for purposes of the NLRA. The RNs follow doctors' orders and perform tasks such as administering medication, running blood tests, taking vital signs, observing patients, and processing admissions and discharges. They sometimes direct less-skilled employees to feed, bathe, and walk patients and to perform doctor-ordered tests. Twelve RNs serve as charge nurses on every shift they work, while some RNs take turns serving as charge nurse, and others never take on the duty. [The union (P) argued that all the charge nurses should be included in the bargaining unit, and the employer argued that all the charge nurses should be excluded.]

ISSUE: Are registered nurses who serve as charge nurses on a permanent basis, and in that capacity regularly assign other personnel to specific patients and exercise independent judgment in doing so—as opposed to those who undertake charge nurse duties on a rotating basis, supervisors for purposes of the National Labor Relations Act?

HOLDING AND DECISION: [Board member who wrote the decision not stated in casebook excerpt.] Yes. Registered nurses who serve as charge nurses on a permanent basis, and in that capacity regularly assign other personnel to specific patients and exercise independent judgment in doing so—as opposed to those who undertake charge nurse duties on a rotating basis, are supervisors for purposes of the National Labor Relations Act. Under NLRA Section 2(11), a supervisor is an employee who has the authority to perform any of 12 tasks in the interest of the employer and using independent judgment. A supervisor's responsibilities include "assigning" other employees, responsibly "directing" others, and using "independent judgment." "Assign" is the act of designating an employee to a place, appointing an individual to a time, or giving significant overall duties to an employee. But choosing the order in which the employee will perform discrete tasks within those assignments would not necessarily indicate the authority to assign. For direction to be "responsible," the person directing and performing the oversight of the employee must be accountable for the performance of the task by the other. As for "independent judgment," a judgment is not independent if it is dictated or controlled by detailed instructions, whether set forth in company policies or rules, the verbal instructions of a higher authority, or in the provisions of a collective-bargaining agreement. Rotating charge nurses do not exercise supervisory authority for a substantial part of their work time, and therefore are not supervisors. Charge nurses are supervisors, and are therefore excluded from the bargaining unit.

ANALYSIS

Chairman Robert J. Battista and members Peter C. Schaumber and Peter N. Kirsanow joined in the majority opinion in the case. Members Wilma B. Liebman and Dennis P. Walsh dissented regarding the majority's interpretations of the statutory language and asserted that the RNs who serve as permanent charge nurses as well as those who serve in that capacity on a rotating basis are not supervisors. The ruling is landmark, because the NLRB issued new guidelines for determining who is a supervisor and not entitled to have union representation and engage in collective bargaining, a ruling that could result in removing certain workers in a wide variety of industries from coverage under federal labor law.

Quicknotes

BARGAINING UNIT A community of interest, usually a labor union that is authorized to carry out collective bargaining for workplace benefits on behalf of employees.

COLLECTIVE BARGAINING Negotiations between an employer and employee that are mediated by a specified third party.

Continued on next page.

NATIONAL LABOR RELATIONS BOARD An agency established pursuant to the National Labor Relations Act for the purpose of prohibiting unfair labor practices by employers and unions.

New York University Medical Center and Association of Staff Psychiatrists, Bellevue Psychiatric Hospital

Employees (P) v. Employer (D)

324 N.L.R.B. No. 139 (1997).

NATURE OF CASE: Unfair labor practice charge before the National Labor Relations Board.

FACT SUMMARY: An association that represented, as a union would, employees of a hospital charged that the hospital violated the National Labor Relations Act when it threatened and discharged employees because they engaged in protected activities.

RULE OF LAW

Where there is evidence of animus by an employer toward an association that represents employees as a union, as well as members of that association, and the employer discharges members of the association, the burden shifts to the employer to show that in the absence of the employees' protected concerted activities under the National Labor Relations Act, they would have been discharged.

FACTS: New York University Medical Center and Bellevue Psychiatric Hospital (Hospital) (D) provide mental health services. Six psychiatrists on staff were also members of the executive committee of the Association of Staff Psychiatrists (P), which is a labor organization under the National Labor Relations Act even though it is not a union. The Association (P) dealt with the Hospital (D) on matters of salaries, working hours and conditions, and grievances. When the Hospital (D) changed its policy of allowing some psychiatrists to work six-hour workdays because of budget constraints, the six members of the Association's (P) executive committee protested. The Hospital (D) administrator then indicated that such protests and refusal to cooperate with the new policy would make the protestors likely candidates for layoffs. When the Hospital (D) eventually implemented layoffs, the six Association (P) committee members were among those laid off.

ISSUE: Where there is evidence of animus by an employer toward an association that represents employees as a union, as well as members of that association, and the employer discharges members of the association, does the burden shift to the employer to show that in the absence of the employees' protected concerted activities under the National Labor Relations Act, they would have been discharged?

HOLDING AND DECISION: [Board member not identified in casebook excerpt.] Where there is evidence of animus by an employer toward an association that represents employees as a union, as well as members of that association, and the employer discharges members of the association, the burden shifts to the employer to show that in the absence of the employees' protected concerted activities under the National Labor Relations Act, they would have been discharged. A motivating factor in the discharge of the six committee members was likely their protected concerted activities, because there was "abundant" evidence of animus by the Hospital (D) administration toward the Association (P) and its executive board members, as well as their open opposition to schedule changes. In addition, the Hospital (D) administration made unlawful implicit threats of cutbacks, layoffs, and other consequences if they continued to protest such changes. Finally, the timing of the discharges—shortly after their protected activities—also indicates that the discharges were motivated by animus toward the Association (P). Therefore, the Hospital (D) had to show that even in the absence of their protected activities, the discharges would have occurred. The Hospital's (D) assertion that the layoff was motivated by a reduction in budget mandated by the city is unpersuasive, however.

ANALYSIS: Conclusions by the National Labor Relations Board are usually fact-specific, and do not generally result in changes to the law. Generally, either party retains the right to appeal to a court after a final ruling by the Board. The usefulness of this case is primarily limited to its statement of the rule that the burden of showing that discharges, or any adverse action against an employee who charges the employer with an unfair labor practice, shifts to the employer after the employee shows animus. The other interesting aspect of this case is that non-union associations of employees may bring actions before the Board. The National Labor Relations Board's jurisdiction is not limited to actions involving unions.

Estate of Mauro v. Borgess Medical Center

Employee (P) v. Former employer (D)

137 F.3d 398 (6th Cir. 1998).

NATURE OF CASE: Appeal from summary judgment for defendant.

FACT SUMMARY: When Borgess Medical Center (BMC) (D) laid off Mauro (P) after discovering that he was infected with the human immunodeficiency virus (HIV), Mauro (P) alleged that he had been the victim of unlawful discrimination.

RULE OF LAW

A person with an infectious disease who poses a significant risk of communicating an infectious disease to others in the workplace is not otherwise qualified to perform the job.

FACTS: Mauro (P) was employed as an operating room technician at Borgess Medical Center (BMC) (D) when someone called BMC (D) saying that Mauro (P) had full-blown AIDS. Because of the fear of exposure, a new position was offered to Mauro (P), who was HIV positive. Mauro (P) refused the new position, and he was laid off. Mauro (P) then filed suit, alleging discrimination under section 504 of the Rehabilitation Act and the Americans with Disabilities Act (ADA). The district court found that Mauro's (P) continued employment as a surgical technician posed a direct threat to the health and safety of others and granted BMC's (D) motion for summary judgment. Mauro (P) appealed.

ISSUE: Is a person with an infectious disease who poses a significant risk of communicating an infectious disease to others in the workplace otherwise qualified to perform the job?

HOLDING AND DECISION: (Gibson, J.) No. A person with an infectious disease who poses a significant risk of communicating an infectious disease to others in the workplace is not otherwise qualified to perform the job. The "direct threat" standard applied in the ADA is based on the same standard as "significant risk" applied by the Rehabilitation Act. Courts defer to the reasonable medical judgments of public health officials in determining whether HIV-positive health care workers pose a significant risk or a direct threat in the performance of the essential functions of their jobs. The Center for Disease Control has released a report advising health care institutions to determine which procedures are exposure-prone and recommends that HIV-infected health care workers not perform such functions. Here, Mauro's (P) supervisor explained that a surgical technician may be called upon to assist in the performance of a surgical procedure, though this occurs rarely. The district court did not err in determining that Mauro's (P) continued employment posed a direct threat to others in the workplace. Affirmed.

DISSENT: (Boggs, J.) The chance that Mauro (P) will transmit a lethal disease is small. A full assessment should be conducted of both the risk and the consequence.

ANALYSIS

The surgical worker here had to qualify as a disabled person in order to rely on the ADA or the Rehabilitation Act. Asymptomatic HIV was held to be an impairment because it substantially limited a major life function, that of reproduction. The Center for Disease Control's guidelines have been criticized for not providing more specific information on which activities are "exposure prone."

Quicknotes

AMERICANS WITH DISABILITIES ACT Prohibits discrimination in employment, housing, transportation, and other services on the basis of an individual's physical or mental disabilities.

REHABILITATION ACT OF 1973 Requires that all contracts over $2,500 made by the United States for property or services include a provision requiring the contracting party to take affirmative action to employ handicapped individuals.

CHAPTER 13

The Structure of the Health Care Enterprise

Quick Reference Rules of Law

Stern v. Lucy Webb Hayes National Training School for Deaconesses and Missionaries

Patients (P) v. Hospital trustees (D)

381 F. Supp. 1003 (D.D.C. 1974).

NATURE OF CASE: Class action for breach of fiduciary duties.

FACT SUMMARY: The trustees (D) of the Lucy Webb School, a nonprofit institution that provided health care to the poor, did not invest the school's liquid assets.

RULE OF LAW

Trustees of charitable corporations have a duty to avoid participation in transactions in which they have an interest and must exercise general supervision over investment decisions.

FACTS: The Lucy Webb School was established in 1891 for the purpose of providing health care services to the poor. It was incorporated as a charitable institution, and the Sibley Hospital (D) was built to facilitate its work. The board was to consist of twenty-five to thirty-five trustees who were to meet twice annually. The Board was to handle all financial matters of the school. In fact, from the early 1950s until 1968, two trustees (D) handled all of these matters. The Finance and Investment Committees never met for years at a time. Some of the trustees (D) were associated with financial institutions. The hospital (D) maintained most of its liquid assets in these same institutions in non-interest-bearing accounts. A class action suit was brought against the trustees (D) by patients (P) of the hospital (D) challenging their actions, claiming mismanagement, nonmanagement, and self-dealing.

ISSUE: Do trustees of charitable corporations have a duty to avoid participation in transactions in which they have an interest and to exercise general supervision over investment decisions?

HOLDING AND DECISION: (Gesell, J.) Yes. Trustees of charitable corporations have a duty to avoid participation in transactions in which they have an interest and must exercise general supervision over investment decisions. Both trustees and corporate directors can be liable for losses occasioned by negligent mismanagement of investments. Generally, trustees are held to a higher standard of care and are liable for simple negligence. However, in cases involving trustees of charitable institutions, the gross negligence standard for corporate directors is more appropriate. It is also proper to apply the lower standard with regard to nonmanagement. Trustees of charitable companies should be permitted to delegate investment decisions to a committee as long as the directors assume the responsibility for supervision. For allegations of self-dealing, trustees are not absolutely barred from placing funds under their control in their own institutions. However, there must be full disclosure. In the present case, the trustees (D) failed to exercise any supervision over the investment decisions of the hospital (D). Some of the trustees (D) also knowingly permitted the hospital (D) to enter into transactions with related companies without having disclosed the relationship. Thus, these trustees (D) violated their fiduciary duties to the hospital (D). The appropriate committees are ordered to present to the full board statements concerning the investments of the hospital (D).

ANALYSIS

The court went on to emphasize that management of a nonprofit charitable hospital imposed severe obligations on its trustees. The court ordered that each newly elected trustee read its opinion and order in this case. Section 8.30 of the Revised Model Nonprofit Corporation Act follows this decision and adopts the corporate standard for fiduciary duties of nonprofit trustees.

Quicknotes

CLASS ACTION A suit commenced by a representative on behalf of an ascertainable group that is too large to appear in court, who shares a commonality of interests and who will benefit from a successful result.

FIDUCIARY RELATIONSHIP Person holding a legal obligation to act for the benefit of another.

SELF-DEALING Transaction in which a fiduciary uses property of another, held by virtue of the confidential relationship, for personal gain.

In re Caremark International Inc. Derivative Litigation

Shareholders (P) v. Corporate directors (D)

Del. Ct. Ch., 698 A.2d 959 (1996).

NATURE OF CASE: Pending motion to approve settlement of a derivative action.

FACT SUMMARY: A derivative action was filed on behalf of Caremark International, Inc., to recover losses suffered because of violations of federal and state laws and regulations by employees.

RULE OF LAW

A director's obligation includes a duty to attempt in good faith to ensure that a corporate information and reporting system, which the board concludes is adequate, exists to inform the board of potential noncompliance with applicable legal standards.

FACTS: Caremark International, Inc. (P) provided alternative site health care services as part of its patient care business. Caremark (P) had taken a number of measures to assure compliance with the antikickback provisions of the Medicare fraud and abuse law. When two federal grand juries indicted Caremark (P) and individuals for violations of the antikickback laws, a derivative suit was filed claiming Caremark directors (D) breached their duty of care by failing adequately to supervise Caremark (P) employees. A proposed settlement was reached to recover the corporation's losses against the individuals who constitute its board of directors, and the court must decide whether the proposed settlement appears to be fair to the corporation and the absent shareholders.

ISSUE: Does a director's obligation include a duty to attempt in good faith to ensure that a corporate information and reporting system, which the board concludes is adequate, exists to inform the board of potential noncompliance with applicable legal standards?

HOLDING AND DECISION: (Allen, Chan.) Yes. A director's obligation includes a duty to attempt in good faith to ensure that a corporate information and reporting system, which the board concludes is adequate, exists. In order to show that Caremark directors (D) breached their duty of care by failing adequately to control Caremark employees, the shareholders (P) would have to show either that the directors (D) knew or should have known that violations of law were occurring and, in either event, that the directors took no steps in a good-faith effort to prevent or remedy that situation, and that such failure proximately resulted in the losses complained of. [The Board appears to have been informed by experts that the company's practices, while contestable, were lawful. There is no evidence that reliance on such reports was not reasonable. Here, the record supplies essentially no evidence that the directors (D) were guilty of a sustained failure to exercise their oversight function. The corporation's information systems appear to have represented a good faith attempt to be informed of relevant facts. Given the weakness of the shareholders' (P) claims, the proposed settlement appears to be an adequate, reasonable, and beneficial outcome for all of the parties. Thus the proposed settlement will be approved.]

ANALYSIS

The court in this case noted that director liability for a breach of duty to exercise appropriate attention may arise in two distinct contexts. First, such liability may be said to follow from a board decision that results in a loss because that decision was ill-advised or negligent. Second, liability to the corporation for a loss may be said to arise from a failure of the Board to act in circumstances in which due attention would, arguably, have prevented the loss.

Quicknotes

CORPORATION A distinct legal entity characterized by continuous existence; free alienability of interests held therein; centralized management; and limited liability on the part of the shareholders of the corporation.

DERIVATIVE SUIT Action asserted by a shareholder in order to enforce a cause of action on behalf of the corporation.

DUTY OF CARE A principle of negligence requiring an individual to act in such a manner as to avoid injury to a person to whom he or she owes an obligatory duty.

FIDUCIARY DUTY A legal obligation to act for the benefit of another, including subordinating one's personal interests to that of the other person.

Manhattan Eye, Ear and Throat Hospital v. Spitzer

Hospital (P) v. Attorney General (D)

N.Y. Sup. Ct., 186 Misc. 2d 126, 715 N.Y.S.2d 575 (1999).

NATURE OF CASE: Petition for approval of the sale of a not-for-profit corporation.

FACT SUMMARY: Manhattan Eye, Ear and Throat Hospital (MEETH) (Petitioner) (P) sought approval of its proposed sale of a not-for-profit medical complex pursuant to section 511 [New York Not-For-Profit Law].

RULE OF LAW

In order to approve the sale of a not-for-profit corporation, the corporation must show that the consideration and terms of the transaction are fair and reasonable and that the purposes of the corporation will be promoted by the sale.

FACTS: In 1995, Manhattan Eye, Ear and Throat Hospital (MEETH) (P), a medical complex located on East 64th Street that was world renowned as an acute care specialty hospital, opened an outpatient center in Harlem. MEETH's (P) articles of incorporation identified the corporation's purposes as being: "to establish, provide, conduct, operate and maintain a hospital in the City, County and State of New York for the general treatment of persons suffering from acute short-term illnesses; performing general plastic surgery; treating persons suffering from diseases of the eye, ear, nose or throat; maintaining a school for post-graduate instruction in the treatment of such illnesses, performing such surgery, and the treatment of such diseases, and conducting associated and basic research." In 1999, due to budgetary constraints, MEETH (P) decided to sell its 64th Street complex to Memorial Sloan Kettering Cancer Center (MSKCC) and Downtown Group/Colony Capital (Downtown). The sale would require shutting down its programs at the 64th Street location. MEETH (P) also planned to transform the Harlem clinic into a freestanding Diagnostic and Treatment center (D&T). In addition, there were plans to add further D&T centers in the South Bronx. The property of the 64th Street complex was appraised between $46–$50 million and ultimately MEETH (P) agreed to sell the complex for $41 million to MSKCC and Downtown. MSKCC planned to use the portion of the real estate it purchased to expand its cancer treatment and research, while Downtown planned to use its portion to build an apartment complex. There was also discussion by the board of directors to revise the corporation's purpose to that of its "original" purpose, which was serving the poor in under-serviced areas in the City. However, the articles of incorporation were never amended. MEETH (P) had planned to time its petition for approval of the sale to follow the Department of Health's (DOH) approval for creation of the D&T centers and after the hospital had been closed. However, this timing did not work out and the petition was filed prior to DOH approval and the facilities were still partially operational at the time the court was evaluating the sale.

ISSUE: In order to approve the sale of a not-for-profit corporation, must the corporation show that the consideration and terms of the transaction are fair and reasonable and that the purposes of the corporation will be promoted by the sale?

HOLDING AND DECISION: [Judge not stated in casebook excerpt.] Yes. In order to approve the sale of a not-for-profit corporation, the corporation must show that the consideration and terms of the transaction are fair and reasonable and that the purposes of the corporation will be promoted by the sale. The evaluation of the first prong of this test, whether the consideration and terms of the transaction are fair and reasonable, requires more than just looking at the market value of the real estate because the sale is linked with the elimination of the medical services that MEETH (P) currently provides. Necessarily, closure of the acute care medical specialty facility will bring about a fundamental change to the corporation's purposes as delineated in the corporation's articles. MEETH (P) has major medical value that is not being preserved under the terms of the proposed transaction. "Monetizing" the value of the physical assets does nothing to capture the full value of its not-for-profit provision of world-renowned medical services. As for the second prong of the analysis, whether or not the corporation's purposes will be promoted, the evidence of MEETH's (P) plan to amend its articles of incorporation to align the corporation's new purposes with the function of its newly proposed D&T centers demonstrates that the corporation was well aware that it was not meeting this requirement under the terms of the transaction. While the definition of "hospital" includes the functions of what the D&T centers would provide in terms of general medical practice, the center's deviation from specialty eye, ear, nose and throat surgery and research cannot be ignored or denied. The transaction before the court can best be summarized as one where an organization sells major assets to solve financial difficulties and then undertakes a completely new mission. MEETH's (P) Board of Directors failed to consider various alternatives that would have preserved the corporation's mission. The proposed transaction fails to meet the two-pronged test of § 511 and the court denies MEETH's (P) petition.

Continued on next page.

ANALYSIS

Procedurally, in the charitable corporations context, there were no shareholders to represent the corporation's interests, so to ensure protection of the interests held by the beneficiaries of the not-for-profit hospital, the court appointed the Attorney General (Spitzer) to represent those interests. A large number of not-for-profit health insurance companies and HMOs have recently chosen to convert to for-profit status. Blue Cross organizations have led the way in this movement. In the typical conversion, the assets are sold to a for-profit entity. To comply with internal revenue laws, the money derived from the sale of the not-for-profit assets is supposed to be distributed to charitable organizations that are eligible pursuant to § 501(c)(3) of the IRC. Many not-for-profits, when making this conversion, intentionally undervalue their assets and purchase the assets for the newly formed for-profit corporation, which is conveniently under the management of the same Board of Directors. The new corporation then has a sale of public stock at a substantial premium above the price paid by the investors. This practice has resulted in a number of lawsuits to retain the actual value of the not-for-profit corporation in the respective communities who had invested goodwill and tax relief with the expectation of receiving the charitable services in return. A number of states also responded to this tactic by amending their not-for-profit corporations law to ensure the sales were not shams—such as the situation in the above case.

Quicknotes

ARTICLES OF INCORPORATION The written instrument that gives rise to the existence of a corporation when filed with the appropriate governmental agency.

CORPORATION A distinct legal entity characterized by continuous existence; free alienability of interests held therein; centralized management; and limited liability on the part of the shareholders of the corporation.

Berlin v. Sarah Bush Lincoln Health Center

Physician (P) v. Hospital (D)

Ill. Sup. Ct., 179 Ill. 2d 1, 688 N.E.2d 106 (1997).

NATURE OF CASE: Appeal from plaintiff's summary judgment in declaratory judgment suit.

FACT SUMMARY: Dr. Berlin (P) sought to have a restrictive covenant prohibiting him from competing with Sarah Bush Lincoln Health Center (D) declared unenforceable.

RULE OF LAW

A duly licensed hospital is authorized by legislative authority to practice medicine by means of its staff of licensed physicians and is excepted from the operation of the corporate practice doctrine.

FACTS: Dr. Berlin (P) was employed by the Sarah Bush Lincoln Health Center (Health Center) (D), a nonprofit corporation duly licensed to operate a hospital, pursuant to a written agreement. Berlin (P) resigned prior to the expiration of his five-year contract, and began working at a nearby clinic. The Health Center (D) sought a preliminary injunction to prohibit Berlin (P) from practicing at the clinic, based on the restrictive covenant in the employment agreement. Berlin (P) filed a complaint for declaratory judgment and a motion for summary judgment seeking to have the restrictive covenant contained in the employment agreement with the Health Center (D) declared unenforceable. The circuit court granted summary judgment, holding that the Health Center (D), as a nonprofit corporation employing a physician, was practicing medicine in violation of the prohibition on the corporate practice of medicine, and a divided appellate court affirmed. The Health Center (D) appealed.

ISSUE: Is a duly licensed hospital authorized by legislative authority to practice medicine by means of its staff of licensed physicians and is it excepted from the operation of the corporate practice doctrine?

HOLDING AND DECISION: (Nickels, J.) Yes. A duly licensed hospital is authorized by legislative authority to practice medicine by means of its staff of licensed physicians and is excepted from the operation of the corporate practice doctrine. The corporate practice doctrine, which prohibits corporations that are licensed hospitals from employing physicians to provide medical services, is not applicable to licensed hospitals in the modern health care industry for public policy reasons. Consequently, the employment agreement between the Health Center (D) and Dr. Berlin (P) was not unenforceable merely because the Health Center (D) was a corporate entity. Reversed.

ANALYSIS

The court in this case found that legislative enactments pertaining to hospitals supported its conclusion that licensed hospitals were excepted from the prohibition. It found that certain statutes clearly authorized, and at times mandated, licensed hospitals to provide medical services despite their corporate stature. It also could find no justification for distinguishing between nonprofit and for-profit hospitals in that regard.

Quicknotes

CORPORATION A distinct legal entity characterized by continuous existence; free alienability of interests held therein; centralized management; and limited liability on the part of the shareholders of the corporation.

RESTRICTIVE COVENANT A promise contained in a deed to limit the uses to which the property will be made.

Utah County v. Intermountain Health Care, Inc.

County tax board (P) v. Hospital operator (D)

Utah Sup. Ct., 709 P.2d 265 (1985).

NATURE OF CASE: Appeal of granting of tax exemption.

FACT SUMMARY: Utah County (P) contended that Intermountain Health Care (D), operating two nonprofit hospitals, was not entitled to tax-exempt status.

RULE OF LAW

A hospital may be considered nonprofit and still not be entitled to a tax exemption.

FACTS: Intermountain Health Care (IHC) (D) operated two hospitals, which were classified as nonprofit. The hospitals were funded almost exclusively through insurance, government assistance, and fees; very little income came from gifts. Income exceeded expenses, and free services amounted to less than 1% of revenue. Employees of the hospitals worked on a voluntary basis, but the hospitals used the services of numerous paid contractors. The Utah County (P) Board of Equalization denied IHC (D) tax-exempt status. The State Tax Commission reversed, and Utah County (P) appealed.

ISSUE: May a hospital be considered nonprofit and still not be entitled to a tax exemption?

HOLDING AND DECISION: (Durham, J.) Yes. A hospital may be considered nonprofit and still not be entitled to a tax exemption. Under the Utah constitution, an entity is entitled to a property tax exemption only if it is a charitable institution. Whether an institution is charitable does not depend on a nonprofit nomenclature. Rather, the workings of the institution must be analyzed against the standard of what constitutes a charitable institution. Factors include: (1) whether the entity provides services without expectation of material reward, (2) the extent to which it is supported by donations, (3) the extent to which recipients are expected to pay for services, (4) whether income exceeds expenses, (5) restrictions upon beneficiaries, and (6) whether financial benefits are available to those involved. Here, free services accounted for less than 1% of the hospital's revenue; only a small amount of revenue came from donations; patients were charged; income exceeded expenses; indigents were discouraged from seeking treatment; and although employees were unpaid, contractors (who often were also employees) were often utilized. In light of these considerations, charitable status appeared inappropriate. Reversed.

DISSENT: (Stewart, J.) The legal concept of charity does not require that an institution incur a deficit. As the evidence shows that not one cent of revenues went toward paying employees, officers, or directors, the hospitals should be entitled to tax-exempt status.

ANALYSIS

In years past, most hospitals were charitable in that they were affiliated with a church or philanthropic organization and were money-losers. In the twentieth century, for-profit hospitals became the norm. While still having indicia of charitable institutions, they are run like businesses. Where charity ends and business begins is not always clear.

Quicknotes

CHARITABLE INSTITUTION A nonprofit organization that offers charity to all who need and apply for it, that does not appear to obstruct in any way the provision of services to those who need and would avail themselves of its charitable services.

TAX EXEMPTION Freedom from the obligation of paying taxes with regard to particular income or property.

IHC Health Plans, Inc. v. Commissioner of Internal Revenue

Health care corporation (P) v. Government agency (D)

325 F.3d 1188 (10th Cir. 2003).

NATURE OF CASE: Appeal from decision of Tax Court.

FACT SUMMARY: Intermountain Health Care Health Plans, Inc. (Health Plans) (P) brought suit in the United States Tax Court (Tax Court) seeking a declaratory judgment to reverse the decision of the Commissioner of Internal Revenue (Commissioner) (D) to revoke their non-profit tax-exempt status.

RULE OF LAW

In order for a health care corporation to qualify for tax-exempt status under 26 U.S.C. § 501(c)(3), it must be an organization operated primarily for charitable purposes.

FACTS: Intermountain Health Care (IHC) formed a subsidiary, IHC Health Services (Health Services), as a Utah non-profit corporation. Health Services operated twenty-two hospitals in Utah and Idaho, and during the years of 1997 through 1999 Health Services provided $1.2 billion in unreimbursed medical care to Medicaid patients and another $91 in unreimbursed care to indigent patients. The Commissioner (D) recognized Health Services as having tax-exempt status under § 501(c)(3). Later, IHC formed three additional subsidiary health care companies: IHC Health Plans (Health Plans) (P), IHC Care, Inc. (Care) and IHC Group, Inc. (Group) to operate as health maintenance organizations (HMOs). The Commissioner (D) would later conclude that none of these three subsidiaries was operating exclusively for exempt purposes pursuant to § 501(c)(3). The Commissioner (D) revoked Health Plan's (P) exempt status and determined that Care and Group were not entitled to the exemption. Health Plans (P), Care and Group brought suit in the Tax Court seeking a declaratory judgment to reverse the Commissioner's (D) ruling. The Tax Court affirmed the Commissioner's (D) ruling in a separate opinion for each of the three corporate entities. Health Plans (P) became the successor in interest to Care and Group and brings this appeal on behalf of all three entities.

ISSUE: In order for a health care corporation to qualify for tax-exempt status under 26 U.S.C. § 501(c)(3), must it be an organization operated primarily for charitable purposes?

HOLDING AND DECISION: (Tacha, C.J.) Yes. In order for a health care corporation to qualify for tax-exempt status under 26 U.S.C. § 501(c)(3), it must be an organization operated primarily for charitable purposes. There is a two-part test for this evaluation. First it must be determined if the purpose of the corporation is "charitable," and second the corporation must operate primarily to serve this purpose. To be "charitable" the corporation must be engaged in activities that convey a benefit to the public. The public benefit is accepted in exchange for lifting the tax burden and is not a benefit the community actually chooses, but rather is one that supplements or advances the work of public institutions already supported by tax revenues. The magnitude of this benefit must give a strong inference that the organization operates primarily for the purpose of benefiting the community. A number of factors are relevant under the "community benefit" analysis including how many people are eligible to receive the benefit, if the benefit provided is free or below-cost, if funds are used for research and education, and if the benefit is provided to persons participating in governmental programs such as Medicare or Medicaid. The court also examines the composition of the corporation's board of trustees when making it determination to see if the Board will represent the community's interests. In this case, Health Plans (P) charges premiums for the medical services it provides to its members. Health Plans (P) HMO membership is offered to a large cross-section of the community, but it is so offered for the purpose of making profits. Care and Group limited their membership to employees working for large employers, which does not provide a widespread community benefit. Health Plans (P) does not engage in any medical research or provide free health education to the public. The Board of Trustees composition had been changed to represent the community, however, given the lack of services provided to benefit the community, this factor becomes irrelevant. The Tax Court's decision to affirm the Commissioner's decision that these three corporate entities do not qualify for exempt status pursuant to § 501(c)(3) is affirmed.

ANALYSIS

Clearly the two-part inquiry to determine tax-exempt status is a fact intensive inquiry that must be implemented on a case-by-case basis. Consequently, the way the health care corporation structures its HMOs can be the determinant factor for qualifying for the exempt status. If an HMO engages in health care research that will ultimately benefit the community and provides subsidized (i.e., below cost) memberships, free health education, indigent emergency services, etc., to a large cross-section of the community, it

Continued on next page.

will likely qualify. IHC's fourth subsidiary, Health Services, retained its tax-exempt status, but it would appear the unreimbursed services offered by Health Services alone could not be used to convey tax-exempt status to Health Plans (P), Care or Group.

Quicknotes

CORPORATION A distinct legal entity characterized by continuous existence; free alienability of interests held therein; centralized management; and limited liability on the part of the shareholders of the corporation.

IHC Health Plans, Inc. v. Commissioner of Internal Revenue

Health care corporation (P) v. Government agency (D)

325 F.3d 1188 (10th Cir. 2003).

NATURE OF CASE: Appeal from decision of Tax Court.

FACT SUMMARY: Intermountain Health Care Health Plans, Inc. (Health Plans) (P) brought suit in the United States Tax Court (Tax Court) seeking a declaratory judgment to reverse the decision of the Commissioner of Internal Revenue (Commissioner) (D) to revoke their non-profit tax-exempt status.

RULE OF LAW

A corporation may qualify for tax-exempt status under 26 U.S.C. § 501(c)(3), when its sole activity is an "integral part" of an exempt affiliate's activities.

FACTS: Intermountain Health Care (IHC) formed a subsidiary, IHC Health Services (Health Services), as a Utah non-profit corporation. Health Services operated twenty-two hospitals in Utah and Idaho, and during the years of 1997 through 1999 Health Services provided $1.2 billion in unreimbursed medical care to Medicaid patients and another $91 in unreimbursed care to indigent patients. The Commissioner (D) recognized Health Services as having tax-exempt status under § 501(c)(3). Later, IHC formed three additional subsidiary health care companies: Intermountain Health Care Health Plans, Inc. (Health Plans) (P), IHC Care, Inc. (Care) and IHC Group, Inc. (Group) to operate as health maintenance organizations (HMOs). The Commissioner (D) would later conclude that none of these three subsidiaries was operating exclusively for exempt purposes pursuant to § 501(c)(3). The Commissioner (D) revoked Health Plan's (P) exempt status and determined that Care and Group were not entitled to exemption. Health Plans (P), Care and Group brought suit in the Tax Court seeking a declaratory judgment to reverse the Commissioner's (D) ruling. The Tax Court affirmed the Commissioner's (D) ruling in a separate opinion for each of the three corporate entities. Health Plans (P) became the successor in interest to Care and Group and brings this appeal on behalf of all three entities.

ISSUE: May a corporation qualify for tax-exempt status under 26 U.S.C. § 501(c)(3), when its sole activity is an "integral part" of an exempt affiliate's activities?

HOLDING AND DECISION: (Tacha, C.J.) Yes. A corporation may qualify for tax-exempt status under 26 U.S.C. § 501(c)(3), when its sole activity is an "integral part" of an exempt affiliate's activities. In order for a health care corporation to qualify for tax-exempt status under 26 U.S.C. § 501(c)(3), it must be an organization operated primarily for charitable purposes. However, several circuits have carved out an exception to the general rule known as the "integral-part doctrine." The exception discounts two basic rules of tax law that corporate entities are separate and distinct taxable entities, and that tax exemptions are narrowly and strictly construed. To qualify for exempt status under this exception, the court looks to the totality of the circumstances, and the corporate entity seeking exempt status must demonstrate that there is a nexus between itself and the tax-exempt affiliate. Under the facts of this case, there is no question that Health Services, one of IHC's four subsidiaries, is engaged in the provision of charitable services. The Commissioner (D) has already recognized Health Services' exempt status. However, Health Services only accounts for the provision of 20 percent of IHC's health care services. The remaining three subsidiaries do not act in any way to further the affiliate's activities, and in fact, are solely engaged in providing health care for a profit. The required nexus is absent. Petitioners do not qualify for the exception and do not qualify for tax-exempt status under § 501(c)(3).

ANALYSIS

To have granted all of IHC's subsidiaries tax-exempt status based upon the action of Health Services would have amounted to the "tail wagging the dog." The integral part doctrine requires the primary activity of the entire corporation to be an integral part of the charitable activities being conducted by the affiliate. It is not sufficient for the profit-making arm of the corporation to finance the not-for-profit arm's activities. There must be a legitimate nexus between the purposes of the affiliates.

Quicknotes

DECLARATORY JUDGMENT A judgment of the court establishing the rights of the parties.

TAX EXEMPTION Freedom from the obligation of paying taxes with regard to particular income or property.

Redlands Surgical Services v. Commissioner of Internal Revenue

Corporation (P) v. IRS (D)

U.S. Tax Ct., 113 T.C. 47 (1999), *aff'd per curiam,* 242 F.3d 904 (2001).

NATURE OF CASE: Appeal from agency decision.

FACT SUMMARY: The Internal Revenue Service (IRS) (D) found that Redlands Surgical Services (RSS) (P) was not a tax-exempt nonprofit organization and RSS (P) appealed.

RULE OF LAW

To qualify for tax-exempt status, an organization must be operated in an exclusively charitable manner.

FACTS: Redlands Surgical Services (RSS) (P) was a nonprofit member corporation that was a parent of a hospital. RSS (P) was also a partner with for-profit businesses that operated a surgery center. RSS (P) alleged that it was entitled to tax-exempt status because its dealings with the for-profit partners had been at arm's length and its goals were charitable. The Internal Revenue Service (IRS) (D) alleged that RSS (P) had ceded effective control over its sole activity—the operation of the surgery center—to the for-profit partners and that this indicated a substantial non-exempt purpose, whereby RSS (P) impermissibly benefited private interests. When the IRS (D) denied tax-exempt status, RSS (P) appealed, asserting that in determining whether an organization's purposes are charitable, the critical test is the sort of conduct in which the organization is actually engaged, not whether a for-profit or not-for-profit entity has control.

ISSUE: To qualify for tax-exempt status, must an organization be operated in an exclusively charitable manner?

HOLDING AND DECISION: (Thornton, J.) Yes. To qualify for tax-exempt status, an organization must be operated in an exclusively charitable manner. To the extent that RSS (P) cedes control over its sole activity to for-profit parties having an independent economic interest in the same activity, and having no obligation to put charitable purposes ahead of profit-making objectives, the IRS (D) cannot be assured that the partnership will in fact be operated in furtherance of charitable purposes. Based on the totality of factors considered, RSS (P) has in fact ceded effective control of the partnerships' and the surgery center's activities to for-profit parties, conferring on them significant private benefits, and therefore was not operated exclusively for charitable purposes. Affirmed.

ANALYSIS

The court here considered three indicia in determining the for-profit control over the partnerships' activities. First, there was no charitable obligation. Second, RSS (P) lacked any formal control. Third, RSS (P) also possessed no significant informal control.

Quicknotes

CHARITABLE INSTITUTION A nonprofit organization that offers charity to all who need and apply for it and that does not appear to obstruct in any way the provision of services to those who need and would avail themselves of its charitable services.

TAX-EXEMPT STATUS Category of property used for educational, religious, or charitable purposes that by law is not subject to assessment for taxes.

CHAPTER 14

Fraud and Abuse

Quick Reference Rules of Law

United States v. Krizek

Federal government (P) v. Psychiatrist (D)

859 F. Supp. 5 (D.D.C. 1994).

NATURE OF CASE: Action for false Medicare and Medicaid billing.

FACT SUMMARY: The federal Government (P) claimed that Krizek (D), a psychiatrist, overbilled and submitted false Medicare and Medicaid claims.

RULE OF LAW

Medicare bills that are submitted with reckless disregard as to their truth are violations of the False Claims Act.

FACTS: Dr. Krizek (D) worked as a psychiatrist treating elderly and poor Medicare and Medicaid patients. His wife (D) was responsible for overseeing the billing operations. Mrs. Krizek (D) used the billing code for a full forty-five to fifty-minute psychotherapy session whenever Krizek (D) saw a patient, without regard to whether Krizek (D) had actually spent that much time working on the case. The result of this system, or nonsystem, was that bills were submitted for time that Krizek (D) could not have possibly spent working. The federal government (P) filed suit under the False Claims Act, claiming that Krizek (D) had overbilled for Medicare payments.

ISSUE: Are Medicare bills that are submitted with reckless disregard as to their truth violations of the False Claims Act?

HOLDING AND DECISION: (Sporkin, J.) Yes. Medicare bills that are submitted with reckless disregard as to their truth are violations of the False Claims Act. The False Claims Act provides that persons who knowingly present fraudulent claims to the government are liable to the government for damages and additional fines. The mental state required for liability is either reckless disregard for the truth of the information, actual knowledge, or acting in deliberate ignorance of the truth. The Act was not intended to apply to mere negligence, but does apply to situations considered gross negligence. In the present case, Krizek (D) submitted claims for payment when he did not provide services for the amount of time billed. The record shows that the submissions were made after Mrs. Krizek (D) had made no effort to establish how much time was actually spent. Krizek (D) himself made no effort to supervise the claims submissions. Accordingly, Krizek (D) was more than negligent and acted with reckless indifference as to the truth of the submissions, thereby violating the False Claims Act. Krizek (D) will be held presumptively liable for claims in excess of nine hours in a single day. Each party may present specific evidence to rebut this presumption. Furthermore, Krizek (D) is enjoined from further Medicare participation until his billing practices are corrected.

ANALYSIS

The decision also dealt with the Government's (P) contention that doctors were not entitled to bill for a full forty-five to fifty-minute session when they spent that much time on a case but did not actually treat or talk to the patient for that long. The court rejected this argument, holding that doctors may reasonably bill for all the time they actually spend working to treat a patient. The court also noted that the amounts paid to doctors under the Medicare and Medicaid plans were minimal and could result in elderly and poor patients receiving inadequate care. Further, the court pointed out several problems it observed with the government's procedures controlling reimbursement that could potentially lead to abuse of the system or lead to physicians restricting the clientele of their practice to exclude Medicaid and Medicare recipients. These observations included: (1) no distinction as to the status of the provider so that any person providing a coded services received equal reimbursement—assistant or physician; (2) Medicaid and Medicare reimbursement so dramatically below the normal charges that a practitioner could not support a medical practice on these payments and might decline to treat patients dependent on these reimbursement systems; (3) restrictions limiting billing to "face time" only is impractical where the provision of services necessarily involves study, research and consultation; and (4) the deceitful practice of requiring separate codes for services when only reimbursing for one of a multitude of services provided. The court added that it hoped the HCFA would reexamine its reimbursement practices and make improvements.

Quicknotes

FEDERAL FALSE CLAIMS ACT Permits the government to recover civil penalties and treble damages from those knowingly submitting false claims under the Medicare or Medicaid program.

United States v. Krizek

Federal government (P) v. Psychiatrist (D)

111 F.3d 934 (D.C. Cir. 1997).

NATURE OF CASE: Appeals from judgment for plaintiff in action alleging violations of federal and common law for false medical claims.

FACT SUMMARY: The Government (P) charged the Krizeks (D), a psychiatrist and his wife, with violation of the False Claims Act (FCA) for overbilling.

RULE OF LAW

A violation of the FCA for "knowingly" filing false claims may be established without reference to the subjective intent of the defendant.

FACTS: The Krizeks (D) requested reimbursement for patient treatment under the Medicare/Medicaid program. The Government (P) brought a civil suit against the Krizeks (D) under the FCA and common law. The district court found the Krizeks (D) liable for knowingly submitting false claims and entered judgment against them for $168,105. The Krizeks (D) filed a cross-appeal, alleging that the district court had assessed civil penalties based on erroneous standards as to whether the defendants filed one claim or many. The court turned to an inquiry on the specific conduct of the defendants to determine whether multiple false claims had been filed.

ISSUE: May an FCA violation for "knowingly" filing false claims be established without reference to the subjective intent of the defendant?

HOLDING AND DECISION: (Sentelle, J.) Yes. An FCA violation for "knowingly" filing false claims may be established without reference to the subjective intent of the defendant. A person acts knowingly if he has actual knowledge of the information, acts in deliberate ignorance of the truth or falsity of the information, or acts in reckless disregard of the truth or falsity of the information. Dr. Krizek (P) delegated to his wife authority to submit claims on his behalf. In failing utterly to review the false submissions, he acted with reckless disregard. The district court erred in its calculation of the civil penalty. Reversed and remanded.

ANALYSIS

The court in this case found that the district court's determination that the Krizeks (D) had acted with reckless disregard was amply supported by the evidence. The doctor was found to be no less liable than his wife. Their actions rose to the level of reckless disregard because there were multiple submissions made with little or no factual basis.

Quicknotes

GROSS NEGLIGENCE The intentional failure to perform a duty with reckless disregard of the consequences.

RECKLESSNESS The conscious disregard of substantial and justifiable risk.

SCIENTER Knowledge of certain facts; often refers to "guilty knowledge," which implicates liability.

United States ex rel. Mikes v. Straus

Physician (P) v. Physician (D)

274 F.3d 687 (2d Cir. 2001).

NATURE OF CASE: Appeal of grant of summary judgment by district court.

FACT SUMMARY: Dr. Patricia S. Mikes (P) brought a qui tam suit against Dr. Marc J. Straus (D), and others, alleging that defendants submitted false reimbursement requests to the government for spirometry services.

RULE OF LAW

A false certification of compliance with a regulation or statute cannot serve as a basis of a qui tam action pursuant to the False Claims Act if payment is not conditioned on that certification.

FACTS: Dr. Patricia S. Mikes (P), a board-certified pulmonologist, was hired by Dr. Marc J. Straus (D) as part of a physician's partnership called Pulmonary and Critical Care Associates. Mikes (P) was specifically hired to provide pulmonary and critical care services, but when she discussed her concerns about invalid spirometry tests being conducted in the office with Straus (D), she was terminated. Spirometry encompasses various breathing tests allowing the doctors to evaluate a patient's overall pulmonary or lung functions. Mikes (P) had observed that the partnership's failure to calibrate the spirometry instruments rendered the results false and unreliable. Mikes (P) filed suit for retaliatory termination and unlawfully withheld wages. Mikes (P) also initiated this qui tam suit pursuant to the False Claims Act (FCA) alleging the partnership had submitted false requests for Medicare reimbursement. The false charges were for the allegedly false spirometry tests as well as false referrals for Magnetic Resonance Imaging (MRI) where the partnership held a financial interest in the facilities providing the testing. The district court granted summary judgment in favor of the defendants finding Mikes's (P) claims failed to satisfy the standard for constituting fraudulent certification and finding that the MRI claims were vexatious. This appeal ensued.

ISSUE: Can a false certification of compliance with a regulation or statute serve as a basis of a qui tam action pursuant to the False Claims Act if payment is not conditioned on that certification?

HOLDING AND DECISION: (Cardamone, J.) No. A false certification of compliance with a regulation or statute cannot serve as a basis of a qui tam action pursuant to the False Claims Act if payment is not conditioned on that certification. See 42 U.S.C. § 424.32, and 42 U.S.C. § 1395y(a)(1)(A). Mikes (P) alleged that the spirometry testing being performed by Straus (D) failed to satisfy the clear medical standard of care for performance of these tests as outlined by the American Thoracic Society (ATS). Mikes (P) maintains that when Straus (D) certified the claims for Medicare reimbursement for having performed these tests that he must have falsified the certification because the testing failed to meet the applicable medical standard. However, to constitute fraud with the certification for Medicare reimbursement it must be demonstrated that the services provided were not medically indicated or necessary. Mikes (P) simply confuses the applicable standards. There is no qualitative standard that applies to the certification for reimbursement, and Mikes (P) fails to establish that the testing ordered was not medically necessary. This distinction is necessary because to hold otherwise would be federalizing medical malpractice actions. Nor can Mikes (P) imply fraud utilizing the Medicare statute by claiming that the charges were not reasonable and necessary for the diagnosis and treatment of the illness or injury pursuant to the Medicare statute. The Medicare statute does add a qualitative standard as to the care actually delivered in 42 U.S.C. § 1320c-5(a). Under that section the care must be medically necessary and the quality of the care must meet the professionally recognized standard. While Mikes (P) may correctly argue that the ATS standard has not been met, the Medicare statute does not condition payment on compliance with § 1320c-5(a) so the billing cannot be constituted as being fraudulent. The government, in its amicus brief, alleges error with the district court's decision for failure to recognize the alternative theory that a claim for a "worthless" service does constitute fraud under the FCA and is not dependent on the false certification theory. Because the spirometry tests were essentially "worthless" due to Straus's (D) failure to ensure their compliance with the applicable standard of care, then he was billing the government for worthless services, which is also fraudulent. The government is correct that the worthless service claim is distinct from the false certification theory. However, such a claim carries with it an element of scienter. The party must knowingly be seeking reimbursement for a worthless test. The claim cannot be predicated on a party's negligence or innocent mistake. Mikes (P) failed to establish that Straus (D) knowingly sought reimbursement for worthless medical testing so this claim also fails. Summary judgment is affirmed.

ANALYSIS

Procedurally, qui tam suits allow a party to raise another party's rights where they would otherwise lack standing to sue. Thus, Mikes (P) could file suit on behalf of the

Continued on next page.

government alleging the government was being defrauded by being charged for services that were not being provided. The False Claims Act allows this procedure to encourage whistle-blowing, and the government can elect to join and prosecute the suit or allow the individual party to proceed. Either way, the whistle-blower is allowed to collect a portion of the monies recovered for the government as an incentive to report the fraud. It has been estimated that up to 10 percent of all money spent on health care annually in this country is collected on the basis of fraud. With 1.5 trillion dollars being spent on health care annually in this country, it means that $150 billion is billed and collected fraudulently by health care providers each year. The standards for violating the FCA and the Medicare statute require there be a showing that the billing itself was somehow fraudulent. No qualitative standard is applied to the delivery of the health care services themselves. The FCA is particularly useful in situations where reimbursement is requested for "ghost patients" or exams, testing, or procedures that were never performed on any patient.

Quicknotes

AMICUS BRIEF A brief submitted by a third party, not a party to the action, that contains information for the court's consideration in conformity with its position.

FALSE CLAIMS ACT Federal act imposing civil and criminal penalties against individuals who knowingly present to the government a false claim or bill or use a false record to reduce an obligation to the government.

FRAUD A false representation of facts with the intent that another will rely on the misrepresentation to his detriment.

QUI TAM An action brought before the court in which the plaintiff sues on behalf of the state as well as for himself, and which provides that part of whatever restitution garnered from penalties imposed as the result of such action will go to the plaintiff and the remainder to the state or some other institution.

United States v. Greber

Federal government (P) v. Osteopath (D)

760 F.2d 68 (3d Cir.), *cert. denied*, 474 U.S. 988 (1985).

NATURE OF CASE: Appeal of conviction for Medicare and mail fraud.

FACT SUMMARY: Greber (D), a specialist, compensated referring physicians in an amount in excess of the work performed by such physicians, with the intent to induce future referrals.

RULE OF LAW

A payment to a referring physician, if done to induce future referrals, is illegal even if the payment is compensatory.

FACTS: Greber (D) was an osteopathic physician who was board certified in cardiology. He organized a company, Cardio-Med, Inc., to provide diagnostic services. Cardio-Med billed Medicare for some such services. The Government (P) eventually charged Greber (D) with Medicare fraud in violation of 42 U.S.C. § 1395nn(b)(2)(B), as well as mail fraud. The charges stemmed from Cardio-Med's practice of paying referring physicians kickbacks from Medicare funds for the purpose of obtaining future referrals. Greber (D) contended that the payments were for work performed by the physicians and that future referrals were only one purpose of the payments. Greber (D) was convicted, and he appealed.

ISSUE: Is a payment to a referring physician done to induce future referrals illegal even if the payment is compensatory?

HOLDING AND DECISION: (Weis, J.) Yes. A payment to a referring physician done to induce future referrals is illegal even if the payment is compensatory. Section 1395nn(b)(2) provides that anyone who knowingly and willfully offers any remuneration to induce the recipient thereof to arrange for such service shall be guilty of a felony. This section clearly provides that, when Medicare is involved, no payment of any kind, either gratuitous or compensatory in nature, can be used with the intent of securing a referral. Such referral need not be the sole reason for the payment; for a violation, it need be only a factor in the payment. Here, that is how the jury was charged, so no error occurred. Affirmed.

ANALYSIS

Earlier versions of § 1395nn(b)(2) only prohibited "kickbacks." The term "kickback" is somewhat imprecise; some courts construed it to refer only to gratuitous payments. In 1982, the word "remuneration" was added, with the intent to cover compensatory payments made to secure referrals.

Quicknotes

MEDICARE FRAUD STATUTE Provides that whoever knowingly and willfully offers or pays any remuneration (including any kickback, bribe or rebate) directly or indirectly to induce such person to order any service or item shall be guilty of a felony.

United States v. Starks

Federal government (P) v. Kickback giver and recipient (D)

157 F.3d 833 (11th Cir. 1998).

NATURE OF CASE: Appeal from convictions under the antikickback provision of the Social Security Act.

FACT SUMMARY: Starks (D) and others were found guilty of giving and receiving kickbacks for patient referrals to a drug treatment program and appealed, alleging that the antikickback statute was unconstitutionally vague, and that the wrong jury instruction was given.

RULE OF LAW

A statute that proscribes conduct that is clearly prohibited or illegal may impose liability on persons engaged in such conduct for acting "willfully," or with the knowledge that such conduct is clearly unlawful, and does not pose a danger of ensnaring persons engaged in apparently innocent activity.

FACTS: Starks (D) was employed by the Florida Department of Health and Rehabilitative Services in a federally funded research project counseling pregnant women about drug abuse treatment. Siegel (D) was the president of a corporation that developed and operated treatment programs for drug addiction. Siegel (D) began giving Starks (D) $250 for each patient she referred to his program. A federal grand jury convicted Starks (D), Siegel (D), and others for conspiring against the United States (P) for offering to pay remuneration for referral of Medicare patients and for soliciting and receiving such referral payments. Starks (D) appealed, alleging that the district court committed reversible error when it refused to instruct the jury that, because of the antikickback statute's mens rea requirement, Starks (D) had to have known that the referral arrangement violated the antikickback statute in order to be convicted, and because the Social Security Act's prohibition on paid referrals, when considered together with the Act's safe harbor provision, was unconstitutionally vague.

ISSUE: May a statute that proscribes conduct that is clearly prohibited or illegal impose liability on persons engaged in such conduct for acting "willfully," or with the knowledge that such conduct is clearly unlawful, and does not pose a danger of ensnaring persons engaged in apparently innocent activity?

HOLDING AND DECISION: (Birch, J.) Yes. A statute that proscribes conduct that is clearly prohibited or illegal may impose liability on persons engaged in such conduct for acting "willfully," or with the knowledge that such conduct is clearly unlawful, and does not pose a danger of ensnaring persons engaged in apparently innocent activity. The district court did not err when it refused to give Starks's (D) requested instruction, and the antikickback statute is not unconstitutionally vague as applied to Starks (D). The antikickback statute is not a highly technical tax or financial regulation that poses a danger of ensnaring person engaged in apparently innocent conduct. The giving or taking of kickbacks for medical referrals is hardly the sort of activity a person might expect to be legal. Such kickbacks are more malum in se, rather than malum prohibitum. Thus we see no error in the district court's refusal to give any additional instruction on mens rea. The statute regulates only economic conduct, and it does not chill any constitutional rights. The knowing and willful conduct mens rea standard mitigates any otherwise inherent vagueness in the statute's provisions. Affirmed.

ANALYSIS

The court in this case explained that since this was not a First Amendment case, the claim of constitutional vagueness had to be evaluated only on an as-applied basis. Starks (D) had claimed that persons working in the medical field could not anticipate what was prohibited under the statute and what was protected under its safe harbor provision. Under the safe harbor provision, the statute's prohibition on referral payments would not apply to any amount paid by an employer to an employee for employment in the provision of covered items and services.

Quicknotes

FIRST AMENDMENT Prohibits Congress from enacting any law respecting an establishment of religion, prohibiting the free exercise of religion, abridging freedom of speech or the press, the right of peaceful assembly and the right to petition for a redress of grievances.

MALUM IN SE An act that is wrong in accordance with natural law, without respect to whether it is prohibited by statute.

MALUM PROHIBITUM An action that is not inherently wrong, but which is prohibited by law.

MENS REA Criminal intent.

SOCIAL SECURITY ACT 42 U.S.C. § 1320a-7b The antikickback statute prohibits the giving or taking of kickbacks for medical referrals.

VAGUENESS AND OVERBREADTH Characteristics of a statute that make it difficult to identify the limits of the conduct being regulated.

CHAPTER 15

Antitrust

Quick Reference Rules of Law

1. **Classic Cartels.** If doctors, in direct competition, conspire to use coercive measures to influence third-party reimbursement policies, such behavior will constitute an improper restraint of trade. (In re Michigan State Medical Society) *136*

2. **Restrictions on Advertising and Dissemination of Information.** Quick look analysis is appropriate when the great likelihood of anticompetitive effects can be easily ascertained. (California Dental Association v. Federal Trade Commission) *137*

3. **Private Accreditation and Professional Standard-Setting.** A professional organization's boycott of a class of related service providers constitutes an antitrust violation. (Wilk v. American Medical Association) *138*

4. **Provider-Controlled Networks and Health Plans.** An agreement on maximum fees for specific medical services constitutes a per se antitrust violation. (Arizona v. Maricopa County Medical Society) *139*

5. **Payors with Market Power.** A medical insurer's practice of prohibiting participating physicians from billing patients is not an antitrust violation. (Kartell v. Blue Shield of Massachusetts, Inc.) *140*

6. **Hospital Mergers.** It is a violation of Section 7 of the Clayton Act if an acquisition of a line of commerce has the effect of lessening competition and creating a monopoly. (Hospital Corporation of America) *141*

7. **Hospital Mergers.** Where the government fails to show the existence of a well-defined relevant geographic market, it cannot show that a merged entity will possess market power within that area. (Federal Trade Commission v. Tenet Health Care Corporation) *143*

8. **Hospital Mergers.** Where a healthcare corporation's acquisition of a hospital substantially lessened competition in the Northern Illinois market for acute-care inpatient services, divestiture of the entities is not warranted seven years after the merger. (In the Matter of Evanston Northwestern Healthcare Corp.) *144*

In re Michigan State Medical Society

Insurers (P) v. Medical association (D)

Fed. Trade Commn., 101 F.T.C. 191 (1983).

NATURE OF CASE: Appeal to the Federal Trade Commission from an administrative finding of restrained trade.

FACT SUMMARY: Doctors, acting through Michigan State Medical Society (D), a professional association, conspired to influence insurance reimbursement policies.

RULE OF LAW

If doctors, in direct competition, conspire to use coercive measures to influence third-party reimbursement policies, such behavior will constitute an improper restraint of trade.

FACTS: The Michigan State Medical Society (D) was composed of doctors practicing in Michigan, most in direct competition with each other. The Society (D), frustrated with reimbursement policies of Blue Cross and Blue Shield, solicited letters of withdrawal from all of its members. The letters were then used to intimidate Blue Cross and Blue Shield, which eventually backed down from its position in a dispute. An administrative law judge found the behavior of the Society (D) to be an unlawful conspiracy in restraint of trade. The Society (D) appealed to the Federal Trade Commission.

ISSUE: If doctors, in direct competition, conspire to use coercive measures such as group boycotts to influence third-party reimbursement policies, does such behavior constitute an improper restraint of trade?

HOLDING AND DECISION: (Clanton, Commr.) Yes. If doctors, in direct competition, conspire to use coercive measures to influence third-party reimbursement policies, such behavior will constitute an improper restraint of trade. A concerted refusal to deal may be characterized as an unlawful boycott where the target is a supplier of the combining parties participating in the boycott. In this case, Blue Cross and Blue Shield reimburses the doctors in the Society (D). Whether the Society (D) successfully manipulated the third-party insurers is not a relevant issue. The very fact that doctors in direct competition with each other conspired to restrain trade is sufficient to find an unlawful restraint of trade in this case.

ANALYSIS

Price fixing is generally analyzed as a per se violation. However, in this case, it is not clear that the boycott was an effort to fix prices. The Society (D) argued that its goal was to negotiate reimbursement policies, not to set the reimbursement level. While anticompetitive behavior often appears to have a price-fixing component, it is often difficult to prove the intent.

Quicknotes

SHERMAN ACT § 1 prohibits any contract, combination, or conspiracy in restraint of trade or commerce.

California Dental Association v. Federal Trade Commission

Professional organization (P) v. Federal agency (D)

526 U.S. 756 (1999).

NATURE OF CASE: Review of agency decision.

FACT SUMMARY: The Federal Trade Commission's (FTC) (D) holding that the California Dental Association's (CDA) (P) advertising restrictions violated antitrust laws was upheld on appeal.

RULE OF LAW

Quick look analysis is appropriate when the great likelihood of anticompetitive effects can be easily ascertained.

FACTS: The Federal Trade Commission's (FTC) (D) held that advertising restrictions imposed by the CDA (P) on its members violated antitrust laws. The Ninth Circuit sustained the FTC's (D) jurisdiction and concluded that an abbreviated or "quick look" rule of reason analysis was proper in this case. The CDA (P) appealed, claiming a more thorough inquiry into the consequences of the advertising restraints was warranted.

ISSUE: Is quick look analysis appropriate when the great likelihood of anticompetitive effects can be easily ascertained?

HOLDING AND DECISION: (Souter, J.) Yes. Quick look analysis is appropriate when the great likelihood of anticompetitive effects can be easily ascertained. The plausibility of competing claims about the effects of the professional advertising restrictions rules out the indulgently abbreviated review to which this matter was treated. CDA's (P) advertising restrictions could plausibly have a net procompetitive effect or possibly no effect at all on competition. The obvious anticompetitive effect that triggers abbreviated analysis has not been shown. Vacated and remanded.

CONCURRENCE AND DISSENT: (Breyer, J.) The FTC (D) has jurisdiction over this case, but I would affirm the FTC (D) just as the court of appeals did below. I hope the courts' effort to blend the procompetitive objectives of the law of antitrust with administrative necessity has not been abandoned.

ANALYSIS

On remand, the Ninth Circuit dismissed the case. That Court relied on expert testimony. The Ninth Circuit did not remand the case back to the FTC (D) for further proceedings.

Quicknotes

ANTITRUST LAW Body of federal law prohibiting business conduct that constitutes a restraint on trade.

FEDERAL TRADE COMMISSION An agency of the federal government, created in 1914, responsible for the promotion of fair competition in interstate commerce, preventing general trade restraints such as price-fixing agreements, false advertising, boycotts, illegal combinations of competitors, and other unfair methods of competition.

RULE OF REASON The standard for determining whether there has been a violation of § 1 of the Sherman Antitrust Act, requiring a determination of whether the activity unreasonably restrains competition as demonstrated by actual harm.

Wilk v. American Medical Association

Chiropractor (P) v. Professional medical organization (D)

895 F.2d 352 (7th Cir.), *cert. denied*, 498 U.S. 982 (1990).

NATURE OF CASE: Appeal of injunction against anticompetitive activities.

FACT SUMMARY: Wilk (P) contended that the American Medical Association's (AMA) (D) boycott of chiropractors constituted an antitrust violation.

RULE OF LAW

A professional organization's boycott of a class of related service providers constitutes an antitrust violation.

FACTS: From 1966 through 1980, the American Medical Association's (AMA) (D) official position was that chiropractic care was an unsound medical technique. AMA (D) rules forbade its members from dealing with chiropractors in any manner, such as in referring, lecturing, or sharing data. This policy officially ended in 1980, but the AMA (D) did not promulgate the change, and most of its members were unaware of the change. Wilk (P), a chiropractor, brought an antitrust action against the AMA (D). The district court held that § 1 of the Sherman Act had been violated and issued an injunction mandating that the AMA (D) notify its members that they were free to deal with chiropractors as they saw fit. The AMA (D) appealed.

ISSUE: Is a professional organization's boycott of a class of related service providers an antitrust violation?

HOLDING AND DECISION: (Manion, J.) Yes. A professional organization's boycott of a class of related service providers constitutes an antitrust violation. Section 1 of the Sherman Act prohibits unreasonable restraints on trade. Whether such restraint exists depends upon whether a defendant has significant market power and whether it exercised that power in an anticompetitive fashion. Here, if the AMA (D) could show that its anticompetitive acts were out of a genuine concern for patient care, a valid defense would be shown. The district court found that the AMA (D) had a powerful market share in the health industry, a point which hardly seems debatable. The court also found that the AMA's (D) acts were in fact anticompetitive, in that it interfered with consumer choice and raised chiropractors' costs of doing business, a holding supported by the record. Finally, the patient care defense was rejected by the district court, which found that the concern professed by the AMA (D) was not reasonable because it did not consider evidence of the benefits of chiropractic and because the AMA (D) had not considered a less restrictive means of ensuring quality patient care. Again, this finding was supported by the record. Affirmed.

ANALYSIS

Private credentialing organizations occupy a sort of netherworld in antitrust law. On the one hand, antitrust laws do apply to them. On the other hand, they could not function without some exclusionary ability. Consequently, courts have fashioned some defenses for them not available to a standard business. The patient care defense analyzed here is an example of this.

Quicknotes

ANTITRUST LAW Body of federal law prohibiting business conduct that constitutes a restraint on trade.

BOYCOTT A concerted effort to refrain from doing business with a particular person or entity.

FEDERAL TRADE COMMISSION An agency of the federal government, created in 1914, responsible for the promotion of fair competition in interstate commerce, preventing general trade restraints such as price-fixing agreements, false advertising, boycotts, illegal combinations of competitors and other unfair methods of competition.

SHERMAN ACT Prohibits unreasonable restraint of trade.

Arizona v. Maricopa County Medical Society

State (P) v. Nonprofit corporation (D)

457 U.S. 332 (1982).

NATURE OF CASE: Appeal from denial of summary judgment in action challenging a medical fee schedule.

FACT SUMMARY: Arizona (P) challenged the schedule of fees of two doctor groups.

RULE OF LAW

An agreement on maximum fees for specific medical services constitutes a per se antitrust violation.

FACTS: The Maricopa Foundation for Medical Care (D) was an Arizona corporation composed of doctors engaging in private practice. About 70% of Maricopa County's doctors were members. The Pima Foundation (D) was a similar corporation consisting of 400 doctors. Both organizations had adopted a schedule of fees imposing a maximum amount that member doctors could charge. This practice was challenged by Arizona (P) as price-fixing in violation of the Sherman Act. This district court, declining to apply a per se rule of illegality, denied Arizona's (P) motion for summary adjudication. The Ninth Circuit affirmed, and the Supreme Court granted review.

ISSUE: Does an agreement on maximum fees for specific medical services constitute a per se antitrust violation?

HOLDING AND DECISION: (Stevens, J.) Yes. An agreement on maximum fees for specific services constitutes a per se antitrust violation. Most actions in restraint of trade are subject to a "rule of reason" requiring extensive inquiry into their purposes and effects. However, some categories of restraint have been deemed so inherently anticompetitive that a per se rule of illegality applies. Horizonal price-fixing is one such category. Here, horizonal price-fixing is what is being affected, so the per se rule would at first glance appear applicable. However, Maricopa (D) and Pima (D) argued that an agreement to fix maximum rather than minimum prices is not anticompetitive. This is not true. Price ceilings and price floors may have different economic consequences, but price ceilings still have anticompetitive effects, as they may severely intrude upon the ability of competitors to survive in the market. Maricopa (D) and Pima (D) also argued that the health care field should not be included in the per se rule. This Court is unconvinced. The economic analysis for the medical profession is essentially the same as for business in general. For these reasons, the courts below were incorrect in failing to apply the per se rule. Reversed.

DISSENT: (Powell, J.) The term "price fixing" is not to be applied in a talismanic fashion to every agreement restricting prices. The system here appears to benefit consumers and should be analyzed under the rule of reason.

ANALYSIS

At first glance, price ceilings do not have the sinister, conspiratorial air that price floors do. However, price ceilings can have anticompetitive effects which in the long run will harm consumers. Generally speaking, restrictions on price lead to decreases in supply, which in turn lead to shortages, which certainly don't help the public.

Quicknotes

PER SE RULE Once an arrangement has been labeled a "price fixing," it is to be condemned.

Kartell v. Blue Shield of Massachusetts, Inc.

Physicians (P) v. Insurance company (D)

749 F.2d 922 (1st Cir. 1984), *cert. denied*, 471 U.S. 1029 (1985).

NATURE OF CASE: Appeal of finding of antitrust violation.

FACT SUMMARY: The practice of insurer Blue Shield of Massachusetts, Inc.'s practice (D) of prohibiting participating physicians from billing patients was challenged as an antitrust violation.

RULE OF LAW

A medical insurer's practice of prohibiting participating physicians from billing patients is not an antitrust violation.

FACTS: Blue Shield of Massachusetts, Inc. (D) provided medical insurance. It insured, either partially or fully, 56% of the Massachusetts population. Blue Shield (D) conditioned payment for services on physicians' accepting Blue Shield's (D) decision as to the appropriate fee for any specified service and not billing patients for any balance above Blue Shield's (D) payment. This rule was challenged by several physicians as an antitrust violation. The district court so held, and Blue Shield (D) appealed.

ISSUE: Is a medical insurer's practice of prohibiting participating physicians from billing patients an antitrust violation?

HOLDING AND DECISION: (Breyer, J.) No. A medical insurer's practice of prohibiting participating physicians from billing patients is not an antitrust violation. The proper analysis for such a situation is to view the insurer as a direct market participant, i.e., a buyer, and not some sort of third force intervening between buyers and sellers. The insurer purchases services for its members and, as a buyer, is perfectly free to try to strike the best deal it can. There is nothing in this that constitutes an antitrust violation. The fact that Blue Shield (D) buys not on its own behalf but for its members is of no moment; so long as such an entity is not a sham organization operating as a front for otherwise competitive entities will an antitrust issue arise. Such is not the case here. Blue Shield's (D) market power is likewise irrelevant. Market power, in itself, is not an antitrust violation. It is the agreement against competition, not present here, that constitutes an antitrust violation. Kartell (P) points to anticompetitive results of Blue Shield's (D) practices, such as discouraging start-up practices and the offering of premium services. Again, this is answered by the commonsense argument that a buyer buys what it wants, not what the seller, here, the medical community, wants it to. For these reasons, no antitrust violation exists in the practices challenged here. Reversed.

ANALYSIS

This case demonstrates that the result in an antitrust action often depends upon how the court chooses to characterize the parties. Here, the court characterized Blue Shield (D) as a simple buyer, and the court's ruling necessarily flowed from that depiction. However, Blue Shield (D) could also be likened to a distributor that sets the prices of its independent retailers. Such a characterization would raise serious antitrust implications.

Quicknotes

ANTITRUST LAW Body of federal law prohibiting business conduct that constitutes a restraint on trade.

SHERMAN ACT Prohibits unreasonable restraint of trade.

Hospital Corporation of America

Health care corporation (D) v. FTC (P)

Fed. Trade Commn., 106 F.T.C. 361 (1985).

NATURE OF CASE: Appeal of an administrative order.

FACT SUMMARY: Hospital Corporation of America (HCA) (D) appeals the decision of an Administrative Law Judge (ALJ) ordering HCA (D) to divest ownership of two unlawfully acquired hospitals.

RULE OF LAW

It is a violation of Section 7 of the Clayton Act if an acquisition of a line of commerce has the effect of lessening competition and creating a monopoly.

FACTS: Hospital Corporation of America (HCA) (D), the largest proprietary hospital chain in the United States, acquired Hospital Affiliates International (HAI) and Health Care Corporation (HCC) through stock transactions. The net effect that these acquisitions had on the geographical area of Chattanooga, Tennessee, was to give HCA (D) ownership and/or management of five of the total eleven acute care hospitals in the Chattanooga urban area (CUA) and seven of the total fourteen acute care hospitals in the six-county region known as the Chattanooga Metropolitan Statistical Area (CMSA). The Federal Trade Commission (FTC) (P) brought a complaint against HCA (D), alleging violation of the Clayton Act. The ALJ ordered HCA (D) to divest itself of ownership of two hospitals and provide notification to the FTC (P) prior to making further acquisitions. HCA (D) appeals the ALJ's (P) ruling.

ISSUE: Is it a violation of Section 7 of the Clayton Act if an acquisition of a line of commerce has the effect of lessening competition and creating a monopoly?

HOLDING AND DECISION: (Calvani, Commr.) Yes. It is a violation of Section 7 of the Clayton Act if an acquisition of a line of commerce has the effect of lessening competition and creating a monopoly. To analyze an alleged violation of the act, the commission must identify and examine the product market, the geographical area in which competition could be harmed and the effect the acquisitions have on that line of commerce in that geographical area. The relevant product market, or line of commerce, is the provision of acute inpatient hospital services and emergency services provided to the critically ill. The FTC (P) only examines the geographic market in relation to the area where competition could be harmed and, in this instance, the relevant market is that of the CUA, not the CMSA. There is no distinction between the hospitals owned by HCA (D) and those managed by HCA (D) because all of these hospitals have effectively been taken out of the independent marketplace.

There is no question that HCA's (D) acquisition subjects the market to collusive forces and is likely to harm competition in the relevant geographical area. However, the court must also evaluate mitigating market factors, because absent any barriers to entry, new firms could enter the market and balance the collusive forces of HCA (D). The protracted and expensive process of obtaining a Certificate of Need (CON), and the ability of existing hospitals to forestall an increase in the number of hospitals in the geographical area, serves as a significant barrier to increase competition in the area. Additionally, with the elasticity of demand being low for hospital services, the potential for price manipulation is high. Discrimination against different insurance groups, and thus different consumer groups, is also highly possible. Whether hospitals are for-profit or not-for-profit entities makes absolutely no difference in terms of market collusion given the fact that area hospitals have historically coordinated their services.

It must be remembered that a violation of Section 7 of the Clayton Act need only be "incipient" or reasonably probable and actual anti-competitive effects need not be demonstrated. The decision of the ALJ is affirmed.

ANALYSIS

The number of hospitals in any given geographical area is not solely determinate to the issue of competition. Looking at the total number of hospital beds, the services provided and the relative size of the health care corporations are also significant factors as they reflect any corporation's ability to control pricing per unit of service provided. The strategy to avoid sanctions by the FTC (P) for corporations like HCA (D) is to attempt to dilute either the market product classification by factoring in outpatient services and alternative sources of health care, or by expanding the relevant geographical area to shrink the appearance of their actual market control. HCA (D) attempted both of these tactics in this case by arguing the need to include outpatient services and utilize the CMSA geographical area. Both of these attempts failed.

Quicknotes

CLAYTON ACT, § 7 Prohibits the acquirement of stock or assets if the effect of such acquisition is to substantially lessen competition or create a monopoly.

Continued on next page.

MONOPOLY A privilege or right conferred upon an individual or entity granting it the exclusive power to manufacture, sell and distribute a particular service or commodity; a market condition in which one or a few companies control the sale of a product or service thereby restraining competition in respect to that article or service.

Federal Trade Commission v. Tenet Health Care Corporation

Federal agency (P) v. Health care corporation (D)

186 F.3d 1045 (8th Cir. 1999).

NATURE OF CASE: Appeal from an order enjoining the merger of two hospitals.

FACT SUMMARY: The district court found a substantial likelihood that the merger of a Tenet (D) hospital with another hospital would substantially lessen competition between acute-care hospitals in Poplar Bluff, Missouri.

RULE OF LAW

Where the government fails to show the existence of a well-defined relevant geographic market, it cannot show that a merged entity will possess market power within that area.

FACTS: Lucy Lee Hospital and Doctors' Regional Medical Center are the only two hospitals in Poplar Bluff, aside from a veterans' hospital. Tenet Healthcare Corporation (Tenet) (D) owns Lucy Lee Hospital (Lucy Lee), a general acute care hospital that provides primary and secondary care services in Poplar Bluff. Lucy Lee has 201 licensed beds and operates ten outpatient clinics in the surrounding counties. Doctors' Regional Medical Center in Poplar Bluff is also a general acute care hospital providing primary and secondary services. Doctors' Regional has 230 beds and also operates several rural health clinics in the area. Tenet (D) entered into an agreement to purchase Doctors' Regional for over forty million dollars, to operate it as a long-term care facility and to consolidate inpatient services at Lucy Lee. The hospitals filed a premerger certification with the Federal Trade Commission (FTC) (P). Shortly thereafter, the FTC (P) filed a complaint alleging that the hospitals' merger would lessen competition for primary and secondary inpatient hospitalization services in the area.

ISSUE: Where the government fails to show the existence of a well-defined relevant geographic market, can it show that a merged entity will possess market power within that area?

DECISION AND HOLDING: (Beam, J.) No. Where the government fails to show the existence of a well-defined relevant geographic market, it cannot show that a merged entity will possess market power within that area. A relevant market, consisting of a product market and a geographic market, must be defined before a court finds an antitrust violation. The FTC (P) in this case proposes a relevant geographic market that matches its service area. A service area and a merging firm's geographic market are not necessarily the same, however. Because the FTC (P) failed to demonstrate a well-defined relevant market, it failed to show that the merged entity would possess market power. Patients may use hospitals outside the service area that may be closer to such residents or provide higher quality services in the patients' minds. Also, the potential efficiencies gained by the merger in this case should have been examined by the lower court to determine if this might have enhanced competition in the greater Southesat Missouri area.

ANALYSIS

The FTC (P) has played a major role in subjecting the health care industry to antitrust scrutiny.

Quicknotes

ANTITRUST Body of federal law prohibiting business conduct that constitutes a restraint on trade.

ENJOIN The ordering of a party to cease the conduct of a specific activity.

In the Matter of Evanston Northwestern Healthcare Corp.

Health care corporation (D) v. FTC (P)

Fed. Trade Commn., August 6, 2007.

NATURE OF CASE: Appeal of administrative law judge's order to divest merger.

FACT SUMMARY: An administrative law judge found that Evanston Northwestern Healthcare Corp. (ENH) (D) violated federal antitrust law when it acquired Highland Park Hospital, because the transaction substantially lessened competition in the Northern Illinois market for acute-care inpatient services. The ALJ ordered ENH (D) to divest itself of Highland Park Hospital. ENH (D) appealed.

RULE OF LAW

Where a healthcare corporation's acquisition of a hospital substantially lessened competition in the Northern Illinois market for acute-care inpatient services, divestiture of the entities is not warranted seven years after the merger.

FACTS: Prior to the merger, Evanston Northwestern Healthcare Corp. (ENH) (D) owned Evanston Hospital and Glenbrook Hospital, both in Cook County, Ill. In January 2000, ENH (D) acquired Highland Park, the nearest hospital to the north. There are other hospitals in the area, including nine facilities that are closer to Evanston, Glenbrook, or Highland Park than they are to each other, but no other hospital exists within the triangle formed by the three ENH (D) hospitals. The Federal Trade Commission (FTC) (P) filed a complaint in February 2004, arguing that ENH's (D) merger with Highland Park resulted in less competition and higher prices for insurers and health care consumers for general acute-care inpatient services sold to managed care organizations in the relevant geographic market. In October 2005, an administrative law judge found that ENH (D) exercised its enhanced power to obtain price increases significantly above its premerger prices and substantially larger than price increases obtained by other comparison hospitals. ENH (D) was ordered to divest of Highland Park.

ISSUE: Where a healthcare corporation's acquisition of a hospital substantially lessened competition in the Northern Illinois market for acute-care inpatient services, is divestiture of the entities warranted seven years after the merger?

HOLDING AND DECISION: [Commissioner not stated in casebook excerpt.] No. Where a health care corporation's acquisition of a hospital substantially lessened competition in the Northern Illinois market for acute-care inpatient services, divestiture of the entities is not warranted seven years after the merger. The evidence shows that the transaction enabled the merged firm to exercise market power that was not offset by merger-specific efficiencies, that senior officials at Evanston and Highland Park anticipated that the merger would give them greater leverage to raise prices, that the merged firm did raise its prices immediately and substantially after completion of the transaction, and that the same senior officials attributed the price increases in part to increased bargaining leverage produced by the merger. It is clear that ENH (D) violated Section 7 of the Clayton Act, and an administrative law judge reasonably ordered that divestiture of Highland Park from ENH (D), because divestiture is the preferred remedy for challenges to unlawful mergers. But it is impractical seven years after the merger, because substantial costs would be incurred to effect divestiture, and it would upset the efficiencies now in place in the combined facility. A better, if inferior, remedy at this point is to require ENH (D) to establish independent negotiating teams—one for ENH's (D) Evanston and Glenbrook hospitals, and another for Highland Park—to allow managed care organizations to negotiate separate contracts for the hospitals. The injunction remedy is not ideal, but it will allow managed care organizations to negotiate separately again for these competing hospitals, thus re-injecting competition between them for the business of managed care organizations.

ANALYSIS

The traditional remedy in a merger case is divestiture, and the proposed remedy—independent contract negotiating teams—could be impractical, because of difficulties associated with to protecting against sharing of information, inadvertent or not, about the separate managed care contracting efforts. Nevertheless, the FTC (P) arguably had no choice but to reject divestiture. It would have been a real challenge to unwind the merger after seven years.

Quicknotes

DIVESTITURE The divestment of an interest in a corporation pursuant to court order.

INJUNCTION A court order requiring a person to do, or prohibiting that person from doing, a specific act.

CHAPTER 16

Reproduction and Birth

Quick Reference Rules of Law

Roe v. Wade

Woman seeking abortion (P) v. Texas attorney general (D)

410 U.S. 113 (1973).

NATURE OF CASE: Review of challenge to state abortion law.

FACT SUMMARY: A state law absolutely prohibiting elective abortions was challenged as unconstitutional.

RULE OF LAW

A state may not, consistent with the Constitution, absolutely prohibit elective abortions.

FACTS: Roe (P) was threatened with prosecution under a Texas law which prohibited all abortions other than those necessary to save a mother's life. Roe (P) later challenged the law as unconstitutional. The district and appellate courts held the law constitutional, and the Supreme Court granted review.

ISSUE: May a state constitutionally prohibit all elective abortions?

HOLDING AND DECISION: (Blackmun, J.) No. A state may not, consistent with the Constitution, absolutely prohibit elective abortions. State abortion laws do not enjoy the historical pedigree some believe. For the most part, they were passed in the second half of the nineteenth century, as a response to the high mortality rate of abortions in those days, a concern that is no longer relevant today. The Constitution gives no express right of privacy, but that right has been recognized since perhaps 1891. This right exists as a corollary to provisions of the First, Ninth, and Fourteenth Amendments. This Court believes that this right encompasses that of a woman to elect to terminate a pregnancy. Until such time as a fetus is viable, the state has no interest in the potential life the woman is carrying and cannot prohibit elective abortions. After viability, a state may take steps to protect the fetus, up to and including proscriptions of abortions. Reversed.

ANALYSIS

The instant case represents probably the most controversial Supreme Court decision since the *Dred Scott* decision of the 1850s. It was hailed as a landmark for women's rights by some. It has been attacked from some quarters both for its result and for its reasoning, which pushed the edge of judicial activism. Despite the furor, the opinion has survived numerous legislative and political attacks.

Quicknotes

FIRST AMENDMENT Prohibits Congress from enacting any law respecting an establishment of religion, prohibiting the free exercise of religion, abridging freedom of speech or the press, the right of peaceful assembly and the right to petition for a redress of grievances.

FOURTEENTH AMENDMENT Declares that no state shall make or enforce any law that shall abridge the privileges and immunities of citizens of the United States. No state shall deny to any person within its jurisdiction the equal protection of the laws.

NINTH AMENDMENT The Ninth Amendment to the United States Constitution provides that the enumeration of any rights contained therein is not to be construed as denying or disparaging other rights retained by the people.

VIABILITY The point at which a newborn child is capable of existing outside the womb.

Planned Parenthood of Southeastern Pennsylvania v. Casey

Abortion provider (P) v. State (D)

505 U.S. 833 (1992).

NATURE OF CASE: Appeal from the judgment upholding a state law regulating abortion in an action challenging the constitutionality of the law.

FACT SUMMARY: Responding to Pennsylvania's (D) enactment of its Abortion Control Act, Planned Parenthood of Southeastern Pennsylvania (P), among others, challenged the constitutionality of five provisions of the Act.

RULE OF LAW

A state may regulate abortion only when such regulation does not place an undue burden on a woman's ability to make a decision to terminate her pregnancy before viability.

FACTS: A number of cases challenging the constitutionality of five provisions of the Pennsylvania Abortion Control Act of 1982 were consolidated on appeal. The Act required that a woman seeking an abortion give an informed consent to the procedure and specified that she be provided with certain information at least 24 hours before the procedure was performed. A minor had to have the informed consent of one of her parents, although a judicial bypass option was provided. A married woman seeking an abortion had to notify her husband of the intended abortion. Compliance with the three previous requirements would be exempted in the event of a medical emergency as defined by the statute. Finally, the Act imposed certain reporting requirements on facilities that provided abortion services.

ISSUE: May a state regulate abortion only when such regulation does not place an undue burden on a woman's ability to make a decision to terminate her pregnancy before viability?

HOLDING AND DECISION: (O'Connor, J.) Yes. A state may regulate abortion only when such regulation does not place an undue burden on a woman's ability to make a decision to terminate her pregnancy before viability. An undue burden exists if a statute's purpose or effect is to place a substantial obstacle in the path of a woman seeking an abortion. If the information required to be made available to the woman is truthful and not misleading, it is not a substantial obstacle to obtaining an abortion, even where it expresses the state's preference for childbirth. Further, requiring a doctor to provide the information is not an undue burden. While the 24-hour waiting period is troubling in some respects, it has not been demonstrated that the waiting period constitutes an undue burden. Nor does the statute's definition of a medical emergency impose an undue burden on a woman's right to an abortion. However, because the spousal notification requirement is likely to prevent a significant number of women who are victims of regular physical and psychological abuse at the hands of their husbands from obtaining an abortion, it is an undue burden and therefore invalid. A state may require a minor seeking an abortion to obtain the consent of a parent or guardian so long as there is an adequate judicial bypass procedure. Finally, the statute's record-keeping and reporting requirements are valid except for the provision requiring the reporting of a married woman's failure to give her husband notice.

CONCURRENCE AND DISSENT: (Rehnquist, J.) Because *Roe v. Wade*, 410 U.S. 113 (1973), was wrongly decided, it can and should be overruled, consistent with this Court's traditional approach to stare decisis in constitutional cases. The challenged provisions of the statute should be upheld in their entirety.

CONCURRENCE AND DISSENT: (Scalia, J.) States may, if they wish, permit abortion-on-demand, but the Constitution does not require them to do so. By continuing the imposition of a rigid national rule instead of allowing for regional differences, the Court merely prolongs and intensifies the anguish surrounding an issue which arouses deep passions.

ANALYSIS

This opinion represents an unusual approach by the Court, in that the majority opinion was authored by three of the Justices, O'Connor, Kennedy, and Souter, with the other Justices joining in or dissenting from various parts of the opinion. The Court announced it was retaining the essential holding of *Roe v. Wade*. However, the opinion rejected *Roe*'s trimester framework in favor of the "undue burden" standard. While it is the constitutional right of a woman to choose to terminate her pregnancy, the line is drawn at viability, the time at which there is a realistic possibility of maintaining and nourishing life outside the womb.

Quicknotes

STARE DECISIS Doctrine whereby courts follow legal precedent unless there is good cause for departure.

UNDUE BURDEN Unlawfully oppressive or troublesome.

Gonzales v. Carhart

Parties not identified.

127 S. Ct. 1610 (2007).

NATURE OF CASE: Supreme Court review of federal statute banning partial-birth abortions.

FACT SUMMARY: A federal statute was passed that bans so-called partial-birth abortions. Its constitutionality under the Fourteenth Amendment was challenged.

RULE OF LAW
The federal nationwide ban on so-called "partial-birth abortions" is constitutional.

FACTS: After the Supreme Court's ruling in *Stenberg v. Carhart*, 530 U.S. 914 (2000), which struck down the Nebraska law that barred abortions in which the physician delivers a "substantial portion" of the fetus into the woman's vagina for the purpose of performing a procedure that kills the "unborn child" and that lacked a health exception, Congress passed a federal statute, 18 U.S.C. § 1531, that essentially bans partial-birth abortions and addresses the constitutionally offensive portions of the Nebraska statute. Unlike the Nebraska statute, the federal statute defined the prohibited procedure as a deliberate delivery of a "living fetus" to the point that either the entire head (in a head-first presentation) or any part of the fetal trunk past the navel (in a breech presentation) is "outside the body of the mother," followed by an "overt act, other than completion of delivery, that kills the partially delivered living fetus." In addition, the "overt act" requirement distinguishes the intact D&E from the standard D&E because the death-inducing act, such as puncturing the skull with scissors and then vacuuming out the brain, must be separate from the delivery and occur after the delivery to an anatomical landmark. In contrast, in a standard D&E, death occurs in the womb via dismemberment by traction when pieces of the fetus are pulled through the cervix; that is not an overt act or a "delivery" covered by the statute. A third difference between the federal statute and the Nebraska statute is that the federal statute only applies when the physician intends from the outset to employ the prohibited procedure. It would not apply to an "accidental intact D&E" that may occur if the fetus unintentionally slips past one of the anatomical landmarks.

ISSUE: Is the federal nationwide ban on so-called "partial-birth abortions" constitutional?

HOLDING AND DECISION: (Kennedy, J.) Yes. The federal nationwide ban on so-called "partial-birth abortions" is constitutional. The 2003 Partial-Birth Abortion Ban Act avoids vagueness problems by spelling out "anatomical landmarks" on the fetal body and setting physician intent requirements that provide reasonable notice of the particular abortion procedures prohibited. The plaintiffs failed to show "that requiring doctors to intend dismemberment before delivery to an anatomical landmark will prohibit the vast majority of D&E abortions." The statute does apply both previability and postviability because, by common understanding and scientific terminology, a fetus is a living organism while within the womb, whether or not it is viable outside the womb. But, under *Planned Parenthood of Southeastern Pa. v. Casey*, 506 U.S. 833 (1992), which reaffirmed a woman's right to choose a previability abortion, the issue in this facial challenge was whether the statute imposed a substantial obstacle to late-term, but previability abortions. *Casey* recognized the state's regulatory interest "in protecting the life of the fetus that may become a child." That interest allows the state, "in order to promote respect for life," to restrict abortion methods that physicians might otherwise choose. The health exception recognized in *Casey* and *Stenberg* cannot be interpreted in a way to "set at naught" the government's interest in fetal life. Here, there is "documented disagreement whether the Act's prohibition would ever impose significant health risks on women." When medical uncertainty exists, the court defers to legislative choice. In addition, the mother's health exception requirement cannot be interpreted to preclude regulation of abortion methods that further the government's interest in protecting and respecting fetal life when there is only uncertainty in the medical community about whether a particular abortion method is ever medically necessary. Here, Congress sought to promote respect for life by drawing a bright line between abortion and infanticide. The statute also recognizes "the bond of love the mother has for her child" by saving her from the sorrow of undergoing what she may not be told until later is a gruesome procedure.

CONCURRENCE: (Thomas, J.) The opinion "accurately applies" *Casey* and *Roe v. Wade*, 410 U.S. 113 (1973), but those decisions, while "current jurisprudence," have "no basis in the Constitution."

DISSENT: (Ginsburg, J.) The reconstituted court's "alarming" decision disrespected precedent, gutted the long-standing health exception requirement, and showed an unconcealed "hostility" to abortion rights. The ruling "refuses to take *Casey* and *Stenberg* seriously." It ignores district court findings that intact D&E is safer for women with certain conditions and generally offers safety advantages over standard D&E, siding instead with a statute that even the majority recognized contains factual errors. The

Continued on next page.

court deprives women of the right to make an autonomous choice, even at the expense of their safety.

ANALYSIS

Remember that this decision answered a facial attack on the statute, leaving open the possibility that the statute, as applied, may not survive constitutional scrutiny. Medical uncertainty may reverse the direction of this case; if, for example, a partial-birth abortion became medically necessary to save a woman's life, the statute may not withstand constitutional scrutiny.

Quicknotes

FOURTEENTH AMENDMENT Declares that no state shall make or enforce any law that shall abridge the privileges and immunities of citizens of the United States. No state shall deny to any person within its jurisdiction the equal protection of the laws.

Smith v. Cote

Mother (P) v. Physicians (D)

N.H. Sup. Ct., 128 N.H. 231, 513 A.2d 341 (1986).

NATURE OF CASE: Certified legal question in malpractice actions for damages for "wrongful birth" and "wrongful life," respectively.

FACT SUMMARY: Linda Smith (P), claiming that doctors failed to diagnose her condition that led to congenital defects in her daughter (P), brought a "wrongful birth" action, and the daughter (P) brought a "wrongful life" action.

RULE OF LAW

A "wrongful birth" cause of action exists, but a "wrongful life" cause of action does not.

FACTS: Linda Smith (P) became pregnant. In April 1979, she visited her doctors complaining of various symptoms. In August, tests indicated that Linda (P) had been exposed to rubella. In January 1980, she gave birth to Heather (P), who suffered numerous congenital defects due to the rubella exposure. Linda (P) brought a "wrongful birth" action, contending that had she known of the rubella and its potential effects in April, she would have terminated the pregnancy. She requested reimbursement of costs associated with Heather (P). Heather's (P) action was for "wrongful life," which sought damages for the misery she would have to endure as a result of her own existence. The trial court certified to the New Hampshire Supreme Court the issue of whether these causes of action could be maintained.

ISSUE:

(1) Does a "wrongful birth" cause of action exist?
(2) Does a "wrongful life" cause of action exist?

HOLDING AND DECISION: (Batchelder, J.)

(1) Yes. A "wrongful birth" cause of action exists. A wrongful birth action can be devised through recourse to traditional tort principles. Duty and breach thereof present no analytical problem. Medical personnel have a duty to provide accurate diagnoses and treatment. If they fail to do so in a negligent manner, this duty has been breached. Causation is somewhat more difficult, as it requires proof that the mother would have terminated the pregnancy but for the physician's negligence. This is a matter for the jury to decide, and no reason for a per se rule against its presentation exists. As to damages, those extraordinary costs associated with the handicaps (as opposed to those intrinsic to the raising of any child) may be recovered.
(2) No. A "wrongful life" cause of action does not. Regarding "wrongful life," the situation is different. To hold that such an action exists requires a judicial determination that no life is better than impaired life. This is a realm better left to philosophers and theologians than courts. Further, it is contrary to the modern trend of viewing handicapped people as potentially valuable members of society rather than burdens. For these reasons, a wrongful life cause of action will not be recognized.

ANALYSIS

Courts have found the wrongful life cause of action quite problematical. Deciding whether such an action exists requires some fairly heavy inquiry into matters of philosophy and religion that courts are not particularly well qualified to answer. Some states, such as California, have answered the issue legislatively. In states where this has occurred, some have allowed special damages to be recovered. So far, courts seem loath to allow general damages for wrongful life.

Quicknotes

WRONGFUL BIRTH A cause of action brought by the parents of a child born with severe birth defects against a doctor for negligent treatment or advice.

WRONGFUL LIFE A medical malpractice action brought by the parents of a child born with severe birth defects against a doctor, claiming that but for the doctor's negligent treatment or advice they would not have given birth to the child.

In the Interest of K.M.H.

Sperm donor (P) v. Recipient (D)

Kan. Sup. Ct., 285 Kan. 53, 169 P.3d 1025 (2007).

NATURE OF CASE: Appeal from judgment denying paternity rights.

FACT SUMMARY: A woman gave birth to twins conceived through artificial insemination. The sperm donor sought recognition of parental rights, alleging he had an oral agreement with the twins' mother to act as their father. The court upheld the constitutionality of the Kansas Artificial Insemination (AI), which denies paternity rights in such cases unless the parties agree in writing that paternity rights exist. Because there was no written contract, the court held, paternity rights did not exist.

RULE OF LAW

The Kansas AI statute is constitutional under the Equal Protection and Due Process Clauses of the Kansas and federal constitutions.

FACTS: A woman, S.H. (D), gave birth to twins conceived through artificial insemination. The sperm donor, D.H. (P), sought recognition of parental rights, alleging he had an oral agreement with the twins' mother to act as their father. S.H. (D) filed a "child in need of care" petition to establish that the donor had no parental rights under Kansas law. The two are not married. The court upheld the constitutionality of the Kansas AI statute, which denies paternity rights in such cases unless the parties agree in writing that paternity rights exist. Because there was no written contract, the court held, paternity rights did not exist.

ISSUE: Is the Kansas AI statute constitutional under the Equal Protection and Due Process Clauses of the Kansas and federal constitutions?

HOLDING AND DECISION: (Beier, J.) Yes. The Kansas AI statute is constitutional under the Equal Protection and Due Process Clauses of the Kansas and federal constitutions. Kansas' AI statute is based in part on the 1973 Uniform Parentage Act, which did not address the determination of a sperm donor's paternity when an unmarried woman conceives a child through artificial insemination. [Section 5 of the Act states in part that "[t]he donor of semen provided to a licensed physician for use in artificial insemination of a married woman other than the donor's wife is treated in law as if he were not the natural father of a child thereby conceived."] Kansas removed the word "married" from the 1973 Act, so that its statute contained a complete bar to paternity for any sperm donor not married to the recipient, regardless of whether the donor was known or anonymous. But the Kansas legislature also modified the UPA language to provide that a sperm donor and recipient could choose to opt out of the donor paternity bar by written agreement. The Kansas AI statute's allowance for a written agreement to grant a sperm donor parental rights and responsibilities provides an escape clause that in turn provides support for finding the statute constitutional, where an absolute bar to rights might have been unconstitutional. The statute's requirement that any opt-out agreement between an unmarried mother and a known sperm donor be "in writing" does not result in an equal protection or due process violation, either. As to the equal protection claim, even assuming that S.H. (D) and D.H. (P) are truly similarly situations, the statute's gender categorization serves legitimate state interests. It protects men who donate sperm and want to be involved in the lives of the children who are born, and those who do not. It also protects women recipients as well, preventing potential claims of donors to parental rights and responsibilities in the absence of an agreement. As to the due process claim, the requirement of a writing does not transform what is an otherwise constitutional statute into one that violates D.H.'s (P) substantive due process rights. The statute does not cut off rights that already exist, but ensures no attachment of rights. While the law may not be wise, it is constitutional.

DISSENT: (Caplinger, J.) The statute is unconstitutional as applied to D.H. (P) because it violates his fundamental right to parent his children without due process of law. Fundamental rights must be waived, not passively lost because of failure to execute a contract asserting them. D.H. (P) may also have been unaware of his responsibilities under the statute. So here is a case of a putative father who wants to participate in the rearing of his children, and instead of being given protection under the Due Process Clause, he has been subjected to the application of a statute of which he was unaware, which required him to opt in to fatherhood before he even donated his sperm. The case should be remanded to consider all evidence relevant to the existence of an agreement between the parties.

DISSENT: (Hill, J.) Someone needs to speak for the children in these proceedings. The application of this statute is not in their best interests.

ANALYSIS

The court actually considered six issues: (1) whether the district judge erred in ruling that Kansas law would govern, since two inseminations took place in Missouri; (2) whether

Continued on next page.

the district judge erred in finding the Kansas AI statute constitutional; (3) whether the district judge erred in interpreting an applying the "provided to a licensed physician" language of the Kansas AI statute; (4) whether the district judge erred in determining that S.H.'s (D) petition did not satisfy the requirements of a writing in the Kansas AI statute; (5) whether the Kansas AI statute granted D.H. (P) parental rights; and (6) whether equity demanded reversal of the district court. The most important—and most interesting—is the constitutional law question and its interplay with the Statute of Frauds, and your mastery of those issues are necessary.

Quicknotes

ARTIFICIAL INSEMINATION The impregnation of a woman by the injection of semen into the uterus.

DUE PROCESS CLAUSE Clauses found in the Fifth and Fourteenth Amendments to the United States Constitution providing that no person shall be deprived of "life, liberty, or property, without due process of law."

DUE PROCESS RIGHTS The constitutional mandate requiring the courts to protect and enforce individuals' rights and liberties consistent with prevailing principles of fairness and justice, and prohibiting the federal and state governments from such activities that deprive its citizens of a life, liberty or property interest.

EQUAL PROTECTION CLAUSE A constitutional provision that each person be guaranteed the same protection of the laws enjoyed by other persons in like circumstances.

PUTATIVE FATHER The supposed father of an illegitimate child.

Davis v. Davis

Husband (P) v. Wife (D)

Tenn. Sup. Ct., 842 S.W.2d 588 (1992).

NATURE OF CASE: Appeal from reversal of a judgment awarding custody of frozen embryos to defendant.

FACT SUMMARY: When Junior Davis (P) filed for divorce, Mary Sue Davis (D) sought control of the seven frozen embryos stored in a fertility clinic.

RULE OF LAW

When the party seeking control of preembryos intends merely to donate them to another couple, the objecting party has the greater interest and should prevail.

FACTS: In attempting a much-wanted pregnancy, Mary Sue (D) and Junior (P) Davis, through in vitro fertilization (IVF), produced a number of preembryos, seven of which had been cryogenically frozen for later transfer to Mary Sue's (D) uterus. When Junior (P) began a divorce action, Mary Sue (D) asked for control of the "frozen embryos" to attempt a postdivorce pregnancy. Junior (P) objected. They agreed upon all terms of dissolution except for disposition of the embryos. After both parties later remarried, Mary Sue (D) wanted to donate the embryos to a childless couple. Junior (P) adamantly objected. The trial court, determining that the embryos were "human beings" from the moment of fertilization, awarded "custody" to Mary Sue (D). The court of appeals reversed, giving the parties joint control and equal voice over the disposition of the embryos. Mary Sue (D) appealed.

ISSUE: When the party seeking control of preembryos intends merely to donate them to another couple, does the objecting party have the greater interest and should that party prevail?

HOLDING AND DECISION: (Daughtrey, J.) Yes. When the party seeking control of preembryos intends merely to donate them to another couple, the objecting party has the greater interest and should prevail. The constitutional right to individual privacy encompasses the right of procreational autonomy, including the right to procreate and the right to avoid procreation. Preembryos are neither persons nor property but occupy an interim category, entitling them to special respect because of their potential for human life. Furthermore, the state's interest in potential human life is insufficient to justify an infringement on the procreational autonomy of the individuals providing the gametes. Mary Sue's (D) interest in donation is not as significant as Junior's (P) interest in avoiding parenthood. The case would be closer if Mary Sue (D) were seeking to use the preembryos herself. Affirmed in Junior's (P) favor.

ANALYSIS

The court noted that its rule did not create an automatic veto. To resolve disputes involving the disposition of preembryos, courts should first look to the preferences of the progenitors. Where there is a dispute, any prior agreement concerning disposition should be enforced, but where no agreement exists, the interests of the parties must be weighed. Ordinarily, the party wishing to avoid procreation should prevail.

Quicknotes

LIBERTY INTEREST A right conferred by the Due Process Clauses of the state and federal constitutions.

ZYGOTE Union of two gametes forming a cell, especially a fertilized ovum before cleavage.

In the Matter of Baby M

Natural father (P) v. Surrogate mother (D)

N.J. Sup. Ct., 109 N.J. 396, 537 A.2d 1227 (1988).

NATURE OF CASE: Appeal of child custody determination.

FACT SUMMARY: Surrogate mother Whitehead (D) declined to turn her baby over to the Sterns, despite having contracted to do so.

RULE OF LAW
A surrogate mother contract is unenforceable.

FACTS: The Sterns were an infertile couple, Mrs. Stern being incapable of bearing children. They contracted with Whitehead (D) for the latter to be inseminated with sperm from Mr. Stern (P), carry the baby to term, and then surrender the baby upon birth. This was done for monetary consideration. After the baby was born, Whitehead (D) refused to hand it over. A custody hearing was held. The trial court enforced the surrogacy contract and ordered Whitehead (D) to surrender the baby, which she refused to do. An appeal of the custody order was taken.

ISSUE: Is a surrogate mother contract enforceable?

HOLDING AND DECISION: (Wilentz, C.J.) No. A surrogate mother contract is unenforceable. Private placement of children, though not illegal, is highly disfavored as a matter of public policy. Beyond that, a surrogacy contract runs afoul of state laws prohibiting the use of money in connection with adoptions, laws requiring proof of parental unfitness prior to termination of parental rights, and laws making surrender of custody and consent to adoptions revocable in private placement adoptions. In a surrogacy contract, money is the sine qua non of the contract, and this clearly violates legislatively expressed policy. Further, a surrogacy contract allows the termination of parental rights without a finding of lack of fitness, which is precisely what happened to Whitehead (D) here. Finally, the surrogacy contract removes the legislatively mandated revocability requirement, which Whitehead (D) certainly would have exercised here. Beyond the statutory issues, the constitutional right to procreate is not involved, as this consists merely of bringing a child into existence. After birth, other state-interest issues may intrude into the analysis, as they have done here. For these reasons, surrogacy contracts are invalid, as is the one at issue here. [The court, employing a best interests of the child test, awarded Mr. Stern (P) custody but reinstated Whitehead's (D) parental rights, and remanded for a visitation decree.]

ANALYSIS

Surrogacy contracts have met for the most part with disfavor. The main reason is that it is perceived to degrade women, making them into incubators. Surrogacy agreements have also been criticized as baby selling. Finally, some have even said that the contract is not unlike an indentured servitude agreement that would be illegal under the Thirteenth Amendment.

Quicknotes

SINE QUA NON Without which not; a necessary element or requirement.

SURROGACY CONTRACT An agreement between parties that sets forth the parental rights and responsibilities of each party according to the role it has played in the life of the child.

THIRTEENTH AMENDMENT The constitutional provision which abolished slavery in the United States.

Johnson v. Calvert

Surrogate mother (D) v. Contracting parents (P)

Cal. Sup. Ct., 5 Cal. 4th 84, 851 P.2d 776 (1993).

NATURE OF CASE: Appeal from judgment terminating the visitation rights of a surrogate mother.

FACT SUMMARY: After Johnson (D) served as a surrogate mother for the Calverts (P), she refused to give up the child, who was not genetically related to her since the child was developed from gametes donated by both of the Calverts (P).

RULE OF LAW
When a zygote formed from the gametes of a husband and wife is implanted in the uterus of another woman, resulting in a child genetically unrelated to her, the husband and wife are the child's natural parents.

FACTS: Because the Calverts (P) could not have children after Crispina's (P) uterus was removed, they turned to surrogacy. Since Crispina's (P) ovaries could still produce eggs, the Calverts (P) signed a contract with Johnson (D), providing that an embryo created by Mark's (P) sperm and Crispina's (P) egg would be implanted in Johnson (D). Johnson (D) relinquished all parental rights to the child, agreeing to accept payment for her services in a series of installments. Johnson (D) later demanded the balance of the payments due, refusing to give up the child otherwise. The Calverts (P) filed suit, seeking a declaration that they were the legal parents of the unborn child. After the child's birth, although blood test results excluded Johnson (D) as the genetic mother, she was granted temporary visitation rights. The trial court ruled that the Calverts (P) were the child's genetic, biological, and natural father and mother and terminated Johnson's (D) visitation rights. The court of appeal affirmed, and Johnson (D) appealed.

ISSUE: When a zygote formed of the gametes of a husband and wife is implanted in the uterus of another woman, resulting in a child genetically unrelated to her, are the husband and wife the child's natural parents?

HOLDING AND DECISION: (Panelli, J.) Yes. When a zygote formed of the gametes of a husband and wife is implanted in the uterus of another woman, resulting in a child genetically unrelated to her, the husband and wife are the child's natural parents. Presentation of blood-test evidence and proof of having given birth are both means of establishing maternity. However, when the two means do not coincide in one woman, the one who intended to bring about the birth of a child whom she intended to raise as her own is the natural mother under state law. From the outset, Crispina (P) intended to be the child's mother. It is safe to say that Johnson (D) would not have been given the opportunity to gestate or deliver the child had she, prior to implantation of the zygote, manifested her own intent to be the child's mother. Affirmed.

DISSENT: (Kennard, J.) The majority's resort to "intent" to break the "tie" between the genetic and gestational mothers is unsupported by statute and is ill-advised. The standard that should be applied, and which is most protective of child welfare, is the best interests of the child. Application of the majority's rule of intent will not serve the child's best interests in every case. The judgment of the court of appeal should be reversed.

ANALYSIS

In its discussion, the majority applied, through analogy, certain portions of the Uniform Parentage Act and the Evidence Code to make its parentage determination. The court saw no clear legislative preference in the Act between blood-testing evidence and proof of having given birth as a means of determining parentage. Despite advances in reproductive technology rendering a different outcome biologically possible, California law recognizes only one natural mother. The court declined to accept the contention of amicus curiae, namely, that the court should find that the child has two mothers.

Quicknotes

AMICUS CURIAE A third party, not implicated in the suit, which seeks to file a brief containing information for the court's consideration in conformity with its position.

GAMETE A cell capable of reproduction, such as a sperm or egg.

UNIFORM PARENTAGE ACT Imposes duty of child support upon both parents without according the father a right to decide that the fetus should be aborted or to avoid child support obligations by showing he offered to pay for an abortion.

ZYGOTE Union of two gametes forming a cell, especially a fertilized ovum before cleavage.

Prato-Morrison v. Doe

Patient (P) v. Patient (D)

Cal. Ct. App., 103 Cal. App. 4th 222 (2002).

NATURE OF CASE: Appeal of order of the family law court to dismiss parentage action.

FACT SUMMARY: Dona Prato-Morrison (P) brought a parentage suit against Doe (D) alleging custody of twins born from genetic material misappropriated by a fertility clinic.

RULE OF LAW

When an original document is missing, and secondary evidence is offered to prove its content, the secondary evidence must be admissible.

FACTS: Dona Prato-Morrison (P) and her husband Robert Morrison attempted to conceive a child by the process of in vitro fertilization at the Center for Reproductive Health (CRH) at the University of California at Irvine (UCI). Their attempts at conception failed and they, along with many other patients, assumed that any remaining genetic materials collected from them, i.e., sperm and eggs, would be destroyed. It was discovered later that doctors at CRH "stole" their genetic material and that it may have been used by Judith and Jacob Doe (D) in the conception of twins. Prato-Morrison (P) settled a claim for money damages with UCI and CRH, but brought a parentage action against Doe (D) to determine parentage and visitation rights of the twins. Doe (D) moved to dismiss alleging that Prato-Morrison (P) lacked standing to sue. The trial court granted Prato-Morrison (P) a continuance to try to establish standing for her claim of being the genetic mother. Prato-Morrison (P) produced a handwritten list and declaration from Teri Ord, a fertilization biologist, stating the she participated in the transfers of genetic material at UCI and that by reviewing laboratory records she determined that Doe (D) had received sixteen of Prato-Morrison's (P) eggs with a twin pregnancy resulting. UCI's original records, however, were unavailable because the FBI had confiscated them. Doe (D) moved to exclude the evidence as being hearsay. The trial court sustained the motion and granted the Does' (D) motion to quash. Prato-Morrison (P) now appeals.

ISSUE: If an original document is missing, and secondary evidence is offered to prove its content, must the secondary evidence be admissible?

HOLDING AND DECISION: (Vogel, J.) Yes. When an original document is missing, and secondary evidence is offered to prove its content, the secondary evidence must be admissible. Ord's declaration and list was allegedly compiled from unidentified laboratory documents and she claims not to have had personal knowledge of the transmission of the genetic material in question. While those laboratory documents could be subject to the business record exception to the hearsay rule, Ord's list and declaration, which are mere secondary evidence, have no foundation or substantiation and hence are inadmissible hearsay. Prato-Morrison (P) also argues that DNA evidence should be obtained from Doe (D) because her right to discover parentage supercedes Doe's (D) right as the presumed parent. Doe's (D) right to privacy will not be violated by parties lacking standing to proceed. Prato-Morrison's (P) rights were properly addressed in the action against CRH and UCI. Lacking any other evidence of parentage, the case was properly dismissed. Affirmed.

ANALYSIS

This case presents a mix of fundamental rights, property law, family law and the rules of evidence. It also illustrates the complex issues surrounding reproductive rights and how health care facilities must protect the privacy, and property, of their patients. Prato-Morrison (P) was able to exercise her property rights and receive compensation from UCI for the unauthorized conversion of her property, but her attempts to claim the alleged tangible product of her property, the twins, required a higher standard of proof beyond the speculation of one witness. Without proper documentation, the court was unwilling to invade Doe's (D) privacy rights to substantiate Prato-Morrison (P) claim of property rights, especially since the property had allegedly been transformed from haploid genetic material into that of two living beings.

Quicknotes

CONVERSION The act of depriving an owner of his property without permission or justification.

MOTION TO QUASH To vacate, annul, void.

SECONDARY EVIDENCE Evidence that is not primary or the actual thing or document itself and which nonetheless may be admissible at trial under certain circumstances.

STANDING Whether a party possesses the right to commence suit against another party by having a personal stake in the resolution of the controversy.

In re A.C.

Medical personnel (P) v. Comatose pregnant woman (D)

D.C. Ct. App., 573 A.2d 1235 (1990).

NATURE OF CASE: Appeal of order mandating Caesarian section upon a terminally ill pregnant woman.

FACT SUMMARY: A court ordered that A.C. (D), pregnant and dying, undergo a Caesarian section to save the baby.

RULE OF LAW

A court may not order an individual to undergo a Caesarian section to save the baby's life.

FACTS: A.C. (D), a chronic cancer patient, became pregnant. When she was 25 weeks pregnant, she entered a hospital, complaining of pain. Tests revealed an inoperable tumor, and she was diagnosed as terminal. Based on conversations with doctors, she agreed to undergo a Caesarian section at 28 weeks. However, her condition rapidly worsened, and by 26 weeks she had begun lapsing into and out of consciousness. Medical personnel believed that the only way to save the baby was an immediate C-section. However, they were not able to obtain A.C.'s (D) consent, as she was mostly unconscious and not lucid when she was conscious. A court hearing was rapidly convened to determine what to do next. The court engaged in a balancing test between the state's interest in the fetus, the fetus's interests, and A.C.'s (D) interests. The court ordered the C-section; unfortunately, the baby died, as did A.C. (D) two days later. The district court of appeals reviewed the case.

ISSUE: May a court order an individual to undergo a Caesarian section to save the baby's life?

HOLDING AND DECISION: (Terry, J.) No. A court may not order an individual to undergo a Caesarian section to save the baby's life. It is a well-grounded common-law rule that an individual is under no duty to take steps to save another's life. For instance, a person cannot be compelled to donate blood or an organ to save another's life. This rule applies with equal force in the context of a dying woman and her fetus: the woman cannot be compelled to undergo a procedure to save the fetus's life. Consent is required. If the woman is no longer competent, a court may hold an inquiry as to whether her consent would have been given were she competent. However, the scope of inquiry can only go so far as consent; the fetus's interests are not to be considered, nor those of the state, except perhaps in extraordinary circumstances. As the court considered those interests, it erred. Reversed.

CONCURRENCE AND DISSENT: (Belson, Assoc. J.) The interests of the state and fetus are entitled to more weight than the court here gives them. In some cases, they may outweigh those of the mother.

ANALYSIS

When a person is not capable of giving consent, it may be that the person had appointed a representative while they were still competent. If not, a court must try to divine what that person would have wanted. This requires an examination of all relevant circumstances, such as statements that the person might have made, as well as her value system. This inquiry is called "substituted judgment."

Quicknotes

DOCTRINE OF INFORMED CONSENT Consent to a particular occurrence requiring full notification as to the consequences of that consent.

State v. Wade

State (P) v. New mother (D)

Mo. Ct. App. 232 S.W.3d 663 (2007).

NATURE OF CASE: Appeal by the state of judgment dismissing felony charge.

FACT SUMMARY: A trial court found that the child endangerment statute did not apply to a fetus.

RULE OF LAW

The state of Missouri cannot intervene through the criminal justice system to protect an unborn child from its mother's misconduct.

FACTS: Janet Wade (D) gave birth to her son, T.L.W., and the following day, both tested positive for marijuana and methamphetamine. The state of Missouri filed a felony information charge against Wade (D) for first-degree child endangerment. The trial court found that the child endangerment statute did not apply to a fetus.

ISSUE: Can the state of Missouri intervene through the criminal justice system to protect an unborn child from its mother's misconduct?

HOLDING AND DECISION: (Hardwick, J.) No. The state of Missouri cannot intervene through the criminal justice system to protect an unborn child from its mother's misconduct. The child endangerment statute's definition of the word "child" does not contemplate children in utero, and its overall context indicates that it applies only to children who have already been born. While some courts have relied on Section 1.205—which provides that the life of a human beings begin at conception, and that unborn children have protectable interests in life, health, and well-being—to determine that an unborn child is a person for purposes of applying criminal and civil liability statutes, there is an exception to Section 1.205 that precludes efforts to prosecute a mother who causes indirect harm to her fetus by failing to properly care for herself. The legislature had determined that mothers of unborn children who fail to properly care for themselves are better handled through social services.

ANALYSIS

Arguably, a state could punish prenatal misconduct that is unlawful, such as the use of illegal drugs. Even though that crime is already punishable, there is nothing to stop the legislature from allowing a concurrent charge of "illegal endangerment of a fetus."

Quicknotes

FELONY A criminal offense of greater seriousness than a misdemeanor; felonies are generally defined pursuant to statute as any crime that is punishable by death or by a term of imprisonment exceeding one year.

Wixtrom v. Department of Children and Family Services (In re J.D.S.)

Petitioner for guardianship (P) v. State (D)

Fla.Ct. App., 864 So. 2d 534 (2004).

NATURE OF CASE: Appeal of denial of guardianship appointment.

FACT SUMMARY: A woman sought to be appointed guardian of a fetus carried by a mentally challenged woman whose medical interests might conflict with the interests of the fetus.

RULE OF LAW

The fetus of a physically and mentally incapacitated woman who was raped while living in a group home is not entitled to appointment of a separate guardian in the state's action for protective services for the woman.

FACTS: The Department of Children and Family Services filed a petition seeking an order authorizing emergency adult protective services for J.D.S. because it had a report she was pregnant as a result of a sexual battery while residing in a group home. The petition stated that J.D.S. was a 22-year-old woman suffering from severe mental retardation, cerebral palsy, autism, and seizure disorder, and that she was unable to adequately provide for her own care and protection. The petition also stated that she was nonverbal, unable to make decisions, and unable to comprehend her own mental, physical, or environmental limitations. The petition further alleged that J.D.S. was taking numerous medications that could be detrimental to the fetus. It requested appointment of a guardian for J.D.S. and protective supervision for her. The department also petitioned for appointment of a separate guardian for J.D.S.'s fetus, alleging that her interests and needs were potentially adverse to those of the fetus. It stated that J.D.S.'s guardian was required to avoid conflicts of interests, but that a conflict of interest was likely because her medications could be detrimental to the fetus. After the trial court denied a petition for appointment of a temporary guardian for J.D.S., Jennifer Wixtrom (P) petitioned to be appointed guardian of the fetus. Wixtrom (P) alleged that the appointment was essential because J.D.S. lacked the mental capacity to provide proper prenatal care and to make necessary decisions for the protection and enhancement of the fetus during its formative months. The trial court ultimately found J.D.S. to be totally incapacitated and ordered the appointment of a plenary guardian for her. After Wixtrom's (P) motion for rehearing was denied, she filed a notice of appeal. Thereafter, the trial court entered an order stating that J.D.S.'s guardian had created a plan for J.D.S. which stated that an abortion would not be performed on her.

ISSUE: Is the fetus of a physically and mentally incapacitated woman who was raped while living in a group home entitled to appointment of a separate guardian in the state's action for protective services for the woman?

HOLDING AND DECISION: (Thompson, J.) No. The fetus of a physically and mentally incapacitated woman who was raped while living in a group home is not entitled to appointment of a separate guardian in the state's action for protective services for the woman. Chapter 744 of the Florida statutes, which governs guardianship, does not provide for the appointment of a guardian for a fetus, and the absence of a provision for fetuses means that the protection of the statute does not extend to fetuses. This is supported by the fact that the legislature had, in other contexts, explicitly provided protection for fetuses. In addition, Fla. Stat. § 744.102(8) defines a "ward" as "a person" for whom a guardian has been appointed, and it therefore follows that a fetus must be considered a "person" to be appointed a guardian. No Florida statute or case law has determined a fetus to be a person. Finally, as to Wixtrom's (P) concern that J.D.S.'s guardian could have authorized an abortion of the fetus, Florida law provides safeguards to ensure that a guardian does not act capriciously or cavalierly when considering the health of an incapacitated mother and fetus.

CONCURRENCE: (Orfinger, J.) The legislature is the proper forum to address the issue.

DISSENT: (Pleus, J.) Wixtrom's (P) petition was for appointment as a plenary guardian under Chapter 744 and not as a guardian ad litem, and under Chapter 744, a trial court has full authority to appoint a plenary guardian for an unborn child because the child is a "minor" as the term is used in the statute.

ANALYSIS

Particularly in the areas of the law that pertain to pregnancy and abortion, much of the contentiousness among the different sides of the issues has more to do with the fact that the law does not always accommodate the various belief systems of a diverse population. Consider that the way one characterizes the fetus—as "fetus" or as "unborn child"—can influence a reading of the law. Justice Pleus's argument is solid, if one assumes his alternative name for "fetus"—"unborn child." A child is undoubtedly a person, and a fetus is an unborn child; therefore, a guardian can be appointed for this unborn child. One might argue that Justice Pleus's assumption—that a fetus is an unborn person—is incorrect, but one cannot find his reasoning, based on that assumption, incorrect. It is unfortunate, in a

Continued on next page.

sense, that the law is subject to sometimes opposing but equally reasonable interpretations, because it seems to perpetuate the very divisiveness it strives to abolish.

Quicknotes

GUARDIANSHIP A legal relationship whereby one party is responsible for the care and control over another and his property due to some legal incapacity on the part of the ward.

CHAPTER 17

Legal, Social and Ethical Issues in Human Genetics

Quick Reference Rules of Law

Safer v. Pack

Daughter of cancer patient (P) v. Father's physician (D)

N.J. Super. Ct. App. Div., 291 N.J. Super. 619, 677 A.2d 1188 (1996).

NATURE OF CASE: Appeal from an order dismissing a complaint that alleged professional negligence.

FACT SUMMARY: Safer (P), the daughter of a man who died of colon cancer, was not warned by the doctor (D) who treated her father that she was also at risk.

RULE OF LAW

A physician has a duty to warn the child of a patient of a genetic risk.

FACTS: Donna Safer's (P) father suffered a protracted bout with severe colon cancer. The cancer spread and killed him when Donna (P) was ten years old. Dr. Pack (D) never told Donna (P) of her heightened genetic risk for colon cancer. At the age of thirty-six, Donna (P) was diagnosed with colon cancer. She lost a majority of her bowel and one ovary. Donna (P) sued, alleging professional negligence, but the trial court dismissed her complaint. Donna (P) appealed.

ISSUE: Does a physician have a duty to warn the child of a patient of a genetic risk?

HOLDING AND DECISION: (Kestin, J.) Yes. A physician has a duty to warn the child of a patient of a genetic risk. Knowledge of a genetic risk is logically no different from knowledge of a risk of an infectious disease. Since a duty exists to warn of the risk of infectious diseases, the same duty, as a matter of law, should require a warning for genetic risks. In this case, it was clear that Donna (P) faced a heightened risk of colon cancer. Whether liability existed, and if so, what damages are appropriate are matters better decided at trial. Reversed.

ANALYSIS

Saying a legal duty exists in theory and proving the breach of such a duty are quite different propositions. The difficulty in showing a duty to warn of genetic risks hinges in part on proving the level of heightened risk. If the risks are not well known, then applying a high-level duty is an unfair standard.

Quicknotes

DUTY OF CARE A principle of negligence requiring an individual to act in such a manner as to avoid injury to a person to whom he or she owes an obligatory duty.

DUTY TO DISCLOSE The duty owed by a fiduciary to reveal those facts that have a material effect on the interests of the party that must be informed.

Greenberg v. Miami Children's Hospital Research Institute

Research collaborator (P) v. Research hospital (D)

264 F. Supp. 2d 1064 (S.D. Fl. 2003).

NATURE OF CASE: Appeal of grant of a motion to dismiss.

FACT SUMMARY: Greenberg (P) brought suit against Miami Children's Hospital Research Institute (MCHRI) (D), and others, alleging multiple claims of conversion and misappropriation by MCHRI (D) for having patented the research results obtained through donated tissue samples.

RULE OF LAW

Property rights are not retained in body tissue and genetic matter if they are voluntarily donated for research.

FACTS: Greenberg (P) and the Chicago Chapter of the National Tay-Sachs and Allied Diseases Association, Inc. (NTSAD) made contact with Dr. Matalon, a research physician affiliated with the University of Chicago, to obtain assistance with treatment of Canavan's disease. Canavan's disease is a genetically inherited fatal progressive brain degenerative disorder afflicting children of eastern and central European Jewish decent. Most of the afflicted children do not survive past the age of ten. Greenberg (P) and the NTSAD provided financial support for Dr. Matalon's research and convinced parents of children with Canavan's disease to provide tissue samples including blood, urine, and autopsy samples. A confidential database was compiled registering the epidemiological and medical information of all of the families participating. Greenberg (P), the NTSAD, and the other family members involved understood that any research and treatment developed in association with this collaboration would remain in the public domain and be provided to those afflicted with Canavan's at an affordable and accessible cost. Dr. Matalon became associated with Miami Children's Hospital Research Institute (MCHRI) (D), and it was there that research discovered the gene responsible for Canavan's disease. This discovery directly resulted from the use of the tissue samples and the confidential pedigree information contained in the confidential database. Unknown to Greenberg (P), Dr. Matalon applied for and received the patent for the genetic sequence that was discovered. The patent allowed the doctor and MCHRI (D) to restrict any activity related to the Canavan's disease gene, including all testing and treatment. Matalon and MCHRI (D) began selling licenses to perform testing and research, restricting public access to any information unless royalty fees were paid, and threatened enforcement actions. Greenberg (P) sued, alleging: (1) lack of informed consent; (2) breach of fiduciary duty; (3) unjust enrichment; (4) fraudulent concealment; (5) conversion; and (6) misappropriation of trade secrets. Greenberg (P) sought a permanent injunction to prevent enforcement of the patent rights, and alleged that MCHRI (D) and Matalon were unjustly enriched from the royalties they were charging for testing and from federal research grants that followed the discovery. The trial court dismissed and Greenberg (P) appeals.

ISSUE: Are property rights retained in body tissue and genetic matter if they are voluntarily donated for research?

HOLDING AND DECISION: (Moreno, J.) No. Property rights are not retained in body tissue and genetic matter if they are voluntarily donated for research. The use of the results from medical research is not conversion because the donors of the tissue lose their property interest in the tissue after the donation, regardless if the receiving party gathers information from that tissue and sells it as a commodity on the open marketplace. Florida's law on genetic testing, Fla. Stat. § 760.40, does not assist the plaintiffs with their claims, because while this statute gives persons contributing genetic material for research ownership rights in the results of the research, the only remedies provided in the statute lie in lack of disclosure or of informed consent. Here the parties knowingly gave their tissue samples to promote the result that was accomplished. The conversion theory was properly dismissed. However, to support a claim for unjust enrichment, Greenberg (P) must plead and prove: (1) that plaintiff conferred a benefit upon the defendant; (2) that the defendant voluntarily accepted and retained the benefit; and (3) that under the circumstances it would be unjust or inequitable for the defendant to retain the benefit without paying for it. While MCHRI (D) has invested in the research, so have Greenberg (P), the family donors, and the NTSAD. The facts demonstrate a continuing research collaboration and MCHRI (D) cannot seek refuge in U.S. Patent Law from disavowing that relationship and the benefits gained. Claim dismissed.

ANALYSIS

The court "split the baby." Courts have traditionally been reluctant to extend property rights to donated tissues for fear of chilling research and development of new medical treatment. The classic case on this issue is *Moore v. Regents of the University of California*, 51 Cal. 3d 120 (1990). *Moore* demonstrates just how far courts have been willing to go to block causes of action against researchers. In *Moore*, the physician involved deceived the patient as to why he was taking tissue samples and never informed him of the research he was conducting.

Continued on next page.

Moore was not a willing or informed participant in the medical research, yet the court still dismissed his claims. The Florida court recognized the significant financial gain the defendants were now receiving from royalties and recognized that the defendants could not have been so enriched had it not been for the donation of tissue, monies, and private familial pedigree information from the plaintiffs. Consequently, the court allows the unjust enrichment theory to proceed, while giving the defendants the property rights to the results of the research.

Quicknotes

CONVERSION The act of depriving an owner of his property without permission or justification.

DOCTRINE OF INFORMED CONSENT Consent to a particular occurrence requiring full notification as to the consequence of that consent.

FIDUCIARY RELATIONSHIP Person holding a legal obligation to act for the benefit of another.

FRAUDULENT CONCEALMENT The concealing of a material fact which a party is under an obligation to disclose.

CHAPTER 18

Defining Death

Quick Reference Rules of Law

1. **Anencephalic Infants.** An anencephalic newborn is not "dead" for purposes of organ donation solely by reason of its congenital deformity. (In re T.A.C.P.) *166*

2. **Anencephalic Infants.** Once an individual has been diagnosed as presenting an emergency medical condition, a hospital must provide stabilizing treatment necessary to prevent the material deterioration of the individual's condition or provide for an appropriate transfer to another facility. (In re Baby K) *167*

In re T.A.C.P.

Parents (P) v. Health care providers (D)

Fla. Sup. Ct., 609 So. 2d 588 (1992).

NATURE OF CASE: Review of order certified by the appellate court.

FACT SUMMARY: The parents (P) of an anencephalic child sought to have their child declared dead so that her organs could be donated.

RULE OF LAW

An anencephalic newborn is not "dead" for purposes of organ donation solely by reason of its congenital deformity.

FACTS: The parents (P) of the child T.A.C.P. were informed that their child would be born without an upper brain, or anencephalic. The parents (P), hoping to offer some benefit to others in the face of their loss, sought a declaration that the child was "dead," so that her organs could be donated. The health care providers (D) refused out of fear of liability. The parents (P) then sought a legal ruling on the matter. The question of the definition of death was certified by the appellate court and forwarded to the Supreme Court of Florida.

ISSUE: Is an anencephalic newborn considered "dead" for purposes of organ donation solely by reason of its congenital deformity?

HOLDING AND DECISION: (Kogan, J.) No. An anencephalic newborn is not "dead" for purposes of organ donation solely by reason of its congenital deformity. Florida generally defines death as cardiopulmonary failure. An exception exists for whole-brain death when the heart is kept operable by artificial means. In this case, the anencephalic infant fits neither of these definitions. Though lacking an upper brain, the child's heart will operate for a short time, and some primordial brain function exists. While this is a policy issue of tremendous import, there is no sufficiently sound reason under the current law to extend the definition of death to include anencephaly. Because the newborn was not dead, donation of her organs was illegal.

ANALYSIS

There is no hope for the survival of an anencephalic infant. They are not conscious and most likely do not have any pain response. The need for infant organs makes it very difficult to avoid considering anencephalic infants as a source for these organs. A medical council concluded in 1995 that it was ethical to use organs from an anencephalic infant who was not yet dead so long as parental consent was obtained, along with other precautionary measures.

In re Baby K

Hospital (P) v. Parents (P) of anencephalic infant (P)

16 F.3d 590 (4th Cir. 1994).

NATURE OF CASE: Appeal from judgment in a hospital's request for declaratory relief concerning its treatment obligations under federal law.

FACT SUMMARY: The Hospital (P) sought a declaratory judgment that it was not required to provide treatment other than warmth, nutrition, and hydration to Baby "K" (D), an anencephalic infant.

RULE OF LAW

Once an individual has been diagnosed as presenting an emergency medical condition, a hospital must provide stabilizing treatment necessary to prevent the material deterioration of the individual's condition or provide for an appropriate transfer to another facility.

FACTS: When Baby "K" (D) was born with anencephaly, she was missing a major portion of her brain. Most such infants die within a few days of birth due to breathing difficulties and other complications. Rejecting the Hospital's (P) recommendation that Baby "K" (D) only be provided with supportive care such as nutrition, hydration, and warmth, Ms. H (D) insisted that her child be provided with mechanical breathing assistance when necessary. When the Hospital (P) sought to transfer the infant, no other hospital in the area would agree to take her. After Baby "K" (D) was transferred to a nursing home and readmitted to the Hospital (P) a number of times due to breathing difficulties, the Hospital (P) instituted this action against Ms. H (D), Baby "K" (D), and Mr. K (D), seeking a declaratory judgment that it was only required to provide warmth, nutrition, and hydration to Baby "K" (D). The district court denied the Hospital's (P) request, concluding that the Emergency Medical Treatment and Active Labor Act (EMTALA) gave rise to a duty to provide respiratory support to Baby "K" (D). The Hospital (P) appealed.

ISSUE: Once an individual has been diagnosed as presenting an emergency medical condition, must a hospital provide stabilizing treatment necessary to prevent the material deterioration of the individual's condition or provide for an appropriate transfer to another facility?

HOLDING AND DECISION: (Wilkins, J.) Yes. Once an individual has been diagnosed as presenting an emergency medical condition, a hospital must provide stabilizing treatment necessary to prevent the material deterioration of the individual's condition or provide for an appropriate transfer to another facility. The Hospital (P) concedes that when Baby "K" (D) is presented in respiratory distress, a failure to provide immediate medical attention would reasonably be expected to cause serious impairment of her bodily functions. Thus, her breathing difficulty qualifies as an emergency medical condition, triggering the Hospital's (P) duty to provide her with stabilizing treatment or to transfer her to another facility. Since transfer is not an option available to the Hospital (P) at this time, it must stabilize Baby "K"'s (D) condition. Affirmed.

DISSENT: (Sprouse, J.) Tragic end-of-life hospital dramas such as this one do not represent phenomena susceptible to uniform legal control. Anencephaly, not the subsidiary respiratory failure, is the condition that should be reviewed in order to judge the applicability of the rule.

ANALYSIS

The rule applied by the majority is found in the Emergency Medical Treatment and Active Labor Act (EMTALA). Congress enacted EMTALA in response to its concern that hospitals were "dumping" patients who were unable to pay by either refusing to provide emergency medical treatment or transferring patients before their emergency conditions were stabilized. In this decision, the court recognized the dilemma facing physicians who are requested to provide treatment they considered morally and ethically inappropriate, but the court could not transcend its judicial function by ignoring the statute's plain language. Congress, not the courts, must redress the Hospital's (P) policy concerns.

Quicknotes

EMTALA Requires hospitals to treat individuals presenting an emergency medical treatment in order to stabilize the condition or transfer the individual to another facility for appropriate treatment in accordance with the statute.

CHAPTER 19

Life and Death Decisions

Quick Reference Rules of Law

CHAPTER 19

Cruzan v. Director, Missouri Department of Health

Parents (P) v. Health department (D)

497 U.S. 261 (1990).

NATURE OF CASE: Review of state court decision regarding the provision of life-sustaining medical treatment.

FACT SUMMARY: Missouri's rule prohibiting the cessation of life support to permanently comatose patients without clear and convincing evidence of the patient's consent was challenged as unconstitutional.

RULE OF LAW

A state may require clear and convincing evidence of a comatose patient's consent prior to cessation of life support.

FACTS: The Cruzans (P), whose daughter was involved in a traffic accident that left her permanently comatose, requested that life support be withdrawn. The facility giving care refused to do so without court approval. The Missouri Supreme Court considered evidence that the Cruzans' (P) daughter had once mentioned to a housemate that she would not want to live if she couldn't take care of herself, but it ruled that this did not meet Missouri's (D) statutory requirement that life support could not be terminated without clear and convincing evidence that this comported with the patient's wishes. The Supreme Court granted review.

ISSUE: May a state require clear and convincing evidence of a comatose patient's consent prior to cessation of life support?

HOLDING AND DECISION: (Rehnquist, C.J.) Yes. A state may require clear and convincing evidence of a comatose patient's consent prior to cessation of life support. Assuming for the sake of argument that the U.S. Constitution secures a right to refuse lifesaving medical care, the question becomes whether a state can impose a burden of proof of clear and convincing evidence of a incompetent's wishes prior to the withdrawal of such care. This requires a balancing of the individual's liberty interests with the state's interests. The state has a profound interest in protecting its citizens' lives. In a situation involving an incompetent who relies on medical care to survive, the potential for abuse by relatives or others who may find the incompetent an inconvenience or burden is clear. Further, an erroneous decision to terminate life support is irrevocable. These dangers argue in favor of the legitimacy of a state imposing a clear and convincing evidentiary standard prior to cessation of life support. Here, the Missouri Supreme Court found the evidence of the incompetent's wishes not to meet this standard, and this was within its discretion. Affirmed.

CONCURRENCE: (O'Connor, J.) The right to refuse medical treatment flows from liberty interests against involuntary invasions of bodily integrity. In addition, it should be emphasized that the court today does not address the role of a surrogate decision-maker.

CONCURRENCE: (Scalia, J.) No federal constitutional issue is involved here. The Due Process Clause of the Fourteenth Amendment has no substantive component with respect to this situation.

DISSENT: (Brennan, J.) The liberty interest of avoiding unwanted medical care should be recognized as a fundamental right. State abridgements of fundamental rights are to be strictly scrutinized, rather than given the deferential treatment accorded by the court.

DISSENT: (Stevens, J.) Missouri's (D) objections subordinate the incompetent's body, her family, and the significance of her life to the state's abstract, undifferentiated interests.

ANALYSIS

This case was closely watched, as it was anticipated that it would settle the question of whether the federal Constitution contained a "right to die clause." The Court's opinion dis-appointed such observers. The opinion dealt more with procedure than substance, and whether such a right exists was a question left open.

Quicknotes

DUE PROCESS CLAUSE Clauses found in the Fifth and Fourteenth Amendments to the United States Constitution providing that no person shall be deprived of "life, liberty, or property, without due process of law."

FOURTEENTH AMENDMENT No person shall be deprived of life, liberty, or property, without the due process of law.

LIBERTY INTEREST A right conferred by the Due Process Clauses of the state and federal constitutions.

RIGHT TO DIE Proposed legislation which would decriminalize doctor-assisted suicide that has been rejected by federal courts but is being pursued through continuing ballot initiatives at the state level. Some states have passed so-called "Death with Dignity" acts (e.g., Oregon), but they are being challenged in appeals.

Bouvia v. Superior Court

Quadriplegic patient (P) v. Court (D)

Cal. Ct. App., 179 Cal. App. 3d 1127 (1986).

NATURE OF CASE: Appeal of denial of injunction compelling the cessation of medical treatment.

FACT SUMMARY: Bouvia (P), not terminally ill but forced to eat through intubation, requested that feeding be stopped.

RULE OF LAW

A competent adult may refuse force-feeding done to sustain life, even if not terminally ill.

FACTS: Elizabeth Bouvia (P), suffering from cerebral palsy and arthritis, slowly lost the use of her body to the point that she could not use her limbs. She lived off government assistance in a public hospital. Wishing to die, she refused food. Medical personnel responded by feeding and hydrating her through a stomach tube inserted through her nose. She sought an injunction compelling removal of the tube. Finding that Bouvia (P) could live indefinitely in her state, not being terminally ill, the trial court denied the injunction. Bouvia (P) appealed, petitioning for a writ of mandamus.

ISSUE: May a competent adult refuse force-feeding done to sustain life, even if not terminally ill?

HOLDING AND DECISION: (Beach, J.) Yes. A competent adult may refuse force-feeding done to sustain life, even if not terminally ill. A competent adult has the right to refuse any sort of medical treatment. This includes force-feeding through tubes. Whether or not a person is terminally ill is irrelevant to that person's rights. The amount of time a person receiving medical treatment may be expected to live simply is not relevant. A decision to forgo medical treatment belongs to the patient alone, and is not to be second-guessed by judges or doctors. Here, there is no question but that Bouvia (P) is of sound mind, and her desire to cease treatment must be respected. Writ issued.

ANALYSIS

The court's position on this issue is by now so well-accepted as to not be controversial. The concurrence's point of view, however, is something else. Medically assisted suicide has generated a good deal of controversy, as demonstrated by the 1992 events surrounding Dr. Jack Kevorkian, a Michigan pathologist who assisted several individuals who wished to die. He was prosecuted, but charges were dismissed when the court found that he broke no law. Michigan's legislature responded by passing a law criminalizing assisted suicide as of April 1993. The Netherlands, on the other hand, enacted about the same time a euthanasia law, permitting physician-assisted death under strict controls.

Quicknotes

WRIT OF MANDAMUS A court order issued commanding a public or private entity, or an official thereof, to perform a duty required by law.

Application of the President and Directors of Georgetown College, Inc.

Hospital (P) v. Patients (D)

331 F.2d 1000 (D.D.C. 1964).

NATURE OF CASE: The court ordered the injection of blood into a critically ill woman whose religious beliefs prohibited the injection of blood.

FACT SUMMARY: A patient who is a member of the Jehovah's Witnesses sect, which prohibits the injection of blood into the body, was brought to a hospital for emergency care. The patient had lost two-thirds of her own blood supply. The hospital's application to the district court for permission to administer blood was denied.

RULE OF LAW
Permission may be granted by a court to a hospital to administer blood to a critically ill patient whose competence is compromised by her illness, even though her religious beliefs prohibit such treatment.

FACTS: Mr. Jones (D) brought Mrs. Jones (D) to the hospital (P) for emergency care after she had lost two-thirds of her body's blood supply due to a ruptured ulcer. Both Mr. and Mrs. Jones are Jehovah's Witnesses, the teachings of which prohibit the injection of blood into the body. When death was imminent, the hospital (P) applied to a federal court for permission to administer blood. The district court denied the application and the hospital (P) appealed.

ISSUE: May permission be granted by a court to a hospital to administer blood to a critically ill patient whose competence is compromised by her illness, even though her religious beliefs prohibit such treatment?

HOLDING AND DECISION: (Wright, J.) Yes. Permission may be granted by a court to a hospital to administer blood to a critically ill patient whose competence is compromised by her illness, even though her religious beliefs prohibit such treatment. Several considerations support this conclusion. Both Mr. Jones and Mrs. Jones indicated that if the court ordered the transfusion, it would not be their responsibility. In addition, the right to practice freely does not include freedom to expose the community or a child to communicable disease or to death, and while those circumstances are not present in this case, they provide a useful analogy because Mrs. Jones (D) was not coherent enough, due to her illness, to make a competent choice about treatment. Also, if a parent has no power to forbid the saving of a child's life, then the husband of the patient has no right to order the doctors to allow his wife to die. Furthermore, granting permission for treatment protected the hospital and doctors from possible liability. But the most compelling reason for granting permission was that a life hung in the balance, and there was no time for research or reflection.

ANALYSIS

The court said that the husband and wife both indicated that if the court ordered treatment, the matter would be out of their hands. A fair interpretation of the facts as written would be that they wanted the court to make the decision, and take the matter out of their hands, so that the wife's life could be saved. Jehovah's Witness religious authorities say that the faith requires not only that consent to a transfusion be denied, but that the patient actually avoid having one. In that case, and given the patient's protests (even though weak and arguably misleading), they might have a valid cause of action.

Public Health Trust of Dade County v. Wons

Hospital operator (P) v. Jehovah's Witness (D)

Fla. Sup. Ct., 541 So. 2d 96 (1989).

NATURE OF CASE: Question certified on appeal in an action to compel medical treatment.

FACT SUMMARY: Wons (D), a Jehovah's Witness, refused to consent to a blood transfusion while still conscious and competent.

RULE OF LAW

A competent adult has a lawful right to refuse, for religious reasons, blood transfusions without which death may result.

FACTS: Wons (D) refused to consent to a blood transfusion due to her religious beliefs as a Jehovah's Witness. At the time she refused, she was competent to make the decision. While unconscious, the Public Health Trust of Dade County (P) obtained a court order allowing the transfusion. When she awoke, Wons (D) appealed the order. The district court held that Wons's (D) rights of religion and privacy could not be overridden and reversed the order.

ISSUE: Does a competent adult have a lawful right to refuse, for religious reasons, a blood transfusion without which death may result?

HOLDING AND DECISION: [Judge not stated in casebook excerpt.] Yes. A competent adult has a lawful right to refuse, for religious reasons, blood transfusions without which death may result. The constitutional guarantees of religious freedom and privacy are sacred. Although the nurturing and support of Wons's (D) two minor children by their mother is important to their development, it is not sufficient to override fundamental constitutional rights. In this case, Wons (D) made an informed choice, based upon her religious beliefs, that the transfusion was not desired. Absent a compelling state interest to the contrary, she has the right to so choose. Affirmed.

ANALYSIS

A patient may not be prevented from undertaking risky activities. The logical difference between refusing a medical treatment and climbing Mount Everest is minimal when evaluating the risk to the parent's life. Inconsistent state intervention cannot be easily tolerated when it tends to isolate specific groups on the basis of religious beliefs.

Quicknotes

LIBERTY INTEREST A right conferred by the Due Process Clauses of the state and federal constitutions.

In re Eichner

Incompetent's representative (P) v. Hospital (D)

N.Y. Ct. App., 52 N.Y.2d 363, 420 N.E.2d 64 (1981).

NATURE OF CASE: Review of lower court decisions in application for injunction to terminate life support.

FACT SUMMARY: Eichner (P) sought, as representative of incompetent Fox, to have the latter's life support removed, citing Fox's prior pronouncements that he did not desire extraordinary medical care.

RULE OF LAW

A representative of an incompetent may authorize removal of life support if such removal comports with the incompetent's wishes.

FACTS: Fox, a member of a Roman Catholic religious order, suffered cardiac arrest during an operation. Loss of oxygen to the brain rendered him permanently comatose. Eichner (P), the head of Fox's order, requested, as Fox's representative, that medical personnel (D) discontinue life support. They refused. A petition for an injunction ordering such cessation was made. Evidence at the hearing demonstrated that Fox had clearly stated that he did not wish to be kept alive on life support. [The casebook opinion did not state the trial court's or appellate division's decisions.] The New York Court of Appeals granted review.

ISSUE: May a representative of an incompetent authorize removal of life support if such removal comports with the individual's wishes?

HOLDING AND DECISION: (Wachtler, J.) Yes. A representative of an incompetent may authorize removal of life support if such removal comports with the incompetent's wishes. When it is clear that the incompetent had indicated during his competency that he would not wish extraordinary measures taken to preserve his life, medical personnel should respect his wishes. Here, it was clear that this was indeed Fox's wishes, so the injunction compelling cessation of treatment should issue. So ordered.

ANALYSIS

It is important to differentiate a patient's own wishes from substituted judgment, i.e., the belief of one person regarding what is best for another when the latter's wishes are unknown. The present case was an example of the former category. The latter is less well accepted as a basis for withdrawing life support. New York, for instance, flatly rejects it unless the patient has formally expressed his desires at an earlier time.

Quicknotes

INCAPACITY Lack of capacity or ability to function legally, physically or mentally.

INJUNCTION A court order requiring a person to do or prohibiting that person from doing a specific act.

RIGHT TO DIE Proposed legislation which would decriminalize doctor-assisted suicide that has been rejected by federal courts but is being pursued through continuing ballot initiatives at the state level. Some states have passed so-called "Death with Dignity" acts (e.g., Oregon), but they are being challenged in appeals.

In re Conroy

Patient's representative (P) v. Hospital (D)

N.J. Sup. Ct., 98 N.J. 321, 486 A.2d 1209 (1985).

NATURE OF CASE: Review of order involving request to cease life support.

FACT SUMMARY: Conroy, mentally incompetent and in pain, sought through her representative (P) to have life support removed.

RULE OF LAW

An incompetent's life support may be removed if doing so is demonstrably in the incompetent's best interests.

FACTS: [The casebook opinion limited its facts to reciting that Conroy was incompetent and in pain, and that she sought through a representative (P) to have life support terminated. The lower court decision was not stated.]

ISSUE: May an incompetent's life support be removed if doing so is demonstrably in the incompetent's best interests?

HOLDING AND DECISION: (Schreiber, J.) Yes. An incompetent's life support may be removed if doing so is demonstrably in the incompetent's best interests. Under what can be called the "limited-objective" test, support may be withdrawn if (1) reasonably trustworthy evidence exists that the incompetent would have so wanted and (2) it is clear that the benefits of life are outweighed by the burdens of treatment. Under another test, the "pure-objective" approach, if the burdens clearly and markedly outweigh the benefits of life, life support may be terminated without evidence that the incompetent would have so wished. [The opinion did not state which test was used here, or the appeal's disposition.]

ANALYSIS

The objective tests are to be used when the incompetent's wishes cannot be clearly ascertained. When they can be, a subjective test is used. Basically, the decision of the incompetent made while competent will control.

Quicknotes

RIGHT TO DIE Proposed legislation which would decriminalize doctor-assisted suicide that has been rejected by federal courts but is being pursued through continuing ballot initiatives at the state level. Some states have passed so-called "Death with Dignity" acts (e.g., Oregon), but they are being challenged in appeals.

Conservatorship of Wendland

Conservator (P) v. Probate court (D)

Cal. Sup. Ct., 26 Cal. 4th 519, 28 P.3d 151 (2001).

NATURE OF CASE: Appeal from the court of appeals decision to reverse the trial court's judgment.

FACT SUMMARY: Rose Wendland (Conservator) (Petitioner) (P) sought an order from the trial court granting her the authority to withdraw or withhold life-sustaining medical treatment from her husband, a conscious but incompetent conservatee.

RULE OF LAW

The conservator of a conscious conservatee cannot withhold artificial nutrition and hydration when the conservatee is not terminally ill, comatose, or in a persistent vegetative state, and has not left instructions for a surrogate to make health care decisions.

FACTS: Robert Wendland (Robert) was involved in a single-vehicle accident resulting in brain injury that left him conscious, but severely disabled. He was dependent on artificial hydration and nutrition, and a feeding tube was placed to provide this life-supporting therapy. After a prolonged recovery period, he was able to regain some basic functioning and was able to operate an electronic wheelchair, draw circles and perform simple two-step commands. He was unable to verbalize and the medical staff was unable to establish a consistent method of communication with him. His medical report noted that he was severely physically and mentally disabled. Robert's wife, Rose, had consented to the placement of a feeding tube on three occasions, but refused a fourth request from the physicians when the tube needed to be replaced. The physicians agreed, but they inserted a nasogastric tube for feeding until the hospital's ethics committee could make a recommendation. The twenty-member ethics committee unanimously approved of Rose's decision to discontinue the artificial feedings, but when Robert's mother and sister discovered the plan they petitioned the court for a temporary restraining order. The order was granted. Rose petitioned the court to become Robert's conservator and sought an order granting her authority to give informed consent for medical treatment and for withholding life-sustaining medical treatment, including hydration and nutrition. The trial court granted the conservatorship and the authority to consent to receiving treatment, but denied authority for withholding treatment. After a 60-day observation period, during which Robert made no progress, Rose, now Conservator (P), renewed her petition for authority to withhold treatment. The trial court denied Conservator's (P) request, finding insufficient evidence to meet the "clear and convincing" evidentiary standard that Robert, now incapacitated, would have wanted life-sustaining treatment to be discontinued under these circumstances. The court of appeals, however, reversed, acknowledging the evidence that Robert had made statements that he would not want to live as a vegetable, or in a comatose state, or in a manner in which he could not perform basic activities of living such as feeding himself and communicating. This appeal followed.

ISSUE: Can the conservator of a conscious conservatee withhold artificial nutrition and hydration when the conservatee is not terminally ill, comatose, or in a persistent vegetative state, and has not left instructions for a surrogate to make health care decisions?

HOLDING AND DECISION: (Werdegar, J.) No. The conservator of a conscious conservatee cannot withhold artificial nutrition and hydration when the conservatee is not terminally ill, comatose, or in a persistent vegetative state, and has not left instructions for a surrogate to make health care decisions. There is no question that a competent adult has the right to refuse medical treatment, even life-sustaining treatment. This right springs from the rights of informed consent and privacy, as well as a liberty interest granted in our Constitution. A conservator can only make decisions in accordance with the conservatee's wishes when those wishes are known. No assumption or presumption can be made that a conservator has been given the authority to end the life of the conservatee in accordance with his or her wishes. The risk of error is simply too high. Consequently, Conservator (P) was required to meet the higher "clear and convincing" evidence standard to obtain the authority to withdraw life-sustaining treatment as opposed to the "preponderance" standard used for other conservatorship duties. The evidence does not support the conclusion that Robert, who is still conscious and not in a persistent vegetative state, would want to die under these circumstances. All of Robert's pre-accident statements regarding his wishes not to receive treatment referenced a much greater incapacity. Nor does the "best interests" standard aid Conservator's (P) position. This standard, while appearing in the Probate Code for ordinary decisions involving a conservatee, is not applicable when the decision contemplated is threatening the conservatee's fundamental rights to life and privacy. The court of appeals' decision is reversed.

ANALYSIS

While courts have universally recognized a right to life, the right to death is viewed with trepidation. The California

Continued on next page.

Supreme Court, however, did make note of what it was not deciding in this case. The court emphasized that the clear and convincing evidence standard did not apply to most conservatorship decisions, but only to those involving the withdrawal of life-support. The court also distinguished the "narrow class" of persons affected by the decision—those who had not left formal directives on their health care prior to their incapacity and who were not comatose or in a persistent vegetative state. As elevated evidentiary standards have evolved for surrogates making life and death health care decisions, the need for clear advanced health care directives or living wills has gained prominence. The high-profile nature of these cases has assisted with informing the public that once a person becomes incapacitated, it is too late to provide the quantum of evidence necessary to sustain a choice to remove life support if those desires have not been adequately articulated prior to the incapacitation.

Quicknotes

CONSERVATOR A court-appointed custodian of property belonging to a person found to be unable to manage his/her property.

INCAPACITY Lack of capacity or ability to function legally, physically or mentally.

Guardianship of Schiavo

Parties not identified.

Fl. Ct. of App., 780 So. 2d 176 (2001).

NATURE OF CASE: Appeal of decision authorizing the discontinuance of artificial life support.

FACT SUMMARY: Michael Schiavo (Guardian) (Petitioner) (P), husband and guardian of Theresa Schiavo (Theresa), petitioned the court for authorization to discontinue Theresa's artificial life support, and Theresa's parents (Parents) (D) challenged the court's decision.

RULE OF LAW

The clear and convincing standard of proof permits a decision in the face of inconsistent or conflicting evidence.

FACTS: Theresa married Michael Schiavo (P) in 1984. In 1990, she suffered a cardiac arrest and, although she was rushed to the hospital, she suffered brain injury and has never regained consciousness. Current CAT scans reveal that the majority of Theresa's cerebral cortex is now gone and has been replaced with cerebral spinal fluid. She is in an incurable persistent vegetative state. She is totally dependent upon others to perform all of her activities of daily living, including feeding her by the use of tubes. She exhibits no awareness. With good nursing care, she could continue to survive in this state. Michael (P) received enough funds from an underlying medical malpractice action to pay for the continued care. After ten years without improvement, but facing only continual deterioration, Michael, as Guardian (P), petitioned the court for an order to terminate artificial life support. The trial court granted the order and Parents (D) now appeal.

ISSUE: Does the clear and convincing standard of proof permit a decision in the face of inconsistent or conflicting evidence?

HOLDING AND DECISION: (Altenbernd, J.) Yes. The clear and convincing standard of proof permits a decision to terminate life support in the face of inconsistent or conflicting evidence. The default in such instances is to err on the side of life. As an initial matter, there is no merit to the Parents' (D) argument that Guardian (P) has a conflict of interest regarding inheriting the remaining settlement funds. In this instance, Guardian (P), instead of deciding the issue himself, chose to present the evidence to the court, and, after hearing contrary evidence from Parents (D), the trial court became the surrogate decisionmaker when granting the order to terminate life support. No conflict of interest exists between the decisionmaker and Theresa's wishes. Moreover, the fact that sufficient funds exist from the settlement of the medical malpractice suit to continue to provide futile care does alter the quantum of evidence presented regarding Theresa's wishes not to receive that care. Secondly, Parents (D) challenge the social science evidence presented by Beverly Tyler, the executive director of Georgia Health Decisions, as being prejudicial. The evidence presented from this expert witness concerned studies on American values, and opinions and attitudes concerning the decision to discontinue life support. After a thorough review of the record we find no evidence that the trial judge gave any undue weight to this evidence that would have prejudiced his decision. The testimony in this case established that Theresa was very young at the time of the tragedy, was without children, and had not contemplated drafting a will. However, statements Theresa made to her friends and family, along with other evidence, was sufficient to prove that Theresa would not wish for life support to be continued under the circumstances of her present medical condition. The decision of the trial court is affirmed.

ANALYSIS

While the appellate court found sufficient evidence to affirm the trial court's decision in this case, the court emphasizes the default rule that if enough conflicting evidence exists the clear and convincing evidence standard will not be met. In cases that do not involve life support, this threshold is much lower. This case garnered national attention when Governor Jeb Bush intervened with a freshly passed statute, "Terri's Law," granting him authority to overrule the courts and order the feeding tube replaced. Ultimately, the Florida Supreme Court struck down the law as being a violation of the Separation of Powers Doctrine, but stayed the removal of Theresa's feeding tube pending a ruling by the U.S. Supreme Court on whether or not to hear the case based upon a Fourteenth Amendment Equal Protection claim. The high court declined. Once the Supreme Court denied certiorari, a flurry of court challenges ensued in the state courts of Florida contesting Michael's guardianship and alleging violations of Theresa's rights to due process and religious freedom. All of these challenges were denied, and Theresa's feeding tube was removed by court order on March 18, 2005. On March 20, 2005, in an unprecedented action, Congress attempted to intervene by passing a law extending jurisdiction of the state court's guardianship determination to the federal courts. The federal district court and the United States Court of Appeals for the Eleventh Circuit denied the requested injunctive relief for an order to reinsert the feeding tube. The U.S.

Continued on next page.

Supreme Court again denied certiorari. Theresa passed away on March 31, 2005.

Quicknotes

FOURTEENTH AMENDMENT DUE PROCESS CLAUSE Provides that protections mandated by the Constitution and observed by the federal government are equally applicable, and therefore must be observed by the states.

SEPARATION OF POWERS DOCTRINE Each branch of government is precluded from interfering with the authority of another.

Superintendent of Belchertown State School v. Saikewicz

Residential center (P) v. Incompetent (D)

Mass. Sup. Jud. Ct., 373 Mass. 728, 370 N.E.2d 417 (1977).

NATURE OF CASE: Review of order regarding the provision of medical treatment.

FACT SUMMARY: The issue arose as to whether Saikewicz (D), incompetent from birth, was required to undergo lifesaving medical treatment.

RULE OF LAW

An individual who is incompetent from birth is not required to undergo lifesaving medical treatment.

FACTS: Saikewicz (D), who suffered from severe congenital mental retardation, was legally incompetent. An issue arose as to whether he was required to undergo lifesaving medical treatment. [The casebook opinion did not state the nature of his medical condition, who the actual litigants in the dispute were, or the result in the lower court.]

ISSUE: Is an individual who is incompetent from birth required to undergo lifesaving medical treatment?

HOLDING AND DECISION: (Liacos, J.) No. An individual who is incompetent from birth is not required to undergo lifesaving medical treatment. Principles of equity and respect for all individuals mandate that lifelong incompetents have the opportunity that other citizens have to refuse medical treatment. Since an incompetent cannot choose for himself, the state as parens patriae must attempt to assess, in its substituted judgment, that which is in the best interests of the incompetent. When it appears that those interests are not served by the provision of lifesaving medical care, this care should not be mandated. This should be as subjective a standard as possible, taking into account all relevant factors regarding the incompetent. In this case, the facts on the record support the proposition that Saikewicz (D), if competent, would have declined treatment.

ANALYSIS

The court states that the decision regarding the incompetent should be as subjective as possible. This is conceptually a difficult proposition, for decisions of this nature are largely beyond an incompetent's comprehension. The concept of "substituted judgment" is the court's best answer to this difficult problem.

Quicknotes

GUARDIAN AD LITEM Person designated by the court to represent an infant or ward in a particular legal proceeding.

PARENS PATRIAE Maxim that the government as sovereign is conferred with the duty to act as guardian on behalf of those citizens under legal disability.

In re Storar

Hospital (D) v. Incompetent's mother (D)

N.Y. Ct. App., 52 N.Y.2d 363, 420 N.E.2d 64 (1981).

NATURE OF CASE: Appeal of order denying petition for authorization to perform medical treatment.

FACT SUMMARY: The guardian (D) of lifelong incompetent Storar, who was dying of cancer, declined to authorize blood transfusions which would prevent an earlier death from blood loss.

RULE OF LAW

The guardian of a lifelong incompetent may not withhold medical treatment in a belief that such withholding is in the incompetent's best interests.

FACTS: Storar, fifty-two years of age, had a mental age of eighteen months, having been retarded from birth. He was diagnosed as having terminal bladder cancer. The lesions in his bladder were bleeding, and Storar required transfusions to stay alive. His guardian (D), who was his mother, initially consented to the transfusions, but later withdrew consent. The hospital (P) petitioned for an order authorizing the transfusions. Storar was incapable of comprehending the purpose of the transfusions. The transfusions were painful, but Storar was sedated during the procedures. The trial court denied the petition, and the appellate division affirmed. The New York Court of Appeals granted review.

ISSUE: May the guardian of a lifelong incompetent withhold medical treatment in a belief that such withholding is in the incompetent's best interests?

HOLDING AND DECISION: (Wachtler, J.) No. The guardian of a lifelong incompetent may not withhold medical treatment in a belief that such withholding is in the incompetent's best interests. An incompetent cannot decide for himself with respect to the provision of medical treatment, much as an infant cannot. A parent cannot deprive a child of lifesaving treatment, no matter how well intentioned. So it is with the guardian of an incompetent; consent to lifesaving treatment may not be withheld. Here, Storar is faced with the prospect of death by blood loss, and his guardian may not withhold consent that he be treated. The fact that he will die from cancer within the foreseeable future does not alter this analysis. Reversed.

ANALYSIS

This case should be compared with Judge Wachtler's opinion in *In re Eichner*, 420 N.E.2d 64 (N.Y. 1981), a companion case to the present opinion. There, a guardian was allowed to withhold authorization for treatment. The difference was that Eichner had at one point been competent and had made his wishes known.

Quicknotes

PARENS PATRIAE Maxim that the government as sovereign is conferred with the duty to act as guardian on behalf of those citizens under legal disability.

Newmark v. Williams

Child protective services (P) v. Christian Scientist parents (D)

Del. Sup. Ct., 588 A.2d 1108 (1991).

NATURE OF CASE: Appeal of a petition by the state to compel medical treatment for a child.

FACT SUMMARY: Colin Newmark's parents (D) refused medical treatment for his advanced cancer, preferring instead a course of prayer.

RULE OF LAW

The state's interest in preserving life must be weighed against the constitutionally protected interests of the individual.

FACTS: Colin Newmark suffered from a severe form of cancer that was almost certainly fatal. His parents (D), Christian Scientists, refused chemotherapy for their child. A state law exempted from abuse and neglect statutes those parents who refused treatment for their children for medical reasons. Child Protective Services (P) sought to compel the treatment.

ISSUE: Must the state's interest in preserving life be weighed against the constitutionally protected interests of the individual?

HOLDING AND DECISION: (Moore, J.) Yes. The state's interest in preserving life must be weighed against the constitutionally protected interests of the individual. Parents can choose, for religious reasons, to refuse medical treatment for their children. The parental right to choose for a child can only be invaded for the most compelling of reasons. To determine what is in Colin's best interests, the court must consider the effectiveness of the treatment prescribed for him and the treatment's probable effect on him. In this case, the chemotherapy recommended by his doctor would have subjected Colin to great agony and probably failed in the end. The Newmarks' (D) parental prerogative and Colin's right to some human dignity in the short time left to him, when weighed against futile and painful medical treatments, are paramount.

ANALYSIS

Most states start with an assumption in favor of parental autonomy. Where a compelling reason exists to invade the parental rights, the presumption can be surmounted. Most often the concerns of the state are weighed against the rights and concerns of the parents in selecting the appropriate course of action.

Quicknotes

FUNDAMENTAL RIGHT A liberty that is either expressly or impliedly provided for in the United States Constitution, the deprivation or burdening of which is subject to a heightened standard of review.

Miller v. HCA, Inc.

Parents (P) v. Health care corporation (D)

Tex. Sup. Ct., 118 S.W.3d 758 (2003).

NATURE OF CASE: Appeal from the reversal of verdict for plaintiff.

FACT SUMMARY: Karla and Mark Miller (Parents) (P) brought suit alleging battery and negligence against Hospital Corporation of America, Inc. (HCA) (D) for wrongly resuscitating an infant in distress without consent.

RULE OF LAW

The "emergency circumstances" exception to battery applies in situations where life-sustaining treatment is provided to an infant without the parents' informed consent.

FACTS: Karla Miller (P), approximately 23 weeks into her pregnancy, presented to the hospital with premature labor. Her physicians informed her that she had an infection that could endanger her life and that they may need to induce labor. The physicians also informed the Millers (P) that if they induced labor, there was little chance of the infant surviving, and if it did survive it would suffer from severe impairments, including cerebral palsy, brain hemorrhage, blindness, lung disease, and mental retardation. The physicians then asked the Millers (P) to decide if they wanted life-sustaining measures for the infant if they were forced to induce labor. The Millers (P) decided against having any heroic measures, which they understood to mean no cardiopulmonary resuscitation and no life-support machines. The hospital administrators and physicians then held a meeting to discuss the situation and it was revealed that the hospital had a policy requiring resuscitation for any baby born with a birth weight of greater than 500 grams. The hospital and the physicians decided that a neonatologist would be present at the delivery and evaluate what treatment to give the infant. The hospital administrators then asked the Millers (P) for consent for treating the infant, and they again refused. Ultimately, the infant was born alive with a birth weight of 615 grams. At birth, the infant was in distress and a decision was made by the neonatologist to administer oxygen. Within the first few days of birth, the infant suffered a cerebral hemorrhage resulting in severe mental and physical impairments. In fact, the child suffered the exact impairments that were predicted cerebral palsy, brain hemorrhage, blindness, lung disease, and mental retardation plus seizures and quadriparesis. At the time of trial, the child was seven years old and could not walk, talk, feed herself or sit up. The Millers (P) elected to sue the hospital and HCA (D), the hospital's corporate owner, and declined to sue any of the physicians. HCA's (D) trial was held separately and the jury, finding HCA (D) to be grossly negligent, returned a verdict in favor of the Millers (P). HCA (D) appealed and the court of appeals reversed reasoning that unless the infant's condition was "certifiably terminal" under the Texas Natural Death Act that the Millers (P) had no right to refuse treatment for the infant. This appeal ensued.

ISSUE: Does the "emergency circumstances" exception to battery apply in situations where life-sustaining treatment is provided to an infant without the parents' informed consent?

HOLDING AND DECISION: (Enoch, J.) Yes. The "emergency circumstances" exception to battery applies in situations where life-sustaining treatment is provided to an infant without the parents' informed consent. Prior to the birth of the infant, the parents would have to rely solely on speculation as to what care or treatment would be required. Consequently, the Millers' (P) decision before the birth was not a fully informed one. When the infant was born the neonatologist made a split-second decision to administer oxygen and there was no time to obtain the Millers' (P) consent, or, had consent been denied, to attempt to obtain a court order to challenge the withholding of consent. The Millers (P) predicated their cause of action on a theory of hospital negligence for having policies that led to the negligent battery upon the infant. Because the doctor was responding to emergent conditions there was no battery by virtue of the emergency circumstances doctrine, and because the doctor cannot be held liable for either negligence or battery, HCA (D) cannot be held vicariously liable. Consequently, the court need not reach the other issues presented. Affirmed.

ANALYSIS

The court declined to specifically address the court of appeals reasoning regarding the application of the Texas Natural Death Act. However, in dicta, the court noted that the Act did not supersede any legal right a person has to withhold or withdraw life-sustaining treatment. The court also declined an invitation to examine if the federal "Baby Doe" regulations applied. The court was making it clear that it did not intend to set contrary precedent when there was an existing and less legally offensive method to reach a decision. Frequently, what a state Supreme Court does not decide is just as important as what it does decide. The Millers (P) may have faired better with a claim for wrongful life. But absent pleading a wrongful life claim, the court cannot weigh the benefits of an impaired life compared to

Continued on next page.

no life. It is clear that the courts do not wish to hold health care providers liable in instances where failure to provide emergency treatment could result in a claim of negligent or intentional abandonment. To do so would create a situation where the provider is damned if he does intervene and damned if he does not intervene.

Quicknotes

BATTERY Unlawful contact with the body of another person.

NEGLIGENCE Conduct falling below the standard of care that a reasonable person would demonstrate under similar conditions.

VICARIOUS LIABILITY The imputed liability of one party for the unlawful acts of another.

Washington v. Glucksberg

State (D) v. Patient (P)

521 U.S. 702 (1997).

NATURE OF CASE: Review of a decision that a state statute banning assisted suicide was unconstitutional.

FACT SUMMARY: The Washington assisted suicide statute was challenged as unconstitutional.

RULE OF LAW

The right to assisted suicide is not a fundamental right protected by the Due Process Clause of the Fourteenth Amendment, and any legislation restricting that right will be upheld where the state has an important interest and the statute is reasonably related to its promotion.

FACTS: Glucksberg (P) sued the state of Washington (D), alleging that its prohibition against causing or aiding a suicide offended the Fourteenth Amendment of the United States Constitution. Glucksberg (P) asserted the existence of a liberty interest protected by the Fourteenth Amendment which extends to a personal choice by a mentally competent, terminally ill adult to commit physician-assisted suicide. The district court agreed, and concluded that the statute was unconstitutional because it placed an undue burden on the exercise of that constitutionally protected interest. A panel of the court of appeals for the Ninth Circuit reversed. The Ninth Circuit reheard the case en banc, reversed the panel's decision, and affirmed the district court. The court decided that the statute was unconstitutional as applied to terminally ill competent adults who wish to hasten their deaths with medication prescribed by their physicians. The Supreme Court granted certiorari.

ISSUE: Is not the right to assisted suicide fundamental under the Due Process Clause, and may legislation restrict that right where the state has an important interest and the statute is reasonably related to its promotion?

HOLDING AND DECISION: (Rehnquist, C.J.) Yes. The right to assisted suicide is not a fundamental right protected by the Due Process Clause of the Fourteenth Amendment, and any legislation restricting that right will be upheld where the state has an important interest and the statute is reasonably related to its promotion. That many of the rights and liberties protected by the Due Process Clause sound in personal autonomy does not warrant the sweeping conclusion that any and all important, intimate, and personal decisions are so protected. The history of the law's treatment of assisted suicides in this country has been and continues to be one of the rejection of nearly all efforts to permit it. The asserted "right" to assistance in committing suicide is not a fundamental liberty interest protected by the Due Process Clause. Since Washington's assisted suicide statute implicates a number of state interests, it is rationally related to legitimate government interests. The Washington statute does not violate the Fourteenth Amendment, either on its face or as applied to competent, terminally ill adults who wish to hasten their deaths by obtaining medication prescribed by their doctors. Reversed and remanded.

CONCURRENCE: (O'Connor, J.) There is no generalized right to commit suicide. A patient who is suffering from a terminal illness and who is experiencing great pain has no legal barriers to obtaining medication from qualified physicians or to alleviate that suffering, even to the point of causing unconsciousness and hastening death.

CONCURRENCE: (Stevens, J.) History and tradition provide ample support for refusing to recognize an open-ended constitutional right to commit suicide. The state has a compelling interest in preventing persons from committing suicide because of depression, or coercion by third parties. It is clear that the so-called unqualified interest in the preservation of human life is not itself sufficient to outweigh the interest in liberty that may justify the only possible means of preserving a dying patient's dignity and alleviating her intolerable suffering.

CONCURRENCE: (Souter, J.) The importance of the individual interest here, as within that class of certain interests demanding careful scrutiny of the state's contrary claim, cannot be gainsaid. Whether that interest might in some circumstances, or at some time, be seen as fundamental to the degree entitled to prevail is not, however, a conclusion that I need draw here, for I am satisfied that the state's interests described here are sufficiently serious to defeat the present claim that its law is arbitrary or purposeless. The state claims an interest in protecting patients from mistakenly and involuntarily deciding to end their lives, and in guarding against both voluntary and involuntary euthanasia.

CONCURRENCE: (Breyer, J.) I do not believe that this court need or now should decide whether or not a right to die with dignity is fundamental. The laws of New York and of Washington do not prohibit doctors from providing patients with drugs sufficient to control pain despite the risk that those drugs themselves will kill.

Continued on next page.

ANALYSIS

Although the Supreme Court decided in *Cruzan v. Director, Mo. Dept. of Health*, 497 U.S. 261 (1990), that the Constitution granted competent persons a constitutionally protected right to refuse lifesaving hydration and nutrition, no general "right to die" exists. The Netherlands has recently permitted the practice of euthanasia, but no reliable statistics are yet available to evaluate the results. The court noted that the right to physician-assisted suicide would in effect lead to a much broader license that could prove extremely difficult to police and contain.

Quicknotes

DUE PROCESS The constitutional mandate requiring the courts to protect and enforce individuals' rights and liberties consistent with prevailing principles of fairness and justice and prohibiting the federal and state governments from such activities that deprive its citizens of a life, liberty or property interest.

FOURTEENTH AMENDMENT No person shall be deprived of life, liberty, or property, without the due process of law.

FUNDAMENTAL RIGHT A liberty that is either expressly or implicitly provided for in the United States Constitution, the deprivation or burdening of which is subject to a heightened standard of review.

LIBERTY INTEREST A right conferred by the Due Process Clauses of the state and federal constitutions.

Vacco v. Quill

State (D) v. Patient (P)

521 U.S. 793 (1997).

NATURE OF CASE: Review of appellate decision that New York's statute prohibiting assisted suicide was unconstitutional.

FACT SUMMARY: A state statute forbidding assisted suicide was challenged as unconstitutional under the Equal Protection Clause of the Fourteenth Amendment.

RULE OF LAW

Although a distinction exists between refusing lifesaving medical treatment and assisted suicide, neither violates the Equal Protection Clause since they apply evenhandedly to all.

FACTS: Quill (P) and three gravely ill patients who have since died sued New York State's Attorney General (D). They urged that because New York (D) permits a competent person to refuse life-sustaining medical treatment, and the refusal of such treatment is "essentially the same thing" as physician-assisted suicide, New York's (D) ban on assisting suicide violated the Equal Protection Clause of the Fourteenth Amendment. The district court disagreed, but the court of appeals for the Second Circuit reversed, finding that those in the final stages of fatal illness who were on life-support systems were allowed to hasten their deaths by directing the removal of such systems; but those who were similarly situated, except for the previous attachment of life-sustaining equipment, were not allowed to hasten death by self-administering prescribed drugs. The court of appeals concluded that this supposed unequal treatment was not rationally related to any legitimate state interest. The Supreme Court granted certiorari.

ISSUE: Although a distinction exists between refusing lifesaving medical treatment and assisted suicide, does this distinction operate in violation of the Equal Protection Clause by treating persons wishing to end their lives differently?

HOLDING AND DECISION: (Rehnquist, C.J.) No. Although a distinction exists between refusing lifesaving medical treatment and assisted suicide, neither violate Equal Protection since they apply evenhandedly to all. Logic and contemporary practice support New York's (D) judgment that the two acts are different, and New York (D) may, therefore, consistent with the Constitution, treat them differently. A doctor who assists a suicide must, necessarily and indubitably, intend primarily that the patient be made dead. The law has long used actors' intent or purpose to distinguish between two acts that may have the same result. The overwhelming majority of state legislatures have drawn a clear line between assisted suicide and withdrawing or permitting the refusal of unwanted lifesaving medical treatment by prohibiting the former but permitting the latter. New York's (D) statutes outlawing assisted suicide neither infringe fundamental rights nor involve suspect classifications, and are therefore entitled to a strong presumption of validity. On their faces, neither New York's (D) ban on assisted suicide nor its statutes permitting patients to refuse medical treatment treat anyone differently than anyone else or draw any distinctions between persons. Generally speaking, laws that apply evenhandedly to all unquestionably comply with the Equal Protection Clause. Reversed.

CONCURRENCE: (Souter, J.) The reasons that lead me to conclude in *Glucksberg* that the prohibition on assisted suicide is not arbitrary under the due process standard also support the distinction between assistance to suicide, which is banned, and practices such as termination of artificial life support and death-hastening pain medication, which are permitted.

ANALYSIS

Physicians assisting in their patients' suicides are usually not convicted by juries. Assisted suicide and euthanasia are officially prohibited, but physicians are not criminally prosecuted for either.

Quicknotes

EQUAL PROTECTION CLAUSE A constitutional guarantee that no person should be denied the same protection of the laws enjoyed by other persons in like circumstances.

FOURTEENTH AMENDMENT No person shall be deprived of life, liberty, or property, without the due process of law.

FUNDAMENTAL RIGHT A liberty that is either expressly or implicitly provided for in the United States Constitution, the deprivation or burdening of which is subject to a heightened standard of review.

RATIONAL BASIS REVIEW A test employed by the court to determine the validity of a statute in equal protection actions, whereby the court determines whether the challenged statute is rationally related to the achievement of a legitimate state interest.

CHAPTER 20

Regulation of Research Involving Human Subjects

Quick Reference Rules of Law

Grimes v. Kennedy Krieger Institute, Inc.

Parents of research subjects (P) v. Research institute (D)

Md. Ct. App., 366 Md. 29, 782 A.2d 807 (2001).

NATURE OF CASE: Appeal from the grant of summary judgment.

FACT SUMMARY: The circuit court granted summary judgment to the Kennedy Krieger Institute, Inc. (KKI) (D). Parents (P) of the children subject to the research study conducted by KKI (D) appealed, contending that KKI (D) owed a duty of care based on the nature of its relationship with the parents (P) and the children participating in the study.

RULE OF LAW

Under Maryland law, informed consent agreements in nontherapeutic research projects can constitute contracts and can constitute special relationships giving rise to duties, out of the breach of which negligence actions may lie.

FACTS: The Kennedy Krieger Institute (KKI), a prestigious research institute associated with Johns Hopkins University, created a nontherapeutic research program whereby it required certain classes of homes to have only partial lead paint abatement modifications performed. In at least some instances, including this case, the institute arranged for the landlords to receive public funding by way of grants or loans to aid in the modifications. The research institute then encouraged, and sometimes required, that the landlords rent the premises to families with young children. Children were encouraged to reside in households where the possibility of lead dust was known to the researchers to be likely, so that lead dust content of their blood could be compared with the level of lead dust in the houses at periodic intervals over a two-year period. The continuing presence of children was required in the subject houses in order for the study to be complete. The purpose of the research was to determine how effective varying degrees of lead paint abatement procedures were. The researchers acknowledged that lead paint was particularly hazardous to children, and that lead dust often remained/returned to abated houses over a period of time. The Institutional Review Board (IRB) overseeing this research abdicated its responsibility to review the potential safety and health hazard impact of this nontherapeutic study, instead advising the institute to recast the study so as to obscure such dangers. The research study was sponsored jointly by the EPA and the Maryland Department of Housing and Community Development. The parents (P) of children with elevated blood levels of lead brought this action against KKI (D). KKI (D) moved for summary judgment on the basis that no contract existed between KKI (D) and the plaintiffs, and there was inherently no duty owed to a research subject by a researcher. The circuit court granted KKI's (D) motion. The parents (P) of the child subjects appealed, contending that KKI (D) owed a duty of care based on the nature of its relationship with the parents (P) and the children participating in the study based on a contract between the parties, the voluntary assumption by KKI (D), a special relationship between the parties and federal regulation.

ISSUE: Under Maryland law, can informed consent agreements in nontherapeutic research projects constitute contracts and can the agreements constitute special relationships giving rise to duties, out of the breach of which negligence actions may lie?

HOLDING AND DECISION: (Cathell, J.) Yes. Under Maryland law, informed consent agreements in nontherapeutic research projects can constitute contracts and can constitute special relationships giving rise to duties, out of the breach of which negligence actions may lie. The very nature of nontherapeutic scientific research on human subjects can create special relationships out of which duties arise. Researchers do not have a right to place children in potentially hazardous living situations for nontherapeutic studies such as the one at issue in this case. Additionally, parents, whether improperly enticed by food stamps, money or other items, have no more right to intentionally and unnecessarily place children in potentially hazardous nontherapeutic research settings. IRBs are not designed to be objective, as they are generally internal boards tied as much to the success of a research project as to its ethical implications. This is evident in this case, where the IRB did not ensure the safety of the children subjects, but encouraged researchers to misrepresent the research as therapeutic in nature. Special relationships are created between researchers and their human subjects generally. Finally, government regulations can create duties on the part of researchers toward human subjects out of which special relationships may arise. Special relationships are to be determined on a case-by-case basis. The circuit court erred in granting KKI's (D) motions for summary judgment. Reversed.

CONCURRENCE: (Raker, J.) The majority correctly found that a special relationship existed between the parties giving rise to an action in tort, but went too far when it decided the duty of care was breached in this case.

ANALYSIS

The court in *Grimes* denied a motion for reconsideration in this case. Judge Raker dissented, arguing that the

Continued on next page.

majority's discussion of the ability of a parent or guardian to consent to the participation of a minor child in a non-therapeutic research study in the opinion was a statement of public policy, best left to the Legislature.

Quicknotes

DOCTRINE OF INFORMED CONSENT Consent to a particular occurrence requiring full notification as to the consequences of that consent.

DUTY OF CARE A principle of negligence requiring an individual to act in such a manner as to avoid injury to a person to whom he or she owes an obligatory duty.

NEGLIGENCE Conduct falling below the standard of care that a reasonable person would demonstrate under similar conditions.

Glossary

Common Latin Words and Phrases Encountered in the Law

A FORTIORI: Because one fact exists or has been proven, therefore a second fact that is related to the first fact must also exist.

A PRIORI: From the cause to the effect. A term of logic used to denote that when one generally accepted truth is shown to be a cause, another particular effect must necessarily follow.

AB INITIO: From the beginning; a condition which has existed throughout, as in a marriage which was void ab initio.

ACTUS REUS: The wrongful act; in criminal law, such action sufficient to trigger criminal liability.

AD VALOREM: According to value; an ad valorem tax is imposed upon an item located within the taxing jurisdiction calculated by the value of such item.

AMICUS CURIAE: Friend of the court. Its most common usage takes the form of an amicus curiae brief, filed by a person who is not a party to an action but is nonetheless allowed to offer an argument supporting his legal interests.

ARGUENDO: In arguing. A statement, possibly hypothetical, made for the purpose of argument, is one made arguendo.

BILL QUIA TIMET: A bill to quiet title (establish ownership) to real property.

BONA FIDE: True, honest, or genuine. May refer to a person's legal position based on good faith or lacking notice of fraud (such as a bona fide purchaser for value) or to the authenticity of a particular document (such as a bona fide last will and testament).

CAUSA MORTIS: With approaching death in mind. A gift causa mortis is a gift given by a party who feels certain that death is imminent.

CAVEAT EMPTOR: Let the buyer beware. This maxim is reflected in the rule of law that a buyer purchases at his own risk because it is his responsibility to examine, judge, test, and otherwise inspect what he is buying.

CERTIORARI: A writ of review. Petitions for review of a case by the United States Supreme Court are most often done by means of a writ of certiorari.

CONTRA: On the other hand. Opposite. Contrary to.

CORAM NOBIS: Before us; writs of error directed to the court that originally rendered the judgment.

CORAM VOBIS: Before you; writs of error directed by an appellate court to a lower court to correct a factual error.

CORPUS DELICTI: The body of the crime; the requisite elements of a crime amounting to objective proof that a crime has been committed.

CUM TESTAMENTO ANNEXO, ADMINISTRATOR (ADMINISTRATOR C.T.A.): With will annexed; an administrator c.t.a. settles an estate pursuant to a will in which he is not appointed.

DE BONIS NON, ADMINISTRATOR (ADMINISTRATOR D.B.N.): Of goods not administered; an administrator d.b.n. settles a partially settled estate.

DE FACTO: In fact; in reality; actually. Existing in fact but not officially approved or engendered.

DE JURE: By right; lawful. Describes a condition that is legitimate "as a matter of law," in contrast to the term "de facto," which connotes something existing in fact but not legally sanctioned or authorized. For example, de facto segregation refers to segregation brought about by housing patterns, etc., whereas de jure segregation refers to segregation created by law.

DE MINIMIS: Of minimal importance; insignificant; a trifle; not worth bothering about.

DE NOVO: Anew; a second time; afresh. A trial de novo is a new trial held at the appellate level as if the case originated there and the trial at a lower level had not taken place.

DICTA: Generally used as an abbreviated form of obiter dicta, a term describing those portions of a judicial opinion incidental or not necessary to resolution of the specific question before the court. Such nonessential statements and remarks are not considered to be binding precedent.

DUCES TECUM: Refers to a particular type of writ or subpoena requesting a party or organization to produce certain documents in their possession.

EN BANC: Full bench. Where a court sits with all justices present rather than the usual quorum.

EX PARTE: For one side or one party only. An ex parte proceeding is one undertaken for the benefit of only one party, without notice to, or an appearance by, an adverse party.

EX POST FACTO: After the fact. An ex post facto law is a law that retroactively changes the consequences of a prior act.

EX REL.: Abbreviated form of the term ex relatione, meaning upon relation or information. When the state brings an action in which it has no interest against an individual at the instigation of one who has a private interest in the matter.

FORUM NON CONVENIENS: Inconvenient forum. Although a court may have jurisdiction over the case, the action should be tried in a more conveniently located court, one to which parties and witnesses may more easily travel, for example.

GUARDIAN AD LITEM: A guardian of an infant as to litigation, appointed to represent the infant and pursue his/her rights.

HABEAS CORPUS: You have the body. The modern writ of habeas corpus is a writ directing that a person (body) being detained (such as a prisoner) be brought before the court so that the legality of his detention can be judicially ascertained.

IN CAMERA: In private, in chambers. When a hearing is held before a judge in his chambers or when all spectators are excluded from the courtroom.

IN FORMA PAUPERIS: In the manner of a pauper. A party who proceeds in forma pauperis because of his poverty is one who is allowed to bring suit without liability for costs.

INFRA: Below, under. A word referring the reader to a later part of a book. (The opposite of supra.)

IN LOCO PARENTIS: In the place of a parent.

IN PARI DELICTO: Equally wrong; a court of equity will not grant requested relief to an applicant who is in pari delicto, or as much at fault in the transactions giving rise to the controversy as is the opponent of the applicant.

IN PARI MATERIA: On like subject matter or upon the same matter. Statutes relating to the same person or things are said to be in pari materia. It is a general rule of statutory construction that such statutes should be construed together, i.e., looked at as if they together constituted one law.

IN PERSONAM: Against the person. Jurisdiction over the person of an individual.

IN RE: In the matter of. Used to designate a proceeding involving an estate or other property.

IN REM: A term that signifies an action against the res, or thing. An action in rem is basically one that is taken directly against property, as distinguished from an action in personam, i.e., against the person.

INTER ALIA: Among other things. Used to show that the whole of a statement, pleading, list, statute, etc., has not been set forth in its entirety.

INTER PARTES: Between the parties. May refer to contracts, conveyances or other transactions having legal significance.

INTER VIVOS: Between the living. An inter vivos gift is a gift made by a living grantor, as distinguished from bequests contained in a will, which pass upon the death of the testator.

IPSO FACTO: By the mere fact itself.

JUS: Law or the entire body of law.

LEX LOCI: The law of the place; the notion that the rights of parties to a legal proceeding are governed by the law of the place where those rights arose.

MALUM IN SE: Evil or wrong in and of itself; inherently wrong. This term describes an act that is wrong by its very nature, as opposed to one which would not be wrong but for the fact that there is a specific legal prohibition against it (malum prohibitum).

MALUM PROHIBITUM: Wrong because prohibited, but not inherently evil. Used to describe something that is wrong because it is expressly forbidden by law but that is not in and of itself evil, e.g., speeding.

MANDAMUS: We command. A writ directing an official to take a certain action.

MENS REA: A guilty mind; a criminal intent. A term used to signify the mental state that accompanies a crime or other prohibited act. Some crimes require only a general mens rea (general intent to do the prohibited act), but others, like assault with intent to murder, require the existence of a specific mens rea.

MODUS OPERANDI: Method of operating; generally refers to the manner or style of a criminal in committing crimes, admissible in appropriate cases as evidence of the identity of a defendant.

NEXUS: A connection to.

NISI PRIUS: A court of first impression. A nisi prius court is one where issues of fact are tried before a judge or jury.

N.O.V. (NON OBSTANTE VEREDICTO): Notwithstanding the verdict. A judgment n.o.v. is a judgment given in favor of one party despite the fact that a verdict was returned in favor of the other party, the justification being that the verdict either had no reasonable support in fact or was contrary to law.

NUNC PRO TUNC: Now for then. This phrase refers to actions that may be taken and will then have full retroactive effect.

PENDENTE LITE: Pending the suit; pending litigation underway.

PER CAPITA: By head; beneficiaries of an estate, if they take in equal shares, take per capita.

PER CURIAM: By the court; signifies an opinion ostensibly written "by the whole court" and with no identified author.

PER SE: By itself, in itself; inherently.

PER STIRPES: By representation. Used primarily in the law of wills to describe the method of distribution where a person, generally because of death, is unable to take that which is left to him by the will of another, and therefore his heirs divide such property between them rather than take under the will individually.

PRIMA FACIE: On its face; at first sight. A prima facie case is one that is sufficient on its face, meaning that the evidence supporting it is adequate to establish the case until contradicted or overcome by other evidence.

PRO TANTO: For so much; as far as it goes. Often used in eminent domain cases when a property owner receives partial payment for his land without prejudice to his right to bring suit for the full amount he claims his land to be worth.

QUANTUM MERUIT: As much as he deserves. Refers to recovery based on the doctrine of unjust enrichment in those cases in which a party has rendered valuable services or furnished materials that were accepted and enjoyed by another under circumstances that would reasonably notify the recipient that the rendering party expected to be paid. In essence, the law implies a contract to pay the reasonable value of the services or materials furnished.

QUASI: Almost like; as if; nearly. This term is essentially used to signify that one subject or thing is almost analogous to another but that material differences between them do exist. For example, a quasi-criminal proceeding is one that is not strictly criminal but shares enough of the same characteristics to require some of the same safeguards (e.g., procedural due process must be followed in a parole hearing).

QUID PRO QUO: Something for something. In contract law, the consideration, something of value, passed between the parties to render the contract binding.

RES GESTAE: Things done; in evidence law, this principle justifies the admission of a statement that would otherwise be hearsay when it is made so closely to the event in question as to be said to be a part of it, or with such spontaneity as not to have the possibility of falsehood.

RES IPSA LOQUITUR: The thing speaks for itself. This doctrine gives rise to a rebuttable presumption of negligence when the instrumentality causing the injury was within the exclusive control of the defendant, and the injury was one that does not normally occur unless a person has been negligent.

RES JUDICATA: A matter adjudged. Doctrine which provides that once a court of competent jurisdiction has rendered a final judgment or decree on the merits, that judgment or decree is conclusive upon the parties to the case and prevents them from engaging in any other litigation on the points and issues determined therein.

RESPONDEAT SUPERIOR: Let the master reply. This doctrine holds the master liable for the wrongful acts of his servant (or the principal for his agent) in those cases in which the servant (or agent) was acting within the scope of his authority at the time of the injury.

STARE DECISIS: To stand by or adhere to that which has been decided. The common law doctrine of stare decisis attempts to give security and certainty to the law by following the policy that once a principle of law as applicable to a certain set of facts has been set forth in a decision, it forms a precedent which will subsequently be followed, even though a different decision might be made were it the first time the question had arisen. Of course, stare decisis is not an inviolable principle and is departed from in instances where there is good cause (e.g., considerations of public policy led the Supreme Court to disregard prior decisions sanctioning segregation).

SUPRA: Above. A word referring a reader to an earlier part of a book.

ULTRA VIRES: Beyond the power. This phrase is most commonly used to refer to actions taken by a corporation that are beyond the power or legal authority of the corporation.

Addendum of French Derivatives

IN PAIS: Not pursuant to legal proceedings.

CHATTEL: Tangible personal property.

CY PRES: Doctrine permitting courts to apply trust funds to purposes not expressed in the trust but necessary to carry out the settlor's intent.

PER AUTRE VIE: For another's life; during another's life. In property law, an estate may be granted that will terminate upon the death of someone other than the grantee.

PROFIT A PRENDRE: A license to remove minerals or other produce from land.

VOIR DIRE: Process of questioning jurors as to their predispositions about the case or parties to a proceeding in order to identify those jurors displaying bias or prejudice.

Casenote Legal Briefs

Administrative Law	Breyer, Stewart, Sunstein & Vermeule
Administrative Law	Cass, Diver & Beermann
Administrative Law	Funk, Shapiro & Weaver
Administrative Law	Mashaw, Merrill & Shane
Administrative Law	Strauss, Rakoff, & Farina (Gellhorn & Byse)
Agency & Partnership	Hynes & Loewenstein
Antitrust	Pitofsky, Goldschmid & Wood
Antitrust	Sullivan & Hovenkamp
Bankruptcy	Warren & Bussel
Bankruptcy	Warren & Westbrook
Business Organizations	Allen, Kraakman & Subramanian
Business Organizations	Bauman, Weiss & Palmiter
Business Organizations	Hamilton & Macey
Business Organizations	Klein, Ramseyer & Bainbridge
Business Organizations	O'Kelley & Thompson
Business Organizations	Soderquist, Smiddy & Cunningham
Civil Procedure	Field, Kaplan & Clermont
Civil Procedure	Freer & Perdue
Civil Procedure	Friedenthal, Miller, Sexton & Hershkoff
Civil Procedure	Hazard, Tait, Fletcher & Bundy
Civil Procedure	Marcus, Redish & Sherman
Civil Procedure	Subrin, Minow, Brodin & Main
Civil Procedure	Yeazell
Commercial Law	LoPucki, Warren, Keating & Mann
Commercial Law	Warren & Walt
Commercial Law	Whaley
Community Property	Bird
Community Property	Blumberg
Conflicts	Brilmayer & Goldsmith
Conflicts	Currie, Kay, Kramer & Roosevelt
Constitutional Law	Brest, Levinson, Balkin & Amar
Constitutional Law	Chemerinsky
Constitutional Law	Choper, Fallon, Kamisar & Shiffrin (Lockhart)
Constitutional Law	Cohen, Varat & Amar
Constitutional Law	Farber, Eskridge & Frickey
Constitutional Law	Rotunda
Constitutional Law	Sullivan & Gunther
Constitutional Law	Stone, Seidman, Sunstein, Tushnet & Karlan
Contracts	Barnett
Contracts	Burton
Contracts	Calamari, Perillo & Bender
Contracts	Crandall & Whaley
Contracts	Dawson, Harvey, Henderson & Baird
Contracts	Farnsworth, Young, Sanger, Cohen & Brooks
Contracts	Fuller & Eisenberg
Contracts	Knapp, Crystal & Prince
Contracts	Ayres & Speidel
Copyright	Cohen, Loren, Okediji & O'Rourke
Copyright	Goldstein & Reese
Criminal Law	Bonnie, Coughlin, Jeffries & Low
Criminal Law	Boyce, Dripps & Perkins
Criminal Law	Dressler
Criminal Law	Johnson & Cloud
Criminal Law	Kadish, Schulhofer & Steiker
Criminal Law	Kaplan, Weisberg & Binder
Criminal Procedure	Allen, Hoffmann, Livingston & Stuntz
Criminal Procedure	Dressler & Thomas
Criminal Procedure	Haddad, Marsh, Zagel, Meyer, Starkman & Bauer
Criminal Procedure	Kamisar, LaFave, Israel, King & Kerr
Criminal Procedure	Saltzburg & Capra
Employment Discrimination	Friedman
Employment Discrimination	Zimmer, Sullivan & White
Employment Law	Rothstein & Liebman
Environmental Law	Menell & Stewart
Environmental Law	Percival, Schroder, Miller & Leape
Environmental Law	Plater, Abrams, Goldfarb, Graham, Heinzerling & Wirth
Evidence	Broun, Mosteller & Giannelli
Evidence	Fisher
Evidence	Mueller & Kirkpatrick
Evidence	Sklansky
Evidence	Waltz & Park
Family Law	Areen & Regan
Family Law	Ellman, Kurtz & Scott
Family Law	Harris, Teitelbaum & Carbone
Family Law	Wadlington & O'Brien
Family Law	Weisberg & Appleton
Federal Courts	Fallon, Meltzer & Shapiro (Hart & Wechsler)
Federal Courts	Low & Jeffries
Health Law	Furrow, Greaney, Johnson, Jost & Schwartz
Immigration Law	Aleinikoff, Martin & Motomura
Immigration Law	Legomsky
Insurance Law	Abraham
Intellectual Property	Merges, Menell & Lemley
International Business Transactions	Folsom, Gordon, Spanogle & Fitzgerald
International Law	Blakesley, Firmage, Scott & Williams
International Law	Carter, Trimble & Weiner
International Law	Damrosch, Henkin, Pugh, Schachter & Smit
International Law	Dunoff, Ratner & Wippman
Labor Law	Cox, Bok, Gorman & Finkin
Land Use	Callies, Freilich & Roberts
Legislation	Eskridge, Frickey & Garrett
Oil & Gas	Lowe, Anderson, Smith & Pierce
Patent Law	Adelman, Radner, Thomas & Wegner
Products Liability	Owen, Montgomery & Davis
Professional Responsibility	Gillers
Professional Responsibility	Hazard, Koniak, Cramton & Cohen
Property	Casner, Leach, French, Korngold & VanderVelde
Property	Cribbet, Johnson, Findley & Smith
Property	Donahue, Kauper & Martin
Property	Dukeminier, Krier, Alexander & Schill
Property	Haar & Liebman
Property	Kurtz & Hovenkamp
Property	Nelson, Stoebuck & Whitman
Property	Rabin, Kwall & Kwall
Property	Singer
Real Estate	Korngold & Goldstein
Real Estate Transactions	Nelson & Whitman
Remedies	Laycock
Remedies	Shoben, Tabb & Janutis
Securities Regulation	Coffee, Seligman & Sale
Securities Regulation	Cox, Hillman & Langevoort
Sports Law	Weiler & Roberts
Taxation (Corporate)	Lind, Schwartz, Lathrope & Rosenberg
Taxation (Individual)	Burke & Friel
Taxation (Individual)	Freeland, Lathrope, Lind & Stephens
Taxation (Individual)	Klein, Bankman & Shaviro
Torts	Dobbs & Hayden
Torts	Epstein
Torts	Franklin & Rabin
Torts	Henderson, Pearson, Kysar & Siliciano
Torts	Schwartz, Kelly & Partlett (Prosser)
Wills, Trusts & Estates	Dukeminier, Johanson, Lindgren & Sitkoff
Wills, Trusts & Estates	Dobris, Sterk & Leslie
Wills, Trusts & Estates	Scoles, Halbach, Roberts & Begleiter